UKRAINE, GAZA, TAIWAN...
A World at War

UKRAINE, GAZA, TAIWAN...
A WORLD AT WAR

Revised Edition

Ajay Singh

PENTAGON PRESS LLP

First published in 2024 by

PENTAGON PRESS LLP
206, Peacock Lane, Shahpur Jat
New Delhi-110049, India
Contact: 011-64706243

Typeset in Adobe Garamond, 11.5 Point
Printed by Aegean Offset Printers, Greater Noida, U.P.

ISBN 978-81-968722-1-2 (HB)

www.pentagonpress.in

For Kookie and Ragini……

As is everything else.

And Sushi,

Who sat patiently through it all, barring a few ripped pages

Contents

1

Ukraine, Gaza, Taiwan... A World at War

War in the Middle East

On 7 October 23, the sacred day of Simchat Torah, Hamas terrorists attacked Israel. They broke through the fence surrounding the Gaza Strip and entered Israel by land, sea and air, in a well-planned and precisely coordinated operation. They entered Jewish settlements and military bases, and reached towns and villages almost 30 kilometres deep and in the day long carnage, they killed over 1400 people and took over 240 hostages back to Gaza. It was the largest single day loss of life in Israel's turbulent history, and plunged the nation into another war. The same day Israel, mobilised 300000 reservists and announced a formal declaration of war for the first time in 50 years. Operation 'Swords of Iron' was launched with the aim of eliminating Hamas, getting the hostages back, and creating a new security architecture in Gaza.

After three weeks of air and missile attacks, Israel launched its ground invasion of Gaza – one which has continued for over three months, destroyed 60 percent of Gaza's infrastructure, displaced over 1.5 million people and claimed over 23,000 thousand lives and 56,000 wounded. To put it in perspective, that is three times the casualty count caused by the Russian invasion of Ukraine after two years of war.

Israel's predictable reaction of bombing all suspected Hamas targets in the Gaza strip – irrespective of collateral damage – was expected. World sympathy was initially with Israel, but that dissipated very fast as images of attacks on hospitals, refugee camps and residential areas began flooding the news channels. Israel moved from being a victim to the aggressor in just three short weeks. And its land invasion of Gaza on 28 October merely compounded the issue. They told 1.1 million Gazan living in the north, to vacate their homes and move south of the line Wadi Gaza, as they attacked Gaza City, the capital, where most of the leadership was reportedly sheltering. Israeli tanks surrounded Gaza City, Jabalia refugee camp and other suspected Hamas centres and closed in on their strongholds. But while buildings and complexes were flattened, the loss to actual Hamas members and leaders could never be ascertained. Israel claimed to have killed over 8000 cadres (most presumably buried under rubble) but none of the top leaders were killed or apprehended. The top three of the Hamas leadership – Yahya Sinwar, Mohammed Deif and Marwan Issa – merely disappeared using the famed 'Gaza Metro' – the 515 km long warren of underground tunnels that Hamas had created – and escaped towards the south in the city of Khan Younis.

Israel shifted the focus of operations to the South. Once again the inhabitants of the South were ordered to vacate their homes and move – but where. Once again Israeli tanks and troops surrounded the known locations of the Hamas leadership, but as at the time of writing they are still elusive. Nor were many hostages rescued – the major aim of the operation. Over a hundred were returned in a prisoner swap during a week-long truce, but most remain untraceable. Many were killed by 'friendly fire' – some even as they waved out to approaching Israeli soldiers. So far, Israeli casualties have been comparatively restricted – around 160 soldiers or so till end December – but it is still higher than all their earlier wars with Hamas put together.

This war has drawn other parties into the fray. Hezbollah, the Houthis, and other Iran sponsored groups from Iraq and Syria, have intensified attacks on Israel in solidarity with Hamas. The Palestinians of West Bank have begun attacks on Israeli security forces, forcing a clampdown there. Hezbollah have launched rocket and missiles from Lebanon, and raided Israeli settlements and military camps in the vicinity of the Israel-Lebanon border. In retaliation, Israel has struck Lebanon itself, killing the deputy chief of Hamas, a senior Hezbollah leader, and a Iranian general in the heart of Beirut with drone attacks. This has further inflamed passions. If Hezbollah opens a northern front from Lebanon, the war will widen considerably, sucking in Syria and Iraq as well. And they are three times the size of Hamas. The Houthis too (another Iranian proxy) have launched a flurry of drone and missile attacks from Yemen targeting Israeli shipping in the Red Sea. They widened the scope of attacks to hit all ships, transiting through the Straits of Bab el Mandeb and the Red Sea – and virtually blocked this crucial waterway through which 15 percent of the world's shipping transits. The USA formed a coalition – 'Operation Prosperity Guardian' – to ensure safe passage through the waters. But the coalition has got a lukewarm response. India has not formally joined, but its warships have been in the forefront in protecting and rescuing commercial ships from raiders in these waters.

US bases in Iraq and Syria have also been targeted by Shia militia, with the inevitable US retaliation and missile strikes in both these countries. Iran has not been directly involved, but most of these attacks have been carried out by its proxies which can get USA and Iran dangerously close to open conflict. To add to the complexity of the situation, the ISIS conducted a series of bomb blasts in Iran, killing over 200 Shia mourners, and signalled the resurgence of the Islamic State.

There is no clarity how this war will end. Hamas and its leadership will most probably be eliminated, but they will simply arise in another form. The hostages remain pawns in a larger game, but it would be safer to get them back through negotiations than armed action. And what of Gaza Strip and its 2.3 million occupants? Who is to pay for the estimated $60 billion to rebuild its shattered infrastructure and displaced people? Will Israel occupy Gaza Strip, as they did earlier (only to withdraw disastrously in 2006) or will they hand it over to Palestinian Authority (which is understandably reluctant to take over the war-torn enclave)? And the most important question? Will the Palestinian people finally get their own State as part of the promised "Two-State Solution". Unless these questions are satisfactorily answered, there will be no end to turmoil of the Middle East and it will simply erupt again.

Ukraine

The events of the Middle East have clouded the Russia-Ukraine war, which has now been pushed into the side lines. For much the year, the war was characterised by the much vaunted Ukrainian spring offensive – an offensive which was inordinately delayed and eventually launched only around June-July 2023. The USA and its western allies had pumped in vast amounts of aid and equipment to build up an offensive force of around twelve brigades, equipped with new western equipment. Yet, the much-hyped offensive "to regain the last inch of Ukrainian soil," was poorly planned and executed. The troops were inadequately trained, and the offensive forces dispersed along a 400 kilometre wide front – none strong enough to attain decisive results. The initial Ukrainian attacks were beaten back, as soon as they contacted the first line of Russian defences, with losses to the newly-acquired Leopard and Challenger tanks. After that, the Ukrainian offensive crept forward slowly and timidly, advancing around 500 meters or so on a good day. After five months of operations, the Ukrainians advanced around 11-13 kilometres, and managed to penetrate the first Russian defensive line in only one location – near Tokmuk – before coming to a halt with winter. Even if they do follow up the offensive next year, at this rate, it will take the Ukrainians 103 years to recapture its lost territories. And Russia has consolidated its positions and built up their own forces for their own counter-offensive which could come soon.

To make matters worse, the war in Gaza has diverted attention and aid away from Ukraine. Most of the European nations are now weary of the war and willing to accept a 'land-for-peace' solution. US aid is being diverted to Israel and Joe's Biden's 'blank cheque policy' now finds few takers. Without external aid, Ukraine will be able to fight for just 45 days before it runs out of fuel and ammunition. And Putin is stronger than before. He has promised that the war will continue till "Russia attain its military aims". As Ukraine slips from the world's radar, Russia could well up the ante in the coming year, seize even more Ukrainian territory and simply hold on to it in a *fait accompli*- as they did with Crimea in 2014.

Taiwan

With wars raging in Europe and the Middle East, the attention has been diverted from the main threat – China. China has been ramping its aggression in the China Seas, taking over islands and building bases in the disputed Paracel and Spratly Islands, claiming the area as their own. This has got it on a confrontation course with USA, Japan, Vietnam, Malaysia and a host of Indo-Pacific nations. It has recently ramped up its actions against Philippines, by deliberately ramming their ships, denying access to fishing boats, and even using water cannons to force Filipino ships away from their own waters.

But these are small actions. Their economy is slowing and Xi Jinping's is coming under increasing internal criticism for his policies. He could use the diversion caused by the Gaza and Ukraine wars, to try his own action to reunify Taiwan – something he considers "a sacred duty." He has warned the PLA to be ready for military action if peaceful reunification fails. The PLA has been rehearsing this contingency for years, and though it is expected to be fully prepared only around 2027, he could use the present US preoccupation with the wars in Europe and the Middle East to take a dangerous gamble. The Taiwanese presidential elections of January 24 raises the possibility of a new anti-unification government that favours outright independence, and China may want to act before it slips from its orbit. The USA too has its presidential elections in November 24 and will be internally occupied. Could China use this "once-in-a-century moment" for a military action to reunify the island by force? And if it does happen, will the USA intervene, as President Joe Biden publicly stated it would? Should that happen, it could trigger off a US-China confrontation in the Indo-Pacific which could well be the war for world superpowerdom.

Three wars, the receding one in Ukraine, the spreading one in the Middle East and a looming one in the Indo-Pacific pose the greatest challenge to the world – besides climate change and artificial intelligence. How can we cope with them, and what will be their likely outcomes? The wars, though fought in three different continents with different participants, are interlinked. They impact each other and much of the world. This book tries to explore the three major conflicts that could shape the course of the 21st century and define the new world order.

UKRAINE

Major Characters

UKRAINE

Volodymyr Zelensky

The President of Ukraine was a former comedienne and actor. His inspiring leadership helped Ukraine stand firm in the war. When the US offered him a helicopter to fly him out of Kyiv, his reply "I need ammunition, not a ride" became a wartime classic. His insistence on standing firm and recapturing "every inch of occupied territory" helped stiffen morale. However, as the war continued and Ukraine began suffering reverses, he earned criticism and began losing support from the West.

General Valerii Zaluzhny

Commander in Chief of the Ukrainian Armed Forces, he skillfully coordinated the Ukrainian defense in the initial days of the war, and then counter offensive of 2022. However, the counter offensive of 2023 did not make much progress and he reportedly had differences with Zelensky on the conduct of the war.

'The Ghost of Kyiv'

A MIG 29 fighter pilot who was credited with shooting down six Russian fighter jets in a single day and then went on to get 40 more kills. It was later proved to be fictitious.

RUSSIA

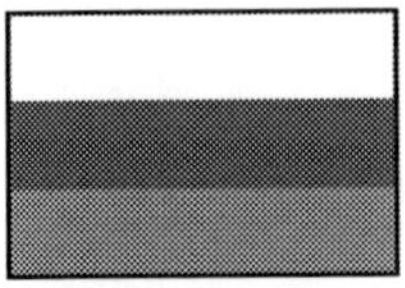

Vladimir Putin

The former KGB spy, who considered the break-up of the Soviet Union to be "The greatest geopolitical catastrophe of the 20th Century". He continued the war with resolve, in spite of western pressure and reverses and his strategy of fighting "a long war of attrition" paid off. He also successfully handled the revolt of the Wagner Group supremo, Prigozhin.

Sergei Lavrov

The Foreign Minister of Russia since 2004, he is reportedly very close to Putin and shares his hard-line views. In spite of criticism because of earlier reverses and casualties, he has managed to hold his position.

Sergei Shoigu

Russia's Defense Minister since 2012. His handling of the war has got him much criticism with one of the senior commanders suggesting, that he should "be shot for incompetence." But he has retained his position due to his proximity to Putin. The Russian staving off of the Ukrainian counteroffensive of 2023, has strengthened his position.

Yevgeny Prigozhin

A Russian oligarch who began his career by opening a hot dog stand and then rose rapidly to become a close confidant of Putin and one of Russia's most powerful men. His Wagner Group captured the town of Bakhmut and earned him fame, but also got him at loggerheads with senior Russian generals. He led his fighters in a famous 'March to Moscow' in May 23, but that mutiny was diffused in just a day. He was killed in an air crash just two months later.

Chronology of Major Events

1991: Russia and Ukraine become separate states after the Soviet Union collapses. The two nations remain close, but Ukraine starts tilting away from Russia and towards the European Union from 2010 onwards.

March 2014: Russia annexes Crimea in light of the pro and anti-Russia protests going on throughout Ukraine.

April 2014 onwards: Fighting between pro-Russian separatists and Ukrainian forces begins in the Donbas region. Russian forces actively aid the separatists, but deny involvement. Over 18,000 fighters killed on both sides in the fighting which continued for over eight years.

2019: Volodymyr Zelensky, a former comic actor is elected President. Promises to join NATO and EU and are enshrined in the Ukrainian constitution.

January 2021: Move to join NATO intensifies. Russia protests and warns Ukraine against it, citing threat to its own security. The warnings are ignored. Russia begins build-up of troops along the border in the guise of 'exercises.'

August-October 2021: Russian troops conduct exercises in Belarus and they continue to remain on Belarus soil. Russia demands that NATO pulls back troops and offensive weaponry from Eastern Europe and provide written guarantees that Ukraine will never become a part of NATO. NATO refuses to accept Russian demands.

November-January 2022: Talks conducted between Russia, Ukraine, and NATO and also between President Biden and Putin. Talks are inconclusive and fail.

24 February 2022: Russia launches 'Special Military Operations' in Ukraine and attacks along three main prongs (with an additional thrust in the Donbas). Kyiv declares Martial Law. Russian airborne operations try to capture Hostomel airport near Kyiv, in the first day of the war itself, but are pushed back by Ukrainian forces with heavy casualties.

28 February 2022: A 64-kilometre-long Russian convoy approaches Kyiv from Belarus. But inexplicably, the column halts for a few days when it is just 30 kilometres away from the capital.

2 March 2022: Kherson surrenders. The first major city to fall. Cities of Kharkiv, Melitopol, Mariupol, Sumy, Chernihev, and others are surrounded and heavily bombarded, but hold on. Russia is unable to capture any other major town, stalling its advance.

First Week, March 2022: The Russian convoy moves again. Russian troops approach Kyiv from the north and north-east in two prongs and begin isolating it from both sides of the Dnieper River. The suburbs of Bucha, Irpin, and Brovary are captured and the city is subjected to heavy artillery and missile strikes.

17 March 2022: Lyiv, a town just 20 kilometres from the Poland border, where Western arms are received, is targeted by air and missile strikes, which destroys vast quantities of newly-received Western equipment. Russia uses Kinzhal hypersonic missiles in a clear warning that it is willing to escalate the conflict.

End March 2022: Russia abruptly announces a withdrawal from the Kyiv sector. Its troops move back from Kyiv with reports of atrocities and mass graves being discovered in the suburbs of Bucha and Irpin. Russia states that it has withdrawn from Kyiv to focus on the Donbas which was "the original aim of the campaign."

First/Second Week April 2022: Russia launches Phase II of the offensive. Operations intensify all along the south and east. In the south the Russians make headway along the entire coastal belt along the Sea of Azov, and surround the port cities of Melitopol, Mariupol, and Mykolaiv. Russian troops reach as far as Zaporizhzhia in the north.

14 April 2022: MOSKVA, the flagship of the Russian Black Sea Fleet is hit by two Neptune anti-ship missiles and sunk. This is a major loss to Russian naval capabilities and prestige.

17 April 2022: Mariupol – the gateway to the south – falls after an 82-day siege. The defenders of the 36 Marine Brigade and the Azov Battalion are forced out of the city and take refuge in the Azovstol Steel Plant till they are forced to surrender on 17 May. This is a major success for the Russians and gives them control over the entire coastal areas up to Kherson.

Mid May 2022: Ukrainian forces counter attack in the north-east and retake the town of Kharkiv, pushing the Russians back across the border. Ukrainian units reach as far as the Russian frontier.

May 2022: Russian attacks intensify all along the Donbas as Russia shifts its focus there.

June-July 2022: Russia gains in the Luhansk province of the Donbas in slow but steady actions, supported by heavy fire power. Advance is only around two or three kilometres per day, but the major towns and vital villages are captured one by one. Izium, Kupyansk, and other communication centres fall into Russian hands.

Early August 2022: Ukrainian troops launch their offensive in the south towards Kherson. It cannot be recaptured, but Russian troops are pushed eastwards behind the Dnieper River. This offensive also draws Russian troops from other sectors towards it.

9 August 2022: Attack on Saki air base destroys eight fighter jets, almost half of Russia's naval aviation resources. This strike, almost 100 kilometres deep in the Crimea is not admitted by Ukraine, but underscores its new-found long-range strike capabilities.

12 August 2022: The area around Zaporizhzhia sees heavy fighting during Ukraine's counter-attack and the nuclear plant comes under artillery fire raising fears of nuclear radiation leak. Both sides accuse the other of the firing.

24 August 2022: Ukraine celebrates Independence Day amidst attacks from Russia. War completes six months.

End August-early September 2022: Ukraine secretly prepares for its own counter-offensive, beefed up by the arrival of trained reservists and sophisticated equipment from the West. US intelligence provides vital information of the gaps in Russian positions. Russia remains unaware of the impending offensive till it is too late.

5 September 2022: Ukrainian counter-offensive begins in Kharkiv region and makes stunning headway. In less than a fortnight, they recapture around 6,000 square kilometres of occupied territory, and retake the important towns of Izium, Kupyansk and Balakliya. Russian troops are pushed back to the line of the Oskil River.

21 September 2022: President Putin orders partial military mobilization to call up 200,000 reservists into service. This leads to thousands of men fleeing Russia to avoid military service.

23-27 September 2022: Russia conducts a referendum in the provinces of Luhansk, Donetsk, Kherson and Zaporizhzhia. As per Russian reports, 93 per cent in Zaporizhzhia, 87 per cent in Kherson, 98 per cent in Luhansk, and 99 per cent in Donetsk voted to join Russia, setting the stage for their formal annexation.

3 October 2022: Putin signs decree to formally amalgamate the regions of Luhansk, Donetsk, Kherson and Zaporizhzhia into Russia. It is not recognized by any other nation.

4 October 2022: Ukrainian troops follow up their counter-offensive with the capture of Lyman, denying the Russians a major logistical base. Offensive in the south also makes headway.

8 October 2022: A truck laden with explosives blows up on Kersh Bridge, the crucial 19-kilometre-long bridge linking Russia with Crimea. Russia responds by carrying out a series of missile and drone attacks in Ukraine targeting their power and water infrastructure. Over 30 per cent of their power stations are destroyed.

End October–Mid November 2022: Both sides consolidate in defensive positions in the areas they hold.

End November 2022: Russian forces launch offensive in the north-east and close in on Bakhmut.

5 December 2022: Drone attack by Ukraine on two Russian airbases – Engels and Dyagilevo – that damaged two bombers and infrastructure.

10-31 December 2022: Intensification of drone and missile attacks by Russia targeting Ukrainian infrastructure, especially water and electrical installations.

13 January 2023: Russians capture Soledar, a small-town north-east of Bakhmut.

Mid-January 2023: Poland, Germany, the UK and the USA agree to provide

Leopard II, Challenger II and M1 Abrams tanks to Ukraine, and facilitate training of crew. A total of 315 tanks are pledged.

Early February 2023: Russian offensive towards Bakhmut gains momentum with the Wagner Group in the forefront. A rift breaks out with Wagner Group leader Yevgeny Prigozhin accusing the Russian army of denying ammunition to his fighters.

25 March 2023: Putin announces that Russia will station Iskander tactical missiles in Belarus. They also refuse to extend the START II Treaty.

April 2023: Heavy fighting in Bakhmut. The town still holds in spite of heavy casualties. Russian forces control over 80 per cent of the town, but the Ukrainians hold on.

3 May 2023: Two drone attacks hit Moscow, striking close to the Kremlin. Russia claimed it was an attempt to assassinate Putin and responded with a volley of drone and missile attacks on Kyiv.

9 May 2023: Victory Day in Moscow to celebrate Soviet victory over Nazi Germany. Ukraine shifts its celebrations to a day earlier. A huge strike by over 60 drones hits Kyiv, but most are reportedly shot down. Ukraine also claims to have intercepted and shot down six Kinzhal hypersonic missiles.

22 May 2023: Wagner Group announces that all of Bakhmut has been captured.

5 June 2023: Ukrainian offensive begins along the south and north-eastern regions. Probing actions all along the front, but little progress.

23 June 2023: Wagner Group warlord, Yevgeny Prigozhin, withdraws his troops from the front lines and marches towards Moscow, against perceived slights to his fighters. Takes over Rostov and Voronezh.

24 June 2023: Around 200 kilometres short of Moscow, Prigozhin calls off the march and turns around, stating he does not want "to spill Russian blood." The deal was apparently brokered by Belarus President Alexander Lukashenko.

17 July 2023: Black Sea grain deal expires. Russia refuses to extend it.

End July 2023: Russia launches a series of drone and missile attacks on Ukraine striking Kyiv, Odessa, Kharkiv, Donetsk and Zaporizhzhia.

Mid-August 2023: Ukraine retaliates with drone and missile attacks inside

Russia, hitting Kursk, Rostov, Belgorod and Moscow. Two TU-22M bombers are reportedly destroyed by a missile attack on a Russian airfield.

23 August 2023: Wagner Group Supremo, Yevgeny Prigozhin, is killed when his private jet crashes shortly after take-off near Moscow. The most likely cause of the crash was an on-board explosion.

First Week September 2023: Ukraine claims to have breached the first line of Russian defences in the Zaporizhzhia region. It also claimed to have recaptured eight square kilometres around Bakhmut.

22 September 2023: The HQ of the Russian Black Sea Fleet is hit by a Ukrainian Storm Shadow missile reportedly killing 34 senior officers and injuring 105 servicemen. The drone and missile attacks by both Russia and Ukraine, deep inside each other's territory intensify.

28 August 2023: Ukrainian forces announce the capture of Robotyne, in the Zaporizhzhia sector which is the only major success of their offensive.

End September 2023: Poland, one of Ukraine's staunchest allies, said that it would be "no longer transfer weapons to Ukraine" in the first signs of rift between Ukrainian allies. Simultaneously, Ukrainian aid was reduced in the US Government Funding Bill in an indicator that US aid could not be indefinitely sustained and could be further reduced.

Early October 2023: Ukrainian offensive seems to be running out of steam. Except for incursions of approximately 11 km deep into Russian defensive lines on the south, and the capture of Robotyne and Verbone, no headway is made.

7 October 2023: Hamas launches an attack on Israel and kills almost 1,400 persons; over 200 taken hostage. The Gaza war begins and diverts attention away from Ukraine.

End October 2023: Russians launch offensive in area of Avdiivha in the Donbas.

10 November 2023: Russia formally withdraws from Treaty on Conventional Armed Forces in Europe. Earlier, it had withdrawn ratification of the Comprehensive Test Ban treaty. NATO too announces the suspension of the Conventional Armed forces Treaty, bringing an end to a vital confidence building measure.

Mid-November 2023: Early December – Missile and drone attacks by both sides intensify, striking cities deep in the rear.

12 December 2023: Zelensky visits Washington and though he got sympathy and assurances of support, only received a watered-down amount of aid. It is an indicator that US support is gradually waning.

14 December 2023: Putin announces in his annual press conference that his goals in Ukraine have not changed and the war would continue unless Kyiv did a deal that took Moscow's security concerns into account. That announcement seemed to open a window for subsequent negotiations.

28 December 2023: Ukraine launches a massive missile and drone attack on the Russian regional capital of Belgorod.

30 December: Russia launches 150 missile and drone attacks on six Ukrainian cities in the largest such attack of the war.

January 2024: Russia makes probing actions towards Avdiivka and in the Kharkiv region using small assault groups for raids and incursion.

8 February 2024: Zelensky replaces the Commander in Chief of Ukrainian forces, General Valerii Zaluzhnyi with General Oleksandr Syrski, amidst reports of growing differences between the two, over Zaluzhnyi's 'over-cautious' style.

17 February 2024: Avdiivka falls to the Russian forces in the first major Russian success after Bakhmut.

End February 2024: Russian forces storm Robotyne in the Zaporizhzhia region. The town had been taken by the Ukrainians during their offensive of Oct 23, and now came back in Russian control.

18 March 2024: President Putin won the Russian elections in a landslide, getting almost 88 per cent of the votes in a largely uncontested election. He enters his fifth term in power, making him the longest serving Russian head since Stalin. This gives him 6 more years in power which will ensure that the war continues on his terms.

22 March 2024: The Crocus City Hall in Moscow attacked by militants of the Islamic State Khorasan Province, killing 133 concert-goers. Russia alleged a Ukrainian hand, but Ukraine denied involvement.

20 April 2024: The US Senate approved $61 Billion aid to Ukraine.

6 May 2024: Russia announced that it would practice the deployment of nuclear weapons in response to the perceived threat from NATO.

10 May 2024: Russia began offensive operations in the Northeastern region of Kharkov. The operation made initial headway, but Ukrainian forces successfully prevented any further ingress. The Kharkov front stabilized around end June.

14 May 2024: Russian Defense Minister Sergei Shoigu replaced by Andrei Belonsov, an economist. Shoigu, a long time Putin loyalist, held the role for over 12 years. His replacement by an economic expert, indicated that Putin wanted to focus on the economic aspects of this long war.

17 May 2024: Vladimir Putin visits Beijing where he is received as a special guest and reaffirms Russia-China ties with 'my old friend' Xi Jinping.

19 May 2024: Ukraine claimed to have sunk the Russian minesweeper 'Kovrovets' and a missile ship in the vicinity of Sevastopol in a strike using unmanned surface vessels and drones. Ukrainian strikes by explosive laden USVs, often operating in tandem with drones, along with long range strikes by drones and missiles were estimated to have damaged over a dozen Russian warships and damaged port facilities. Even though the Ukrainian fleet has been left without a single operating warship, these strikes have curtailed Russian shipping in the Black Sea and the Sea of Azov.

30 May 2024: USA, France, Germany and UK finally gave permission for Ukraine to use their weaponry to strike targets inside Russia. This would aid future Ukrainian action significantly, especially for their subsequent offensive in Kursk in Aug 2024.

15-16 June 2024: Ukraine Peace Summit held in Switzerland with 92 nations participating. Russia and China did not attend. India sent a representative but did not sign on the joint declaration issued at the conclusion of the summit. A 'Zelensky Peace Formula' was announced, which included the withdrawal of Russian forces from Ukraine, war damages and reparation of prisoners. But without the presence of Russia, the Summit had no meaning.

9-11 July 2024: The Washington Summit attended by heads of state of 32 NATO countries held to mark 75 years of the alliance. It was held in the same location where the founding treaty was signed in 1949. As expected, Ukraine's membership was discussed but put off for the future.

13 July 2024: Prime Minister Modi visited Moscow in his first bilateral visit since taking over his third term. The visit re-affirmed India-Russian ties, but also drew criticism from Ukraine and western nations. India however, maintained its independent position in the conflict.

04 August 2024: Ukraine received its first consignment of F-16 fighters and are likely to receive 20 aircraft by the end of the year. Though touted with much fanfare, they would be unlikely to make a significant impact in the immediate battlefield.

06 August 2024: Ukraine launched an incursion into the Kursk-Belgorod area of Russia which took the ground war onto Russian soil for the first time. Using around four brigades the Ukrainians advanced over 30 kilometers deep and occupied 1000 square kilometers of area – including around 28 villages - forcing Russia to evacuate over 1,00,000 civilians from the region. The Russians however continued their own offensive in Kharkiv and Donbas.

24 August 2024: Prime Minister Modi meets Zelensky in Kyiv. Promises help to end the war.

26 August 2024: Russia strikes Ukraine power grid with over 200 missiles and drones in an attempt to coerce Ukraine, following its incursion. Ukraine follows up with long range attacks in Russia.

2

The Backdrop to War

"Not an inch of NATO's present military jurisdiction will spread in an eastern direction. Not one inch."

–US Secretary of State,
James Baker to Mikhail Gorbachev, 1990

The Conjoined History of Russia and Ukraine

When Russia invaded Ukraine at 5 a.m. on 24 February 2022, full-scale conventional war revisited Europe after almost seven decades. At the heart of the war lies the intertwined history and geography of Russia and Ukraine.

Ukraine occupies a unique place in Europe. Second only to Russia in size, it lies in the centre of Europe with the massive land mass of Russia to its east and the states of Poland, Rumania and Moldova to the west. Its unique position gives it control over both Eastern and Western Europe and its shoreline and ports allow it to dominate the Sea of Azov and the Black Sea. Its rich fertile soil provides most of the world's wheat and corn. This rich, culture-filled land provides a buffer between Russia and Western Europe and has been wooed by both – though it has traditionally been part of Russia and inclined towards it.

The two nations have a conjoined history going back to the 10th century. At that time, Russia, Ukraine and Belarus were all part of Kievan Rus – the medieval region comprising the lands of the three nations which was centred around the area of modern-day Kyiv. Kyiv is called "the cradle of Russian civilization" and has influenced Russian culture as much as Moscow itself. In the 18th century, Russia emerged as the strongest imperial power of Europe and formally annexed Ukraine in 1783. Ukraine became part of Russia and with the intermingling of population and culture both literally became one. Even then, the Russian Empire traditionally considered the Ukrainians (and Belarusians) as ethnically Russian and referred to them as "little Russians" – a condescending view that was opposed by many Ukrainians who wanted to preserve their own distinct identity.

With the eruption of the Russian Revolution in 1917-21, the Communist Party of Ukraine, joined hands with the Communist Party of Russia and willingly merged (with other Caucasian states) to form the USSR in 1922. Ukraine, with its rich granaries and mineral wealth was the bread basket of the Soviet Union – but it paid a heavy price for it. In the 'Thirties, Stalin set out to privatize farms and convert its vast agricultural lands for industry, in the process leading to the great famine of 1932-33 which claimed over three million lives in Russia and Ukraine. That holocaust lingers on in the Ukrainian consciousness and even today Ukraine has a name for that – the Holodomor famine, or killing by starvation.

Ukraine was in the front lines during World War II. When the German armies crossed the frontier into the Soviet Union in May 1941, the first battles of the war were fought around the Ukrainian front. German panzers cut through the flat countryside and encircled Kyiv and Kharkiv (then Kiev and Kharkov) in wide envelopments that decimated over 700,000 Soviet soldiers in the first three months of the war. In fact, though we remember the titanic battles of Moscow and Stalingrad, the major battles of the Eastern front were fought on Ukrainian soil (both during the German advance and their subsequent retreat) and it was the Ukrainian people who suffered the most in the carnage. Many of the sites of the present war – Kyiv, Kharkiv, Crimea, the

Dnieper River and others, find an echo in the Great War. In many cases, the two combatants (although one nation then) re-fought the battles on the same soil, on which they had once fought another adversary.

For over 70 years Russia and Ukraine shared a conjoined history as part of the USSR, including the tumultuous days of the post-war era and the Cold War. Then, in 1991, the Soviet Union imploded spectacularly. The 11 states that composed it – including Russia and Ukraine – became independent nations. With the dissolution of the Soviet Union, Ukraine inherited a vast stockpile of nuclear weapons, the third largest in the world with over 1,700 warheads and 3,000 tactical nuclear weapons that were left behind on its soil. It surrendered its entire arsenal in 1994, in return for security guarantees from Russia, Europe and the USA and became a non-nuclear state. The two nations followed their own course – independent but often complementary.

Even though Russia and Ukraine became independent entities, they were still held together by common bonds. Russia was the 'big brother', and in many ways had a say in Ukraine's internal affairs. But in the new millennium, a subtle shift came over Ukraine. It was slowly shedding its pro-Moscow stance and veering towards Europe, hoping to join the European Union. For Russia, that shift was disturbing. They installed their own man as the President – Victor Yanukovych, a staunch pro-Russian – even rigging elections and poisoning his opponent to ensure a win. Yanukovych veered Ukraine back towards Russia. But it was quite apparent that he was "their man" and his decisions were dictated by Moscow. In 2013 he withdrew from an earlier decision to join the European Union and refused to sign the European Union Association Agreement that would have made Ukraine part of the European Union. Instead, he moved back towards Russia and the Eurasian Economic Union.

The movement to join the European Union had been gathering momentum within Ukraine for many years now, especially amongst the younger generation, and this decision was met with widespread protests. A wave of demonstrations and protests broke out in November 2013 in Maidan Nezalezhnosti – Independence Square in Ukraine – which was also called the Euromaidan protests. The protests spread across the country as pro and anti-Russian rallies erupted across the country, reaching as far out as Kharkiv, Odessa and the Crimea. Over 200 demonstrators were killed as government authorities clamped down and that spurred even greater protests. Eventually, the pro-Europe lobby won and Yanukovych capitulated and fled to Russia in February 2014, leaving it in the hands of an interim government. Flush with the victory of the Euromaidan protests, Ukraine tilted even more strongly towards the European Union and proposed joining NATO – an action that would take it away from Russia's orbit, and make it completely entrenched with the West.

The Actions in Crimea and Donbas – 2014-2021

The turn of events in Ukraine was not taken lightly by Russia. The protests had also seen a large number of pro-Russian rallies, especially in the eastern regions of the Donbas and the southern peninsula of Crimea which had a large Russian-speaking population. In February 2014, pro-Russian supporters launched their own violent protests in the Crimea, seized the parliament building and airports and virtually held the local government to ransom. As the local authorities tried to suppress the protestors, Russia used this action as a pretext, and on 27 February sent troops in to "save Russian-speaking people." Russian paratroopers captured strategic sites across Crimea and installed a pro-Russian government in place. Things moved rapidly thereafter. In March, a referendum was held in Crimea, in which an overwhelming 90 per cent of the population voted for independence from Kyiv to join Russia. Crimea was declared 'independent' and formally incorporated into Russia on 18 March 2014.

Russia had been claiming Crimea as "Historically Russian" – as part of the old Russian Empire – since 1991. Its crucial position abutting into the Black Sea was vital to its own maritime interests. The annexation of Crimea was illegal and orchestrated, and though it drew international condemnation and sanctions, it had little effect on an unrepentant Russia. Russian passports were issued, the Hryvnia replaced by roubles, and the process of "Russification" began. In a *fait accompli*, Crimea became part of Russia.

Around the same time, they also incited unrest in the largely Russian-speaking eastern provinces of Donetsk and Luhansk, – which together made up the Donbas – setting off a civil war between the pro-Russian separatists and Ukrainian forces that lasted eight years. This war in the Donbas is the precursor to the war that erupted in 2022.

In April 2014, the activities of the pro-Russian separatist groups in Donbas increased. The ranks of these groups swelled to over 20,000-30000, which included a large number of Russian 'volunteers.' The unrest swelled to a full-fledged insurgency, actively encouraged and abetted by Russia. Although Russia denies it, there is no doubt that it actively participated in the conflict. Russian soldiers and Spetznaz operatives were captured, and units and formations operating there identified – including their elite 76th Guards Air Assault Division. Under the pretext of 'humanitarian aid' large convoys of arms and equipment were sent from Russia to support the separatist groups, who fought under the banner of "Novorossiya" – New Russia. A Russian surface-to-air missile in their hands hit Malaysian Airlines Flight MH-17. which was mistaken for a Ukrainian transport aircraft and crashed, killing all on board. The civil war in Donbas between the Ukrainian forces and separatists raged for eight years with neither side being able to exert control.

In an attempt to stop the fighting, the Minsk Agreement was signed between representatives of Ukraine, Russia, the Luhansk People's Republic and the Donetsk People's Republic along with the Organization for Security and Cooperation in Europe, in September 2014. This initial agreement (also called the Minsk Protocol) failed to stop the fighting and a revised agreement was signed in February 2015 – Minsk II. Both sides agreed to a ceasefire, release of prisoners and granted self-government to certain areas of the Donbas, while recognizing Ukraine's sovereignty over it. In the ceasefire that followed, the fighting subsided, but it never stopped altogether. Donbas became a zone of 'frozen conflict' with tensions rising and ebbing, but never resolved completely.

The platform that Russia had established in the Donbas and Crimea would help them in the invasion, and they would use the same model in this war.

And then in 2019, Volodymyr Zelensky was elected President of Ukraine – ironically on the promise that he would end the fighting. This 44-year-old had no experience of politics and had attained fame as a stand-up comedian and his roles in television comedies. His most remembered role was in the series 'Servant of the People' in which he played the role of a high-school teacher who gets elected as the President of Ukraine through a series of flukes, and then fits into the role with the premise "you only have to be good to lead." The unassuming Zelensky would play the same role in real life and prove his mettle in the war – the same war he hoped to avert – where his leadership would give steel to his countrymen to withstand the Russian invasion that came in February 2022.

On 14 September 2020, President Zelensky approved Ukraine's new National Security Strategy that included "a distinctive partnership with NATO, with the aim of membership." An amendment was made in the Ukrainian constitution that enshrined its decision to join the EU and NATO. Ukraine was now conclusively moving away from Russia and towards NATO. Ukraine applied for full membership of NATO (though it would be refused at this juncture). If Ukraine joined NATO, it would bring the alliance right to Russia's borders. Putin insisted that the clause be withdrawn and demanded guarantees that Ukraine would never join NATO, something that could not be formally given. As round after round of negotiations faltered, Putin ratcheted the pressure, sending troops towards the border. Europe was moving closer and closer towards war.

Russia and NATO

At the heart of the war lie two issues – the Ukrainian decision to join NATO, and the volatile, mercurial personality of Vladimir Putin. This invasion is the brainchild of Putin, a former intelligence officer who ruled Russia with an iron fist since 1999 – first as prime minister and then as president for an unprecedented three terms (after making constitutional changes that virtually made him president for life). This ex-KGB officer saw the break-up of the Soviet Union as "The greatest geo-political catastrophe of the 20th Century" and hoped to take Russia back to the glory and former position of the USSR.

It was in his desire to make Russia take on the mantle of the former USSR that he pushed his ultra-nationalistic agenda ruthlessly. He crushed the Chechen uprising with tanks and heavy artillery, virtually flattening Grozny. Then he took Russia to war with Georgia, which he defeated in 12 short days in August 2008. He also orchestrated the annexation of Crimea in 2014 and the encouragement of separatism in Ukraine's eastern provinces. His engagement in the Syrian civil war in 2015 helped his ally, Assad, to cling on to power, and reasserted Russian influence in the Middle East and also eased out US presence in the region. For good measure, he tried to influence the US presidential elections to ensure that Donald Trump would win; an action that earned him the personal animosity of Joe Biden – Trump's opponent – and the eventual winner.

Under his watch, Russia has grown at an impressive seven per cent, largely due to gas and oil revenues. It had cosied up to China and had begun exerting itself in Afghanistan, Central Asia and Europe. For him, the NATO expansion right up to Russia's border was a direct threat. If Ukraine joined the alliance, NATO troops would be on Russia's flanks, and missiles would take just three or four minutes to hit Moscow. As he himself put it, "Can't they see this? After this we have no place to go. We can't go backwards anymore."

In many ways, he was right. It has been explicitly promised to Mikhail Gorbachev himself that NATO would not expand 'one-inch eastwards' after the dissolution of the Soviet Union. At that time, in 1991, its boundaries stood along the borders of

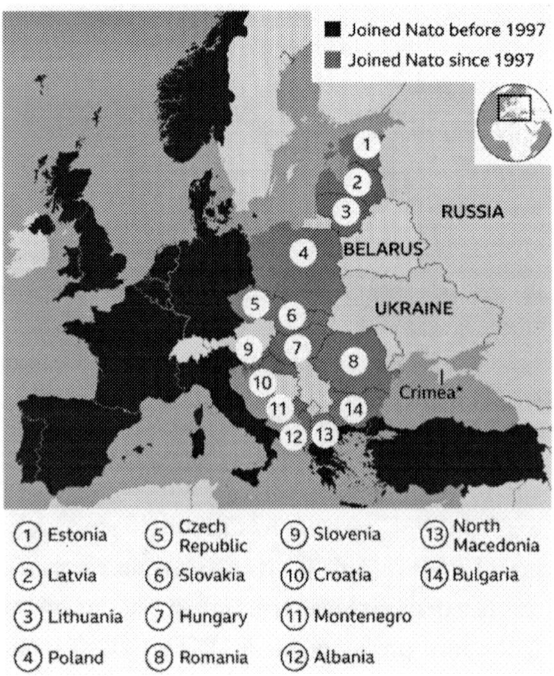

NATO's Expansion since 1997

Germany. In the decades after that, Poland, Hungary, the Czech Republic, Bulgaria, Rumania and the Baltic states of Estonia, Latvia and Lithuania were co-opted into the alliance. When Estonia and Latvia joined in 2004, NATO's borders touched Russia for the first time in its northern areas. If Ukraine joins, NATO would be at Russia's doorstep.

Putin's demand that Ukraine not be given membership of NATO and that NATO's offensive weaponry in the Baltic states bordering Russia be withdrawn, was thus justified. Perhaps Putin's initial posturing was just a way of buttressing his demands. After all, he too would not have wanted a full-scale war that would send the just recovering Russian economy back into the doldrums. But the written guarantees that Ukraine would never join NATO, which was demanded by Putin could not be given, and Europe headed inexorably towards a war that no one really wanted.

The Build-up to War

The first signs of a Russian military build-up came in February 2021 when around 3000 paratroopers were deployed around the Ukrainian border for 'exercises.' Around the same time, the activities of the separatist groups of the Donetsk People's Republic also increased. Small arms and mortar fire on Ukrainian positions began once again – to be followed by retaliatory fire. The ceasefire in the Donbas, always fragile, was effectively breaking up.

At the same time, NATO conducted its DEFENDER EUROPE 21 exercises – one of the largest in decades, which involved 28,000 troops from 27 nations. In response, Russia deployed around 40,000 men along the Ukrainian border, and built up their garrison in the Crimea. Russian ships moved into the Black Sea and the first naval confrontation took place in the Sea of Azov on the night of 15 April 21 when three Ukrainian vessels were blocked from entering the waters of the Kerch Straits which the Russians claimed as theirs, following their annexation of Crimea.

By end April, around 60,000 troops of the 41st and 58th armies were moved from the Siberian frontier towards the Ukrainian border, in the time-honoured garb of exercises. The exercises were conducted perilously close to the border, raising hackles across the world. However, by May, Russia announced that the troops would be withdrawing and returning to their permanent bases. In effect, only around 3,000 or so troops were moved back.

Most of the units were simply moved around laterally, creating the impression of movement, but in effect remaining in the border areas with their heavy equipment and weaponry.

In October, a second, and even more significant, build-up of troops followed. Around 30,000 soldiers were sent on 'exercises' to Belarus – on the northern border of Ukraine – ostensibly to practice with their Belarussian allies. The Russians took great pains to stress that the soldiers were merely exercising and had no offensive intentions. But it was the largest build-up of troops ever seen in Europe since World War II and raised alarms across the world.

By early November, the signs were clear. The 8th and 20th Guards armies and the 4th and 6th Air Defence armies joined the fray, and the concentration along the borders increased to around 110,000-120,000 troops. Additional troops also moved into the Crimea, with heavy offensive weaponry. US intelligence warned of a likely invasion, and estimated that it could take place by January 2022. For a change, the intelligence reports were right, but as is often the case with unpalatable news, were not taken too seriously.

Efforts to defuse the crisis continued. On 7 December 2021, US President Joe Biden and President Vladimir Putin spoke via video conference where Putin demanded "reliable, legal guarantees to preclude NATO from expanding towards Russia or deploying offensive weapons in countries bordering it." Russia also handed over a set of demands that included:

- The USA and NATO would not deploy troops in ex-Soviet states.
- NATO would not expand any further eastwards.
- NATO would not deploy any additional forces in Eastern Europe.
- Refrain from any military activity in Ukraine or other state in Eastern Europe, the Caucasus, and Central Asia.

The demands were actually quite flagrant. It is quite likely that the demand for denial of NATO membership to Ukraine had already been agreed to behind closed doors. But giving written guarantees for the same, and agreeing to Putin's other demands (which were actually not quite unreasonable, seeing the scale of NATO expansionism) would be seen as tantamount to surrender. Another frosty call followed between Biden and Putin on 30 December "to de-escalate tensions" in which Biden warned of "serious costs and consequences" including unspecified sanctions. Further talks followed, including a meeting of NATO-Russia, which got delegates from all 30 NATO countries and Russian representatives to the table. That meeting was a disaster. Russia stuck to its stance of 'written security guarantees'. NATO held on to its position that "Russia does not have a veto on whether Ukraine can become a NATO member. It has to be NATO and Ukraine that decides on membership." The lines were now clearly drawn.

In January 2022, Russia began a gradual evacuation of its embassy staff from Kyiv – another clear indicator of what was afoot. By mid-January, it was estimated that Russia had built up around 127,000 troops along with 35,000 Russian-backed separatists in Donbas and around 3,000 soldiers in rebel-held Eastern Ukraine. It also moved in 36 Iskandar short-range ballistic missiles near the border, many of them within striking distance of Kyiv. By late January, the headquarters of Eastern Military District along with combat units from the 5th, 29th, 35th and 36th Combined Arms Armies along with the 76th Air Assault Division and the 98th Airborne Division moved to Belarus – an indicator that the Russians would use the proximity of Belarus to attack Kyiv from the north. As per US estimates, Russia had assembled 83 battalion tactical groups – almost 70 per cent of their combat strength – for the invasion and predicted the attack to come any time after mid-February. Americans were warned to immediately leave Ukraine. They also correctly assessed that Russia would need 175,000-200,000 troops for the invasion and that the present strength would not be sufficient to capture and hold the large tracts of Ukrainian territory the Russians had set their sights on. That assessment would prove to be right.

As the Russian preparations continued, Ukraine too began mobilizing its forces. As per Oleksii Reznikov, the Minister of Defence, Ukraine held 250,000 troops, of which 125,000 had been deployed in the Donbas conflict since 2014, and were battle hardened. In addition, there were 400,000 veterans, and 200,000 reservists who were willing and available to be inducted with just a short period of training. As events would show later, the ready availability of highly motivated Ukrainian defenders would make all the difference.

The first shipments of foreign arms and aid began arriving. In January, the first consignment of FGM-148 Javelin anti-tank missiles, precision guided munitions, machine guns and small arms and specialized radio and communications equipment reached Lyiv – the trans-shipment hub in Western Ukraine where Western arms were stored and distributed. Stinger surface-to-air missiles, which had played such a vital role in the Afghan Soviet war, also arrived. Other NATO nations also chipped in. Estonia, Latvia, and Lithuania provided anti-tank missiles and air defence systems. Germany, reluctant to get involved in the conflict initially, provided 5,000 helmets – an offering that provoked a derisive snort from Zelensky, "What will they give us next – blankets?" The UK and Canada began a military training program that would train reservists and make them combat ready in a few months; and also provided 2,000 New Generation Light Anti-Tank missiles to help stave off the anticipated Russian armour onslaughts. As the war progressed, newer and more sophisticated weapons would find their way to Ukraine and prove decisive in the battles ahead.

Even as the clock began ticking, NATO began bolstering its eastern flank, by sending 2,000 additional troops to Germany. This was followed by an additional 3,000 troops to Poland, and F-15 jets to Rumania. Spain and the UK sent additional warships to the Mediterranean and the Black Sea, and Eurofighters and F-35s jets were deployed in Bulgaria as part of NATO's expanded air surveillance mission. At the same time, the USA made it clear that it would not get directly involved in the war, but would provide complete support and strike Russia with "sanctions as never before."

Within Russia too, the media began increasing their justification of the coming war. Ukraine was accused of violating the ceasefire agreement in Donbas and "spreading Russophobia as the first step to genocide." The Ukrainian government was "run by neo-Nazis" who had to be removed. 'Demilitarization and denazification' became catchwords, though there was little evidence to justify them.

In the midst of all this, Putin still found time to attend the Winter Olympic Games at Beijing in early February 2022, where he met his ally, Xi Jinping, and was wined and feted as a special guest of honour. It is quite likely that he shared his plans with the Chinese premier and perhaps even got a *de facto* expression of support. Both sides of course deny that but the fact that Xi Jinping was the last major world leader whom Putin met just before launching his invasion is a little too much of a coincidence. In any case, Putin conveniently waited for China to complete its prestigious games before launching his own invasion.

In the Donbas, the fighting escalated. Russia had moved in around 2,000 advisors and trainers to coordinate the actions of the militia, and ramp up their activities. Shelling of Ukrainian positions by the Donetsk and Luhansk militia intensified with almost 60 artillery and mortar attacks being conducted daily. Even as these attacks took place, Russia announced that Ukraine had been attacking civilians with mortar and machine gun fire, forcing them to evacuate their homes and flee to safe zones within Russia. They also claimed that Ukrainian artillery had destroyed a border post inside Russia. The Ukrainians denied these activities and it is quite likely they were mere propaganda or stage-managed by the Russians themselves as part of 'false flag' operations.

Events moved fast thereafter. On 21 February, Putin signed a decree, recognizing the breakaway Donetsk and Luhansk provinces as independent states – paving the way for their ultimate amalgamation into Russia. It also sent Russian troops into the Donbas as a "peacekeeping mission to save the lives of Russians from the neo-Nazis of the Ukrainian government."

It was becoming increasingly clear that Russia was poised to attack. As the last round of negotiations failed on 22 February, a vicious denial-of-services-cyber-attack hit Ukraine's financial and transport networks. Its internet was also downed, breaking communications. All along the border, satellites and local civilians reported an intensification of tank and troop movement, headed towards the border with an ominous 'Z' marked on their sides. This letter would become the symbol of the Russian offensive.

At 5 a.m. on 24 February 2022, Russian troops debouched from their concentration areas along the border and began moving into Ukraine from the north, the east and along the south. Putin's 'special military operation' had started. The war that everyone knew would happen, but still hoped would never take place, had begun.

REFERENCES

"Annexation of Crimea", Uaberexplained.com., 29 March 2022.

"Crimeans vote over 90 % for Russia", *Reuters*, 8 March 2015.

"Don't give Putin a Veto over NATO Expansion", https://www.washingtonpost.com 21 January 2022.

"Euro Maidan Rallies in Ukraine", *Kyiv Post*, 21 November 2013.

"Everything you need to know about the 2014 Ukraine Crisis", Vox ,https://www.vox.com 3 September 2014.

"Invasion of the Soviet Union, June 1941", https://encyclopedia.ushnm.org

Michael Gordon. "Russia moves units into Ukraine, NATO says", *The New York Times*, 5 June 2015.

"NATO conducts 'STEADFAST DEFENDER 21' War Games amidst Tensions" https://m.economictimes.com

"NATO's response to Russia's invasion of Ukraine", https://www.nato.int 23 September 2022.

"Putin Announces Donetsk and Luhansk Recognition", *BBC News*, 22 February 2022.

"Putin says Russia has 'Nowhere to Retreat' over Ukraine", *CNBC*, 21 December 2021.

"Putin wants 'de-Nazification, but how much is Ukraine Nazified?" https://www.indiatoday.in 24 March 2022.

"Putin-Soviet Collapse 'a Genuine Tragedy'", *NBC News*, 25 April 2005.

"Russia issues List of Demands to Lower Tensions", https://www.theguardian.com 17 December 2021.

"Russia's War on Ukraine, Timeline of Cyber-attacks", https://www.europa/.europa.eu 8 June 2022.

"Russian Military Build-up along the Ukrainian Border , https://crsreports.congress.gov, 7 February 2022.

Thomas McCray. "Russia and the Former Soviet Republics". "Ukraine – The Famine of 1932-33 (Holodomor)", https://www.britannica.com

"Timeline of NATO's Expansion since 1949", *ABC News*, 9 May 2022.

"Ukraine – History, Kyivan Rus", *Encyclopaedia Britannica*, 5 March 2020.

"Ukraine and pro-Russian rebels sign Ceasefire Deal", *BBC*, 5 September 2014.

"Ukraine says Donetsk Operations underway", *BBC News*, 15 April 2014.

"Ukraine, Nuclear Weapons and Security Assurances", Arms Control Association, February 2022.

"Xi meets Putin ahead of Beijing Winter Olympic Opening", *South China Morning Post*, 4 February 2022.

3

The War

"Russia and Ukraine at War. It is unimaginable."

—Mikhail Gorbachev

PLANNING AND PREPARATION "The Best Laid Plans"

The War Begins

At 5 a.m. on the morning of 24 February, Russian troops debouched from their assembly areas along the Russian-Ukraine border and entered Ukraine along three main axes – from the north and northeast; from the east; and from the south and southeast. The Russian invasion of Ukraine had begun.

The preparations had begun months earlier. Around 120,000 troops of the 41st Combined Arms Army had been brought from Siberia and concentrated along the border since November. Another 30,000 troops were engaged in 'exercises' in Belarus – a Russian ally – from where they could enter Ukraine rapidly from the north. Around 40,000 troops had already been garrisoned in the Crimea since 2014 – when Russia occupied and took over the peninsula – and were poised to advance northwards. Plus, the Russian-backed separatists in the Donbas region of Eastern Ukraine had been beefed up by additional Russian troops and had stepped up their attacks on Ukrainian positions. As a prelude to war, a vicious information campaign was launched against the Ukrainian leadership and government, ostensibly to justify the coming invasion. Cyber-attacks and denial-of services attacks on government and military sites disrupted finance, transport, and communications services and downed the internet hours before the actual attack – cutting off much of the communications and information networks. The Russian build-up and preparation had been picked up by satellites and Google maps, and was monitored virtually on a real-time basis. But though the invasion was expected, the eventual scale caught many by surprise. Russia attacked virtually all along the Ukrainian frontier in the largest offensive seen in Europe since the Second World War.

On the face of it, it was expected that the Russian Army would sweep through Ukraine and reach all the way to Kyiv in a week or so. After all, the Russians have the fifth-largest army in the world, with 900,000 men in uniform and over two million reservists. Its defence budget of $ 61.7 billion was ten times that of Ukraine's $ 5.9 billion. It held 12,420 tanks, 7,500 artillery pieces and over 1,500 fighter aircraft, against Ukraine's force of around 209,000 active personnel, 2,500 tanks, 2,040 artillery pieces and just around 150 effective fighter aircraft. Like the campaign in Georgia in 2008, it was expected that the Russians would reach their objectives in a fortnight or so – a month at the most. Possibly most of the Russian troops expected to be back home for Easter, just as the German soldiers who had invaded USSR in May 1941 were sure that they would be back home for Christmas.

Ukraine was isolated and alone. No European nation, or the USA was willing to get directly involved, and their support was restricted to military aid and equipment, political and moral support and the exertion of pressure on Russia through sanctions and international isolation. Yet, the Ukrainian Army, hardened by eight years of battling separatism in Donbas, put up a stiff resistance that stalled the Russians at each juncture. They revealed courage and tactical acumen – individually and collectively – that perhaps surprised the Russians themselves, who were half-expecting a walkover. Their leadership too stood up to be counted, and President Zelensky provided an example of wartime leadership that will go down in history. And of course, the Ukrainians held the defender's advantage. They were in their own territory, knew each inch of the land, and were fighting for their homes and hearths. They could replace their losses by calling up reservists, and virtually every able-bodied male joined the war effort. They improvised beautifully too. Distilleries switched from making beer to making Molotov cocktails, pizza delivery drones, and children's quad copters were modified to act as surveillance and early warning drones. They held on with a determination that very few expected. Eventually, after months of dogged defence they followed up with their own counter-offensive in September directed at the northeast and the south, which suddenly changed the complexion of the war.

The Russians made a series of baffling tactical and strategic decisions which prevented them from achieving their aim swiftly. A war, expected to last for a week, went on for months, forcing the Russians to push in even more troops and firepower to achieve their aims and sucked them into a brutal war of attrition. The rapier thrust the Russians hoped to strike became a sledgehammer blow. For starters, the Russians made the cardinal error of moving along too many thrust lines – along the north, the east, and the south – in an area separated by over 1600 kilometres. Perhaps they hoped to emulate the German offensive of 1941 which entered the Soviet Union along three widely spread axes which addressed each part of the country – with one thrust in the north towards Leningrad, one in the centre towards the prized objective, Moscow, and one in the south towards the Caucasus. But unlike the Germans, their thrust lines lacked cohesion. Each thrust line seemed to have its own commander, and it was only in April that General Alexandr Dvornikov was appointed as the overall commander to give coordinated direction to the war. There also seems to have been a measure of overconfidence. The troops were not told their objectives – perhaps for reasons of security, and half-expected to be welcomed as 'liberators.' Perhaps their intelligence got the 'pro-Russian' sentiment wrong, and many of the soldiers were taken by surprise in the initial days when civilians began firing on them. From some accounts, ceremonial uniforms were also recovered in captured tanks and vehicles. Perhaps they were preparing for a victory parade in Kyiv after a short, victorious war. In any case the assessment of the Russian planners – both in terms of their own capabilities and the Ukrainian will to resist - was grossly off the mark.

Plus, the Russians did not even attempt to control the skies – even though they easily out-matched the Ukrainian air force in quality and quantity. It was expected that a 'shock and awe' campaign of air power would be unleashed to suppress the Ukrainian air defence and keep their aircraft on the ground. Surprisingly, only around 75 aircraft were committed – largely Sukhoi-25 ground attack aircraft. There was no determined attempt to destroy the Ukrainian air force and air defence sites, nor were concentrated air strikes made at value targets. Russia never gained control of the skies, nor were their aircraft seen actively in support of ground troops. The neglect of the air war was one of the baffling aspects of their campaign.

Even the timing of the offensive was awry. In February-March, the spring thaw sets in and the snow begins to melt, turning the ground to slush. Surely Putin and his generals would have been aware of that. After, all Russian history is full of stories of how 'Marshall Mud' and 'General Winter' defeated Napoleon's and Hitler's armies, who were traversing along the same route (albeit from opposite directions). Or perhaps the decision was taken by Putin himself, who wanted to postpone the offensive till after China's Olympic Games were over and none of his generals could contradict him. One has to only look back to India's great victory in the 1971 Bangladesh liberation war to realize the impact of timing. Mrs. Indira Gandhi – the then prime minister – had asked the Army Chief to launch an offensive into East Pakistan in April. He refused, on the grounds that the monsoon would be setting in, and the ground of East Pakistan would be flooded – impairing movement. Plus, the passes in the north would be open at this time, which would enable the Chinese to intervene. He requested for time till 15 November to launch the offensive into East Pakistan, and the results, as they say, became history. Perhaps had one of Putin's generals revealed the same professional integrity, the offensive would not have got bogged down the way it did in the initial days. The slushy ground halted all road movement enabling Russian columns to be ambushed. The videos of Russian tanks and trucks being hit by missiles and artillery, while strung out in long lines along the road, showed the effect of the awry timing. In fact, it was only in the later months, when the ground conditions improved that the Russians could make sizeable headway in the south and the east.

Logistics also played a major role. From some accounts, the Russians had faulted in their logistic planning and had not catered for the fuel and ammunition that the campaign would require. The Russian concept of logistics relies heavily on using railroads and pipelines to push forward supplies and their units and formations are notoriously short of trucks. Also, since they were road bound, they had to clear the towns and cities that stood at the road junctions. They were unable to capture most of the major towns in the initial thrust, which also stalled the forward movement of their logistics columns. The capture of the towns and cities thus became increasingly important, and much of the offensive force was sucked in to the battle of the cities which was slow, expensive and more often than not, inconclusive.

Once again, one cannot, but help comparing this offensive to the Indian campaign in East Pakistan in 1971. There too, the Pakistanis had occupied all the major towns and cities as strong points – virtual fortresses that had to be cleared to pass. The Indians then simply bypassed the cities – leaving a small force to contain it – and moved deeper towards Dacca, creating a psychological paralysis in the minds of the defenders. Perhaps the Russians could have taken a leaf out of this book and not got themselves sucked into the battle for the cities. That was what eventually spent the offensive. It is however quite significant that when the Ukrainians launched their own counter-offensive in September, they followed more innovative tactics, in which their mobile forces simply raced ahead to deep objectives, causing psychological dislocation and cutting off their opponents from the routes of withdrawal, while the infantry cleared the by-passed objective. That was one of the reasons for the stunning speed of the Ukrainian counter-offensive and the manner in which it recaptured territory in days, which the Russians had taken weeks and months to occupy.

The Overall Offensive Plan

Ukraine is the second-largest country in Europe; next only to Russia in size, with whom it shares a 2,600-kilometre-long land border. To its north lies Belarus – a Russian ally – and to the south lie the Sea of Azov and the Black Sea. The Dnieper River – which is the lifeline of the country, runs north to

south – flowing through its capital city, Kyiv, and cuts southwards down to the Black Sea. The areas east of the river adjoining Russia comprise some of its richest agricultural and industrial lands – areas that Russia seemed to have its eyes on. By all accounts, Russia hoped to push on towards the line of the Dnieper River and then simply carve the rich territories into their own land.

The long border with Russia has its challenges. Kyiv lies a good 380 kilometres from the Eastern Russian frontier, which forced it to attack the capital from Belarus in the north. In its northeast, Kharkiv, Ukraine's second-largest town, just 80 kilometres from the Russian border along with the towns of Sumy and Chuhiv form the gateway into the heart of Ukraine. To the east, lies the Donbas with its provinces of Luhansk and Donetsk – an area which held a large Russian-speaking population and where a Russian-sponsored insurgency has been raging since 2014. Much of the Russian attention was focused on the Donbas after their attempt to capture Kyiv failed, which they called "the original aim of the campaign". To the south, its 1,600-kilometre-long coastline with its port towns of Mariupol, Mykoliav, Kherson and Odesa, were its most critical areas, essential for maritime trade with the rest of the world. The coastline was broken by the Crimea, a diamond-shaped peninsula that projected into the Black Sea and was vitally important to both the Russians and the Ukrainians. The entire frontier between Russia and Ukraine was over 1,800 kilometres long, but the Russians, in their initial enthusiasm, decided to address all of it virtually simultaneously.

The jury is still out as to what exactly Putin hoped to achieve by this offensive. In many ways, it was a completely needless war. After having recognized the provinces of Luhansk and Donetsk as independent states, he had set the grounds for them to be amalgamated into Russia. Crimea in any case had been annexed in 2014. The main demand of Ukraine not going in for NATO membership had already been agreed to informally. All this would have led to a regime change – which was one of Putin's major aims – in which Zelensky would be replaced with an amenable pro-Russian president. Even if he did want a military action to demonstrate Russian might, he could have gone in for a limited action – focusing only in the Donbas and the southern sector, where his troops could be concentrated, logistic lines would be shorter and the population would not be so hostile. Those aims could have been attained relatively easily.

Instead, he decided to go in for the all-or-nothing option in which the Russian Army attacked virtually along a 1,400-kilometre-long frontage, striking Ukraine from the north towards Kyiv, from the east towards Kharkiv, from the southeast in Donbas and all along the coast line in the south. This ambitious offensive was perhaps designed to reach the line of the Dnieper River and cut off the rich Eastern region from the rest of the country. Simultaneously the capture of the coastal areas would have cut off Ukraine from the Black Sea and the Sea of Azov, crippling its economy. But the focus of the offensive, at least in the initial days, seemed to be Kyiv, whose capture would seize the nerve centre of the government and be the symbol of their complete victory. In conjunction, the three thrust lines would be able to take over the capital, seize the coast and the rich lands east of the Dnieper River, and virtually carve Ukraine into three.

The thrust lines were:

- **The Northern Front.** This offensive was launched from Belarus and directed towards Kyiv, approximately 400 km from the frontier. This offensive actually had two prongs. One – the northern thrust, comprising troops of the Eastern Military District from the 29th, 35th and 36th Combined Arms Armies – moved along highway M01, the main highway from Belarus to Kyiv, keeping east of the Dnieper River (which cut Kyiv in two). Another thrust line – the north-eastern thrust with the 41st Combined Arms Army and the 2nd Guards Combined Arms Army approached from the northeast, keeping east of the River. Both thrust lines were to converge on the town and isolate it.

- **The Eastern Front.** This was a thrust towards Kharkiv (the second largest town in Ukraine) launched by the Central Military District with the 1st Guards Tank Army and the 20th Combined Arms Army. Its aim was perhaps to capture Kharkiv and then head towards the line of the Dnieper River where it would link up with the northern thrust. This thrust actually had two components. The major one came from the northeast towards Kharkiv; and the other from the southeast from the Donbas region with the 8th Combined Arms Army and the 1st and 2nd Army Corps of the Russian separatist forces operating in the Donbas.
- **The Southern Front.** This was launched from Crimea (which was already occupied by around 30,000 Russian troops) by the Southern military district with the 58th and 49th Combined Arms Armies. It moved northwards from Crimea and fanned out along the coast to capture the coastal areas and the port towns of Odessa, Mariupol, Melitopol, and Kherson. It would move almost 200 kilometres deep and also seize the vital town of Zaporizhzhia, where the largest nuclear plant in Europe was located.

Just one glance at the map reveals that the thrust lines were widely separated and not even complementary. In a way, it was akin to the German plan for the invasion of the USSR in 1941, where they attacked on three thrust lines along the entire frontage of the Soviet Union, with the northern thrust heading for Leningrad, the central moving towards Moscow, and the southern towards Crimea and the Caucasus. Like that plan it did divide Ukrainian reaction by forcing them to commit troops virtually along the entire frontier with Russia and its ally, Belarus. But it split the Russian resources along a front almost 2,000 kilometres wide and prevented them from making a decisive thrust along any of them. The greatest weakness of this plan was that it was a little too ambitious, and while all three thrust lines made initial headway, eventually none of them could completely achieve their objectives. We will follow the progress of each of these thrust lines as we go along.

REFERENCES

"2022 Russian Invasion of Ukraine," Wikipedia, https://en.wikipedia.org

"Captured Documents Imply Ukrainian Invasion Planned," https://www.forbes.com, 3 March 2022.

"Road to War: US struggled to convince Allies and Zelensky," https://www.washingtonpost.com, 16 August 2022.

"Russia's Possible Invasion of Ukraine," https://www.csis.org, 13 January 2022.

"Ukraine Reveals Russian Military Plans for 'full-scale' Invasion," https://www.atlanticcouncil.org, 20 April 2022.

"Why has Russia Invaded Ukraine and what does Putin Want?" *BBC News*, https://www.bbc.com, 9 May 2022

THE FIRST PHASE OF THE RUSSIAN OFFENSIVE "At the Gates of Kyiv"

"I don't need a ride. I need ammunition."

—President Zelensky

The three thrusts moved out from the Russian and Belarusian frontiers almost simultaneously. From the very onset, it seemed that Kyiv was the major target. As the capital city and the fact that it housed President Zelensky and his government of 'neo-Nazis', it had an allure that Putin could not resist. A swift capture of Kyiv would have broken Ukrainian morale and brought the war to the swift and complete conclusion that Putin hoped for. But their major thrust emanated from Belarus, a different country altogether, which made problems of communication, coordination, and logistics even more difficult. Plus, it was separated by over 600 kilometres from their eastern thrust line and thus not complementary with the rest of the offensive.

The Russians were well poised to encircle Kyiv from the north and the northeast – if only they moved fast. But Kyiv would not be an easy target. This ancient town, with its spires and cobbled streets, was the largest in Ukraine and covered an area of over 800 square kilometres Its warren of streets and alleys could suck in any attacker, and its underground sewage and subway tunnels enabled defenders to move undetected from one part of the city to another. Most importantly, the Dnieper River ran through the city from north to south, dividing it in neatly in two – the eastern part and the western part. Capturing the city would thus require great coordination and suck up major resources.

The Russians planned their advance along two prongs on either side of the river. From the north, the 29th, 35th, and 36th Combined Arms Army advanced along M01 highway from the Belarus frontier, keeping west of the river. The 41st Combined Arms Army and the 2nd Guards Combined Arms Army moved in from Russia to approach the town from the northeast keeping east of the river. Their move would be more difficult. They had to clear the towns of Sula and Chernihiv en route, and also go through the Pripyat marshes which was notoriously difficult going. The two prongs were to advance simultaneously and encircle the city from both directions, isolate and invest it before its capture. But as time would reveal, the north-eastern thrust would be unduly delayed, and that would eventually delay the isolation of Kyiv and put paid to the plans for a swift capture.

The Russians had an even more ambitious plan to take over the city virtually on the first day of the operations. Air airborne assault was planned to capture Hostomel – a suburb 30 kilometres to the northwest of Kyiv, which held the crucial Antonov airfield. Its capture would give them an airhead to build up troops by air and enable them to seize the town in a swift shock operation. Had that attack succeeded, the war would have taken on an entirely different course.

At 8 a.m. on 24 February, around 30-35 MI-8 troop-carrying helicopters escorted by K-52 'Alligator' attack helicopters flew low across the border and approached Hostomel, carrying soldiers of the elite NVD and Spetznaz special forces. Flying at low levels, they reached Antonov airfield on the outskirts of Hostomel, virtually undetected, and swooped down. Ukrainian air defence guns and MANPADS downed three helicopters, but the Russian paratroopers landed, fanned out, rapidly overcame the members of the National Guard there, and secured the airfield and its runway for the main force that was to follow.

The main force comprising paratroopers of the elite 11 Guards Air Assault Brigade (or 31 Guards Air Assault Brigade (the unit has not been identified) were waiting and ready in their 18 Ilyushin IL-76 aircraft in airfields in Belarus to swoop down and take over the airfield, once it had been secured by the initial pathfinder force. But the Ukrainians responded swiftly. Their 4th Rapid Reaction Brigade based around Kyiv launched a rapid counter-attack with tanks and infantry combat vehicles that eliminated the pathfinder force and prevented the follow-up transport aircraft from landing. The Russian heliborne force, comprising some of their best troops, were cut off and suffered heavy casualties as the Ukrainians closed the pocket and were finally eliminated or captured.

Though the airborne operation had failed, Russian mechanized units were also racing towards the town. The initial plan was perhaps that the mechanized column would link up with the paratroopers at the airfield, secure it for the follow-on main force, and then launch a concerted attack on the town, while it was still relatively unprepared. From the Belarus border, Kyiv was just 180 kilometres away and the route was virtually undefended. Elements of the 37th Guards Motor Rifle Brigade and 6th Guards tank regiment reached Antonov airfield by the evening of 24 February. In the furious fighting that took place – which many describe as the most intense of the war – Antonov airfield changed hands thrice in two days. In the fighting, the world's largest aircraft – the Antonov AN-225 'Mariya' – was destroyed in its hangar. This Soviet-era aircraft was the only one of its kind in the world; a piece of aviation history and source of Ukrainian pride. Hostomel finally came into Russian hands, but the Ukrainians destroyed the runway and made it inoperable – ending any possibility of a Russian airborne attack.

With the airborne assault failing, the onus of capturing Kyiv lay with the large land columns that were closing towards the town from both the north and the northeast. The northern column moved along the M01 highway – the shortest and easiest route to Kyiv. The column from the northeast hit the abandoned town of Chernobyl – the site of the world's largest nuclear disaster. Chernobyl has been abandoned since 1986, its leaking reactor encased in steel and cement, but the movement of tanks and soldiers in the area released increased quantities of radioactivity into the air.

As the Russians were closing in on the capital city, air and missile strikes rained down on Kyiv – perhaps to soften it before the main assault. The TV tower was hit and it collapsed, the power plants were damaged and other key targets hit. Russian saboteurs infiltrated into the city and three paratroopers were killed near the Parliament building, leading to speculation that the Russians intended to assassinate Zelensky himself. Within the city, Mayor Vitali Klitschko called up reservists and all able-bodied males and distributed 18,000 rifles for 'a fight to the finish'. Molotov cocktails were prepared and distributed and anti-tank defences and steel 'hedgehogs' came up on the crossroads and on the main arteries leading into the city. It now seemed a matter of time, before Kyiv would fall, and the USA even offered President Zelensky a helicopter to take him out of the city. His reply, "I don't need a ride, I need ammunition" was a classic of wartime leadership and helped galvanize the defenders. Had Zelensky fled – as did Afghan President Ghani when the Taliban approached Kabul – the story of the war would have been much different.

By 28 February, the situation was dire. A 64-kilometre-long column of tanks and trucks carrying around 30,000 troops was approaching the city along the main road from the north. Another force was closing in from the northeast. It seemed but a matter of time that the two forces would close in and tighten the noose.

And then, inexplicably, the 64-kilometre-long column stopped.

The column had been barrelling down the road from Belarus to Kyiv – undeterred by sporadic air and artillery attacks – when it halted around the evening of 28 February. Even today, it is unclear why the column halted the way it did. The halt has been attributed to faulty logistics. Ostensibly, they ran out of fuel. Russian units and formations are known to be light in load-carrying trucks and can cater for an advance of just around 90 kilometres, before being replenished by follow-on supply units and pipelines. But that seems unlikely. After all, the column would have catered for enough fuel for the advance to contact, and had not fought any major action that would have depleted its fuel or ammunition. In all probability, the column halted while it awaited the thrust line from the northeast to move forward for a coordinated attack on the town.

The North-eastern thrust had more difficult going on the way to Kyiv. It had to clear Sumy and Chernihiv, two border towns along the route. The Russians entered both towns, but were unable to occupy them completely. Very often, the defenders would simply melt away, ambush the vehicles in the narrow roads, and once the Russians withdrew, simply re-occupy the positions.

Though Sumy was almost completely reduced to rubble, Chernihiv held on virtually till the end of the battle – earning the title of 'Hero City' for its staunch defence. The battles were a foretaste of the heavy fighting in built-up areas that awaited the Russians if they entered Kyiv. Yet, in spite of delays, the Russian prong advanced and on 4 March reached Brovary, a suburb around 30 kilometres northeast of Kyiv. Brovary and other suburbs were occupied on 6 March and the Russians started fanning out to isolate the town, as a prelude to its capture.

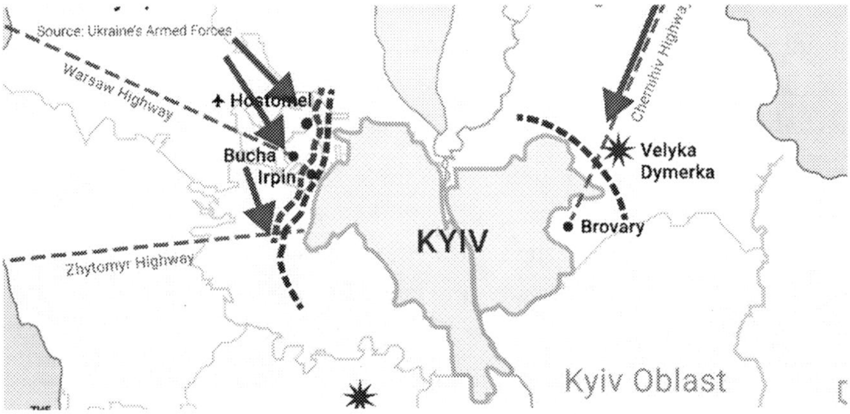

The Russian Advance towards Kyiv

The main column approaching from the north, which had halted 30 kilometres from Kyiv for eight crucial days, finally began moving on 7 March and moved to contact Kyiv. But the halt and needless delay had given the defenders adequate time to prepare obstacles and defensive lines, move up reserves and additional troops into the town. It also allowed the Western countries to fly in much-needed arms and equipment – especially anti-tank missiles and SAMs – to beef up the defences. As the column resumed its move, it approached Kyiv and then fanned out to begin the process of encircling the town and isolating it. The suburbs of Irpin, Bucha and Hostomel were captured as the Russians came within 20 km of Kyiv. In the ast, the suburb of Brovary fell into Russian hands as did other critical townships. Kyiv was being slowly isolated from the northeast and the southwest and the crucial highways leading to it – the Warsaw, Zhytomyr and Chernihiv highways were blocked one by one. Artillery and rocket batteries occupied gun areas, and for the first-time artillery fire hit the outskirts of the town, giving a foretaste of their deadly destructive power. With the Russian concept of massed artillery fire, it was felt they would use their dreaded artillery to simply reduce the town to smithereens before their infantry moved in as it had done in Grozny in 1991 and with some of the Syrian rebel towns in the Syrian war. A psychological campaign was launched on social media and television, calling on the defenders to surrender, and emphasizing that the Russian battle was with the "neo-Nazis of the Government" and not the people. Chechen and Syrian fighters, known for their brutality, were inducted around the town, in a throwback to earlier, more barbaric times, when a besieged town would be threatened with large-scale destruction if they did not surrender early.

But the very capture of the suburbs would have given the Russians an idea of the bitter fighting in built-up areas and all the problems it entailed. Sniping and ambushes took a heavy toll and apparently their logistics too failed to reach the forward troops in time. (To get an idea of the scale of the problems, it required 80 trucks travelling 200 kilometres to carry ammunition for just one artillery salvo). The town itself had a perimeter of around 800 square kilometres and it is unlikely that the Russians would have had the resources to isolate a town of that size effectively. Its capture of course, would have required twice as many troops and the scale of casualties and destruction would have been horrendous. The Russians could never completely isolate Kyiv, and to prove a point Zelensky invited UK Prime Minister Boris Johnson and UN Secretary-General Antonio Guterres to visit the town, which only highlighted Ukrainian resistance.

Though humanitarian corridors were established to permit movement of civilians, there was great damage to civilian lives and infrastructure. Throughout the first two weeks of March, the Russians continued firing and launching missile strikes into the city (as per Russian accounts, the scale of attacks in the city was deliberately reduced to prevent civilian casualties and only 'military targets' were attacked.) but the much-anticipated attack did not come. Perhaps the Russians had already overstretched themselves by then. The Ukrainians took advantage of the lull to launch their own counter-offensive on 22 March and began retaking the lost suburbs one by one. The Russians were gradually pushed back from the outskirts of the town, but surprisingly, the Ukrainians did not meet the kind of resistance they expected. In most cases, the Russians simply withdrew, leaving behind scenes of carnage and destruction. In Irpin and Bucha, bodies of shot civilians and mass graves were found, prompting calls for investigations into war crimes. Slowly, each of the outlying areas were retaken by the Ukrainians as the Russians withdrew.

Then, on 29 March, Russia abruptly announced, that it was withdrawing its forces from the Kyiv area to 'focus on the original aim of the campaign – the Donbas in the East'. That explained the reason for the lack of resistance as the Ukrainians retook the lost areas around the town. The Russians moved back in relatively good order and by 6 April were back across the border. The Ukrainians retook the occupied areas – in spite of the mines and demolitions left in their wake – and the threat to Kyiv receded. Russia claimed that its withdrawal was planned and that there was never any intention to take Kyiv; those actions were merely to draw Ukrainian forces from the area of decision, the eastern front. But that was just a cover up. After all, the Russians would not have committed almost 30,000-35,000 of their best troops had it not been a definite objective. The Russians did have plans for taking over the town, but miscalculated badly in terms of manpower, supplies and resources. Once the air borne assault failed, any hope of a rapid land assault to take the town had little chance of success.

Kyiv was never a viable objective and even had the land offensive not halted the way it did, it is unlikely that the Russians would have been able to capture a town of that size. They would have been sucked into the 'Battle of Zelenskygrad' in much the same way that the Germans were sucked into a needless battle for Stalingrad in the winter of 1942. Even had they entered the town, their troops would have suffered very heavy casualties and would have been in danger of being cut off by a Ukrainian counter-offensive that could sever their supply lines. (Once again, akin to the manner in which the Soviets had trapped the entire German Sixth Army in Stalingrad and then decimated it in detail after its routes of supply and withdrawal were cut off). Their decision to withdraw from Kyiv, though belated, was a correct military decision.

The jury is still out as to what Russia hoped to attain by its actions towards Kyiv. For one, by opening the northern front from Belarus towards Kyiv, the frontage of the offensive increased by over 600 kilometres and became virtually unmanageable. Coordinating the offensive from the soil of a third nation further complicated logistics and control. The force level that the Russians employed would not suffice for a large town like Kyiv. Perhaps they hoped to capture it in the first few hours through its airborne force – and had they succeeded, it would have been a different story. After their airborne operation failed, the ground forces had a far more difficult task ahead, and it was well beyond their capabilities, which they recognized at a belated stage.

Slowly, the action eased around Kyiv. Missile attacks did strike the town from time to time, which virtually continued throughout the war, more as an intimidatory signal than anything else. The town went back to its routine. The trains and trams came back and ran largely on schedule. Traffic and revellers thronged the streets, even though the air raid sirens did go off from time to time. Zelensky and his government continued to oversee the war effort; and he maintained his nightly address to his countrymen, at 9 p.m. on the dot. Visits of world leaders to the town, continued, largely as a symbol of support and solidarity, and gradually the threat to Kyiv receded.

Further to the west, the border town of Lyiv, just 19 kilometres from the Polish border, also received considerable Russian attention. Lyiv was the transit point where Western arms were received, stocked and then sent eastwards for distribution amongst Ukrainian forces. Its warehouses were hit repeatedly by Russian rockets and missiles – including the long-range hypersonic Kinzhal missiles – which destroyed large consignments of newly-received aid and equipment. The strikes on Lyiv were a clear signal that Russia could escalate the war should the Western powers intervene directly, but though it did cause significant damage initially, gradually the attacks reduced as Russia focused its attention on other sectors.

The action now shifted towards the north-eastern front, in the area of Kharkiv; in the eastern sector of the Donbas; and towards the south along the coastal belt and port cities on the Sea of Azov and the Black Sea, where the Russians did make significant gains. We will see how the action unfolded in these sectors, one by one.

REFERENCES

"At the Edge of Kyiv, Ukrainians on the Counter-offensive," *The New York Times*, 26 March 2022.

"Battle of Kyiv – 2022," https://en.wikipedia.org

"Kyiv Region 'Liberated' from Russian Invaders," *Ukrinform*, 2 April 2022.

"Moscow says it will curb Assault on Kyiv: Russian Troops withdrawing," *Times of Israel*, 2 April 2022.

"Russia failed to take Kyiv; was Key Objective," *The Independent*, 30 March 2022.

"Russia forced into Retreat from Ukraine Airport," *The Telegraph*, 31 March 2022.

"Russian Convoy north of Kyiv stretches for 40 Miles–MAXAR" *Reuters*, 1 March 2022.

"Russian Military Convoy advances on Kyiv," *CBC News*, 1 March 2022.

"Ukraine says it Repels Russian Attack on Kyiv Base," *Reuters*, 26 February 2022.

"Why has Russia's 64-kilometer-long Convoy Stopped Moving," *BBC News*, 3 March 2022.

THE NORTH EASTERN FRONT (FEB – MAY 22)
"The Battle of Kharkiv – Again"

German Troops Entering Kharkiv, August 1941

To the northeast of Ukraine, lies Kharkiv – an old town, steeped in over a millennium of history and culture. Ukraine's second-largest town, it is just thirty kilometres from the Russian border and in a way is guard the approach into Ukraine from the northeast. Kharkiv is no stranger to war. During World War II, some of the major battles of took place in and around it, when German and Soviet armies clashed for control of this vital town. (Kharkov, as it was known then). It was captured by the Germans in autumn 1941 when their forces decimated over half a million Soviet soldiers in a classical encirclement around the town. It fell back into Soviet hands in the closing days of 1942, only to be recaptured by a stunning counter-offensive by General Manstien, and then was lost again in the summer of 1943 when the Soviet armies began pushing the Germans slowly but inexorably, from their soil. The town was destroyed in the World War only to be rebuilt back to its former glory once again.

This old and beautiful town was again under attack – this time from the opposite direction, and by a former sibling – the Russians. As in the World War, the town became the site of advances, retreats and counter-offensives that helped decide the outcome of the overall war. On the very first day of the war – 24 February – the town was contacted by Russian forces that had concentrated in the area of Belgorod, and advanced into Ukraine, in conjunction with the other thrust lines. Kharkiv, Ukraine, just 35 kilometres from the Russian border was the gateway to the east, and had to be cleared to enable the Russians to move up to the Dnieper River and the rich lands of Eastern Ukraine.

By 25 February, the Russians reached the northern suburbs and began taking over the villages in the perimeter. The town was subjected to a series of artillery and missile attacks and Kharkiv, along with Mariupol, suffered most extensively at Russian hands. The softening-up process killed an estimated 2,000 residents, including Yevgeny Malyshew, a biathlete, who was a member of the Ukrainian national team. The intensive shelling also killed a 21-year-old Indian student, Naveen, S G, a student of Kharkiv National Medical University, as he stood in line to buy groceries. Almost half the 8,000 Indian students in Ukraine were located in Kharkiv and Sumy, and it is to the credit of the Indian government, that all of them were evacuated safety, except for this one unfortunate casualty.

The Russians made their first major effort to seize the town in the early morning of 27 February as armour and infantry closed in after an intensive artillery barrage. A large column of tanks and military vehicles penetrated the lines and entered the city, almost reaching the town square. This attack was beaten back in a much-publicized ambush with halted the column and attacked them with drones and artillery fire. The remnants were counter-attacked by Ukraine's 92 Mechanized Brigade and forced to withdraw, leaving behind seven tanks and APCs.

Even as Kharkiv was being addressed, further to the northeast, the smaller town of Sumy was similarly contacted by the Russians in the early hours of 24 February. In the surprise of the initial attacks, the Russians captured half the city by 26 February, only to be evicted by a Ukrainian counter-attack by the end of the day. Sumy, like Kharkiv held on, and their stubborn defence largely reduced the Russian threat in the northeast.

Kharkiv remained cut off and settled down to a long hard grind. Raids and attacks on the town continued, virtually on a daily basis. Russian paratroopers launched a major raid on 2 March, but were rapidly counter-attacked and not allowed to establish a foothold. The fighting in Kharkiv became confused street fighting, with individual battles raging at every street and cross road. The Ukrainians held on and succeeded in pushing back each ingress. Even the Russians who entered the city got a rude welcome; not the warm reception, they had been told to expect. Videos emerged of a civilian coolly walking up to a Russian tank, as its crew looked confusedly around, lifting his rocket launcher, firing and destroying the tank and calmly walking away. Two soldiers of the 3rd Motor Rifle Division were killed and 28 others hospitalized when "a kind, elderly lady" handed out cakes to them, which later turned out to be laced with cyanide. The reception at Kharkiv was a foretaste of what was to come in other cities as well.

As attack after attack stalled, Major-General Vitaly Gerasimov, the deputy commander of the 41st Combined Arms Army moved ahead to urge his troops forward, and was killed in a sniper attack. A major factor of this campaign was the inordinately high killing of senior Russian officers – whose locations were detected when they used unsecured communications networks. US intelligence also helped identify and target senior commanders and provided advance information of Russian movements and plans.

For much of March and early April, the city remained besieged. Then in mid-April, the Russians withdrew from the Kyiv sector and renewed their focus in the east. The actions to capture Kharkiv intensified as many of the troops who were released from Kyiv were sent to this sector. Villages around the town changed hands with bewildering frequency, with villages being captured and retaken in the course of a single day. The dreaded Russian artillery and rocket batteries subjected the town to terrible shelling which took a terrible toll of civilian lives. Over 60,000 civilians were evacuated along humanitarian corridors, but those who remained faced the firing virtually daily for over three months.

The tide changed around the first week of May. On 6 May, the Ukrainians launched a counter-offensive along a broad front, north and south of Kharkiv. The offensive – spearheaded by the 92nd and 93rd Mechanized Brigades – successfully recaptured around 40 villages around the town, and forced the artillery batteries to pack up and move away. The Ukrainian offensive advanced east of the town, a manoeuvre that could have cut off the Russians from their supply lines in Belgorod within Russia. By the second week of May, the Russians began withdrawing from Kharkiv, in much the same manner they had withdrawn from Kyiv. By most accounts, the Russians did not fight a delaying battle, but concentrated on preserving their supply lines. The Ukrainians pushed eastwards and reached the line of the Siverskyi Donets River, where, in a major action, they destroyed a Russian pontoon bridge and cut off their routes of retreat. In the chaotic withdrawal that followed, the Ukrainians claimed to have decimated two complete battalion tactical groups and captured much of their heavy equipment. The Ukrainians advanced virtually up to the border and reconnaissance units of the 227 Battalion posted selfies of themselves standing by the border pillars, which were flashed across the world as proof of the Ukrainian victory at Kharkiv.

The Russian pull-back from the Kharkiv region was announced in much the same way as their pull-back from Kyiv. The Russian spokesman of the Defence Ministry simply announced that the Russians were "pulling back to better positions." But it did not hide the fact that along two major fronts – Kyiv in the north and Kharkiv in the northeast – the Russians had been unable to attain any of their objectives and were forced to withdraw. The success of the Ukrainian counter=attack had revealed the vulnerability of the over-extended Russians. In a way, their withdrawal from these areas, shortened the front considerably and they could focus on the prime objectives of Donbas in the east, and the coastal areas of the south.

With the Ukrainian re-taking of the areas around Kharkiv and north-eastern Ukraine, the overall threat reduced considerably. This would have a long-term impact. Later in September, the Ukrainians would use the same area around Kharkiv to launch another counter-offensive and this time the results would be even more decisive. The second Kharkiv counter-offensive of 22 September would perhaps change the course of the entire war.

REFERENCES

"A large column of Russian vehicles pushing in to Sumy", *The Kyiv Independent*, 27 February 2022.

"Ex-Biathlete of Ukrainian National team dies in War", *Odessa Journal*, 1 March 2022.

"Heaviest fighting in Ukraine, in and around Kharkiv", *CNN*, 26 February 2022.

"Indian Student killed in Shelling in Kharkiv", *The New Indian Express*, 2 March 2022.

"More than 60,000 evacuated from Kharkiv, says Governor," *Nova Chas*, 8 March 2022.

"No Indian left in Kyiv," NDTV.com, 2 March 2022.

"On the front lines of the Battle of Kharkiv," *BBC,* 10 May 2022.

"Russian Armoured Vehicles meet tough Resistance in Kharkiv," *Wall Street Journal*, 27 February 2022.

"Russian pullback from Kharkiv," *The New York Times*, 9 May 2022

"*The Battles of Kharkov–1941-43*," Casemate Publishers.

"Ukraine claims it killed Russian General during fighting in Kharkiv." *The Independent*, 8 March 2022.

"Ukraine has won Battle of Kharkiv," *The Guardian*, 14 May 2022.

"Ukrainian soldiers clash in fierce fight near Sumy," *The Kyiv Independent,* 24 February 2022.

Scully Rachel, "2 Russians killed, 28 hospitalized, after being poisoned," *The Hill*, 4 April 2022.

THE SECOND PHASE: RUSSIAN OFFENSIVE IN THE SOUTH AND EAST

"It is not just a Battle for the Coast; it is a battle for Ukraine's future."

The Southern Front

The war in the south actually began when Russia annexed the Crimean Peninsula in March 2014 following the Maidan Protests (See 'The Backdrop to War'). As the protests intensified, pro-Russian supporters (actively aided by Russia) seized the Parliament building. Russia used this act to remove the government council and install a pro-Russian government, conduct a referendum (in which over 90 per cent overwhelmingly voted to join Russia) and formally annexed Crimea into Russia. The annexation was criticized resoundingly by the West, which unleashed a raft of sanctions that had little effect. It did not change the *fait accompli.* Crimea, always considered "historically Russia", came back under Russian sway and soon 20,000 troops were garrisoned there and built up their naval and air elements in the strategic peninsula.

In the winter of 2021 as tensions rose, Russia concentrated its forces for an invasion of Ukraine, and placed an additional 20,000 troops in the Crimea. They would be used for an invasion from the south to seize the critical coastal areas and ports along the Sea of Azov and the Black Sea. Additional troops also built up in the Donetsk region from where they could advance from the east, and trap the Ukrainians in a pincer. The Russian aim seemed to be the seizure of the entire coastline right from Mariupol in the east to Odesa in the west, a swathe of over 400 kilometres. It was an ambitious plan, and if it succeeded it would have cut off Ukraine from the sea, made it landlocked and completely dependent on Russia.

On 24 February, troops of the 58th Army, the 8th Guards Combined Army and the 22th Army Corps moved from their bases in Crimea and advanced northwards towards the Ukrainian mainland. They had to cross the narrow Isthmus of Perekop to enter the mainland and in one of the first actions of the war, the Ukrainians destroyed a vital bridge on the Isthmus to slow the Russian advance. Vitali Shakun, a combat engineer responsible for the demolition, detonated the explosives while on the bridge, killing himself, but denying that vital bridge to the Russians. He was awarded a posthumous 'Hero of Ukraine' – Ukraine's highest award – for his act.

Though delayed, the Russians continued their advance northwards, from the Crimean Peninsula into the mainland. They soon secured the North Crimean Canal – a canal emanating from the Dnieper that supplied 85 per cent of Crimea's drinking water, which had been blocked by Ukraine after Russia took over the Crimea in 2014. The resumption of drinking water into Crimea was heralded as a major victory by Moscow, and a sign that their initial offensive was going well.

The Russian southern offensive moved upwards in three prongs. One moved eastwards towards Mariupol – the vital port town just 30 kilometres away from the Donbas. The thrust towards Mariupol was reinforced by a detachment of Russian troops and fighters from the Donetsk People's Republic, who moved out of Donetsk to approach Mariupol from the east. Another thrust line moved northwards towards Melitopol and then further on towards Zaporizhzhia – the site of Ukraine's largest nuclear power plant. Perhaps that thrust line was designed to link up with the eastern thrust line – a manoeuvre that would carve out the entire eastern areas of Ukraine and bring it under Russian control. The third thrust moved westwards towards the port towns of Kherson and Mykolaiv. Taken together, the three prongs of the southern offensive, would have carved a swathe of land over 200 kilometres deep all along the coast and seized the entire coastline along the Sea of Azov and the Black Sea along with its vital ports.

Further to the west, an ambitious amphibious assault was planned on Odesa, Ukraine's major port on the Black Sea. Half of Ukraine's exports and imports moved through this port and it was the last major city on the coastline. Beyond it, the route was open to Transnistria and Moldova. Russia also had its eyes on the large Russian-speaking population of Transnistria, and perhaps one of the eventual goals of the offensive was to reach it and amalgamate it into Russia like the other Ukrainian regions they had annexed. The loss of Odesa would have been comparable to the loss of Kyiv or Kharkiv and its defences were hurriedly built up as residents sandbagged the perimeter, mined the vulnerable areas along the shore and prepared hedgehog defences along the crossroads. A barrage of 60 missiles hit Odesa which severely damaged its infrastructure in the initial days. Satellite images detected a complete amphibious brigade along with a large naval component which seemed to have assembled for the assault. By some accounts, the assault on Odesa was to have been launched at the very onset of the operation. But the much-anticipated amphibious assault was called off at virtually the last moment.

The Russians set out to dominate the coast by launching missile strikes from their warships in the Black Sea. Islands along the coastline were also seized. Snake Island, a major base, just south of Odesa was approached by MOSKVA – the flag ship of the Black Sea fleet – with an ultimatum to surrender. Its defenders replied with the classic, "Russian warship, Go F—k yourself" – a slogan that emblazoned itself in social media, T-shirts and coffee mugs – even in a postage stamp. Roman Hybov, the soldier of the Ukrainian border guard who reportedly made the defiant statement was later awarded the 'Hero of Ukraine' award. Yet, contrary to the initial reports, the 13 soldiers on the rocky outcrop did not die defending the island to the last man and last round. They surrendered instead and were taken into captivity, to be later released in a prisoner swap.

In the first few days of the war, the Russian advance was rapid. The 22nd army corps moved almost 80 kilometres northwards and on 26 February, laid siege to the town of Enerhodar and occupied the Zaporizhzhia nuclear plant – the largest power plant in Europe. That was a huge blow for Ukraine, and put its largest nuclear power plant in Russian hands. During the cross firing, a fire broke out in one of the training facilities of the complex, but fortunately was controlled in time. None of the stowage buildings or the main reactors were affected and there was no radiation leak. However, throughout the occupation of the plant, fears of inadvertent shelling or damage to the crucial nuclear plant remained.

The Russian thrust line moving westwards, rapidly captured Kherson on 2 March, which became the first major city to be captured. The international airport came into Russian hands, its mayor was arrested, and the municipal administration replaced with a pro-Russian council. Like other towns invested by the Russians, Kherson suffered tremendous damage from the strikes that preceded its capture. Concurrently, the Russians also approached the towns of Melitopol and Berdiansk. Russian forces captured Berdiansk on 28 February 2022, and seized six Ukrainian patrol boats in harbour; one of the major successes of the southern campaign. Melitopol, a vital ship-building centre, was attacked on 25 February and captured after heavy fighting on 1 March. One by one, the port towns began falling into Russian hands as they seized control of the entire coast.

The Russians discovered that occupying a town was a far cry from holding it. The troops were subject to sniper attacks and ambushes. Resentful civilians attacked them with Molotov cocktails and other expedients. One video circulating on social media showed an old woman offering a packet of sunflower seeds to a bewildered-looking Russian soldier telling him to put it in his pocket, so that it would sprout sunflowers when he was killed and buried on their soil. Another video showed a Russian tank approaching a town square with its commander telling the local population to stop resisting. A civilian calmly walked up to the tank with a rocket launcher and fired on the tank setting it ablaze. It seemed that the Russian soldiers were actually taken by surprise at the level of anger and resentment amongst the local population. They were perhaps half-expecting to be greeted as 'liberators.'

The third prong of the southern offensive moved eastwards in the direction of Mariupol, just 30 kilometres from the Donbas. This was launched in conjunction with attacks by the pro-Russian separatists of the Donetsk provinces, who approached it from the east. The Russian offensive was actually remarkably successful. It captured areas along the coast line almost 200 kilometres deep, and took control of most of the major cities – including

The Southern Thrust

Kherson, Mykolaiv, Melitopol, Zaporizhzhia and Berdiansk. Virtually all of Kherson and Zaporizhzhia oblasts were in their hands. From here, they could go westwards towards Odesa, move northwards to link up with their eastern thrust line. and also form a land bridge to connect the Donbas with the Crimea. It was quite a major achievement, but one prize still eluded the Russians. Mariupol, the crucial port town in the east which still held on. The story of its defence and ultimate fall is one of the most stirring stories of the war.

The Battle for Mariupol

Mariupol is the largest city of the Donetsk oblast – the southern province of the Donbas which is largely controlled by Russian-backed separatists of the Donetsk People's Republic (DPR). It is one of the largest Russian-speaking cities of Ukraine. After the siege of the city which destroyed over 95 per cent of its infrastructure and killed an estimated 1400 civilians, most of the Russian-speaking population, switched to Ukrainian, rather than speak the language of 'the invader'.

The city is also a major industrial hub and home to Ukraine's largest steel plant, the Azovstal Iron and Steel Works. Located just 30 kilometres from Donetsk, it is essential to provide a land bridge to the Crimea.

The city was in the forefront of the war since May 2014, when the uprising in Crimea and Donbas began. Militants of the Russian-backed DPR took control of the city and forced Ukrainian troops to abandon it. That very month, Ukrainian troops recaptured the vital city, which then faced repeated attacks by DPR fighters who vowed to capture it. Fighting continued for months till the ceasefire came into place with the signing of the Minsk Accord and the conflict was finally frozen.

One of the major groups involved in the recapture and defence of Mariupol was the Azov battalion, a Ukrainian volunteer militia, with openly neo-Nazi and ultra-nationalistic views. They even sport the SS insignia on their badges and give the Nazi salute. Members of the Azov battalion, along with the 36th Marine Brigade and members of the territorial defence forces held the city even now. As one of Putin's goals of "de-Nazification of Ukraine", Mariupol and its defenders became an important ideological and symbolic target, besides of its strategic importance as the gateway to the Crimea.

On 24 February, Russian artillery pounded the city in a foretaste of what was to come. The same day, Russian forces, along with their supporters of the DPR, advanced from the Donetsk in the east, hoping to capture the border town with a swift land attack. This force was halted near the village of Pavlopil, and in a major encounter was forced to withdraw with the loss of 22 tanks and armoured personnel carriers. At the same time, the Russians launched an amphibious assault around 70 kilometres west of Mariupol on the night of 25 February, deploying around 2,000 marines who established a beachhead and then began moving towards Mariupol.

By 1 March, Russian and DPR forces advancing from the east linked up with the marines moving in from the west and by 2 March, Mariupol was completely surrounded. A naval blockade from the sea completed the encirclement, and slowly the noose around the town tightened. The Russians called on the defenders to surrender – an offer that was rudely rebuffed. The city was rapidly running out of food, fuel and supplies. The last cellular tower was hit and all mobile and internet communication services were completely cut. As the city was being bombarded into submission – an estimated 60-70 artillery and missile strikes were made daily in the worst days of March – the mayor appealed for a humanitarian corridor to enable citizens to leave the war zone. Over 200,000 civilians were evacuated, but most still remained and the war continued around them for months to come.

Throughout March, Mariupol remained under siege, subject to attacks virtually every day. On 20 March, DPR forces broke through the inner line of defences and captured the international airport, cutting off the last tenuous link with the rest of the world. The few supplies that were flown in by air stopped. Russian fighters reached the city centre, and captured the railway station, the radio and television buildings and other important communication centres. Russian units entering the town were soon engaged in house-to-house battles, sniping and bitter street fighting, akin to what must have gone on during the bitter siege of Stalingrad in the winter of 1942. Amongst the over 2,000 Russian casualties in the town, was Major-General Oleg Mityaev, the commander of the 150th Motorized Rifle Division, who was killed trying to lead yet another unsuccessful attack into the town.

By end March, even though Mariupol remained notionally under Ukrainian control, its forces had run out of food and ammunition, medical supplies and even clean drinking water. The situation was dire and on 4 April, 267 marines of the Ukrainian naval forces surrendered *en masse* (The Russians claim that 2,000 had surrendered). This act caused tremendous acrimony amongst the fanatical Azov battalion, whose members accused the marines of cowardice. With this surrender, which was done without informing the defenders still holding out, a vast gap came up in the positions. There was no coordinated line of defence now and the remnants of the marines and the Azov battalion fought in isolated pockets of resistance, with virtually each man for himself.

Mariupol was a shattered city, but the beleaguered defenders still held out desperately. The 36th Marine Brigade tried to break out of the ring around them, but were cut down by fire and many were killed or captured. The remnants, mainly from the fanatical Azov battalion, finally holed out in the Azovstal steel plant – "The Fortress within the City". On 20 April, Putin announced the 'liberation of Mariupol' but refused to order a storming of the plant, choosing instead to exhaust the defenders into submission. Even as the Azovstal steel plant held out, the Russians began clearing the rubble and on 9 May – Russia's Victory Day – held a victory parade in the streets of Mariupol.

The 82-day long battle of Mariupol finally ended on 17 May when the last bastion – the remaining Ukrainians in the Azovstal steel plant – finally surrendered and were led away into captivity in buses emblazoned with the infamous 'Z'. Its stubborn defence was very much like the role the German 6th army played in Stalingrad in the winter of 1942. Though cut off and virtually decimated, the 6th army held on for three months tying down Soviet troops who could have been used elsewhere. Similarly, Mariupol tied down 10-12 battalion operating groups for months and divided the Russian forces east and west of the city.

Mariupol was the city that suffered the most during the war. Over 95 per cent of the town was destroyed and over 20,000 civilians reportedly killed during the fighting for the city. The capture of Mariupol – though at great cost – was one of the notable Russian successes of the war. With this, the land route all along the coast to Crimea was open. It now gave the Russians full control of the Sea of Azov and provided an unbroken stretch of eastern and southern Ukraine around the size of Greece. The area extended 800 kilometres from Luhansk in the east to Kherson on the Black Sea. The Russians set about fortifying the positions, erecting barriers and digging trenches to stave off Ukrainian counter-attacks. They installed pro-Russian mayors and placed their own governing bodies in the captured territories to 'Russify' them.

The Russians also suffered a huge loss of prestige and naval capability when the flag ship of the Black Sea Fleet, – the MOSKVA, was sunk in a missile attack on 14 April. The MOSKVA was patrolling off the Black Sea coast when it was hit by two Neptune anti-ship missiles fired from the coast. The ship caught fire and the crew were evacuated, but it sank while being towed away. The Russians denied that it had been hit by missiles, attributing the loss to an internal fire, but satellite images confirmed that the ship had indeed been hit by missiles. Ironically, the MOSKVA was built in the very same ports of Melitopol and Mykolaiv in 1983 – when Ukraine was part of the Soviet Union – which it now bombed and from where the missiles that sank it were fired. With the loss of the MOSVKA their ships were now forced to keep a considerable distance from the coast – reducing their ability to influence operations on land, or even launch amphibious operations.

With Mariupol under their belt, the Russians now had a base from where they could advance northwards to link up with the eastern thrust, or even develop operations further west along the coast towards the prize of Odesa. Though the south with virtually the entire areas of the Kherson and Zaporizhzhia oblast were under Russian control, it would discover that holding on to an area was even more difficult than capturing it. They would face the brunt of the Ukrainian offensives when they came in September, but for now, they turned their attention to the next major objective of the campaign – Donbas in the east.

REFERENCES

"Fighting reaches Centre of Mariupol," *Radio Free Europe*, 23 March 2022.

"Fourth Russian General killed in Ukraine," *MSN*, 18 March 2022.

"Melitopol city taken by Russian Army," *Marca*, Spain, 26 February 2022.

"Putin calls off plan to Storm Mariupol Plant, opts for Blockade instead," *Reuters*, 21 April 2022.

"Putin reclaims Crimea for Russia and denounces West," *The New York Times*, 18 March 2014.

"Putin signs Russia-Crimea Treaty," *BBC News*, 18 March 2014.

"Russia says Ukrainian Marines surrendered in Mariupol," *Eurasian Times*, 6 April 2022.

"Russia's amphibious Operations Dilemma, www.navalnews.com, 20 March 2022.

"Russian forces unblock water flow of Canal to Crimea, Moscow says," *Reuters*, 1 March 2022.

"Russian Offensive Campaign Assessment," Institute for the Study of War, 28 February 2022.

"Russian troops in Final Stages of Readiness, add to Worries for Ukraine," *The New York Times*, 25 February 2022.

"Russian Troops take Zaporizhzhia Nuclear Plant," *ABC News*, 4 March 2022.

"Russian-speakers in Ukraine are struggling to learn a new tongue," *The Economist*, 27 August 2022.

"Sinking of the MOSKVA: What we Know," https://www.theguardian.com, 15 April 2022

"Strategic port of Mariupol now Surrounded by Russian forces," *BBC News*, 4 March 2022.

"Surrender of last of Azovstal ends Ukraine most Brutal siege," https://atalayar.com, 21 May 2022.

"The Azov Battalion", *CBS News*, 22 March 2022.

"Ukraine gives medal to Soldier who told Russian warship to 'go f—-," https://www.theguardian.com, 29 March 2022.

"Ukraine Marine blows himself to delay Russian Advance," https://www.ndtv.com, 26 February 2022.

"Ukrainian Forces retake Port City from Rebels," *Reuters*, 14 June 2014.

Max Hundar. "Timeline – Russia's siege of Mariupol," *Reuters*, 30 March 2022.

Michael Schwartz. "First Ukraine city falls as Russia Strikes more Civilian Targets," *The New York Times*, 3 March 2022.

THE CAULDRON IN THE DONBAS

"The Donbas has been frothing and fermenting since 2014. But this is unlike anything I have seen before."

—Unknown Ukrainian Soldier

In the winter of 1942, the German Sixth Army was trapped inside the ruins of Stalingrad, surrounded by Soviet forces. The ring of steel around them closed within which Germans units and formations were gradually encircled and destroyed. The Germans called it 'Hexenkessel – a witch's cauldron. A cauldron that frothed and foamed and swirled; and then trapped and consumed all within it till the final denouement.

The Donbas has also earned the moniker 'The Cauldron'. The Russian offensive in the Donbas has seen heavy, confused fighting with immense losses to both sides. The tactics followed by the Russians closely resemble those followed by the Soviet-era armies. Slow advances and encirclements, a massive pounding of the trapped forces by artillery, and then an overwhelming assault to finish off the remnants of the defenders. Like Stalingrad and Kursk, the battles involved a series of skirmishes all along the front, and like those two famous battles, the outcome of the Battle of Donbas had a major impact on the war.

The cauldron in the Donbas has been simmering since 2014. In March 2014, as the Maidan protests rocked the country and a strong pro- and anti-Russian sentiment spread across the nation, the provinces of Luhansk and Donetsk which make up the Donbas too came under the fervour. The population of the Donbas is largely ethnic Russian and a series of pro-Russian riots broke out in the Donetsk and Luhansk oblasts of Eastern Ukraine. These protests coincided with the Russian annexation of Crimea and were undoubtedly orchestrated by Russia. Russian-backed separatists of the Donetsk People's Republic and the Luhansk People's Republic seized government buildings, held officials hostage, and launched a widespread campaign of armed conflict against the Ukrainian forces under the banner of 'Russiyana'.

Ukraine responded by launching what they termed "Anti-Terror Operations" against the separatists' groups in April 2014. Security forces were pushed in, and a series of military operations regained control of the Donbas and pushed the separatists back to the Russia-Ukraine border. With their proxy groups on the back foot, Russia intervened directly. They sent in convoys of 'humanitarian aid' to help the 'oppressed, Russian speaking population". They also pumped in special forces personnel and advisors to help the separatists, along with vast quantities of military aid that was smuggled in the humanitarian convoys. Although Russia staunchly denies it, the presence of 'Little Green Men' operating on Ukrainian soil has been an open secret since 2014.

The Minsk Agreement signed between Ukraine, Russia and the separatist groups finally brought a ceasefire in the Donbas, but it was violated blatantly by both sides. No less than 29 separate ceasefires were signed, but it did stop the fighting. The separatists intensified their activities against Ukrainian forces and both sides fortified their positions by developing a vast network of trenches, bunkers and tunnels in the areas they controlled, creating a *de facto* 'Line of Contact' running between the two sides. The static trench warfare along the Line of Contact, became 'a frozen conflict' which continued at low levels interminably, and claimed a soldier every day or so.

Donbas continued simmering. Then, in 2021, when Russia built up troops along Ukraine's borders, the Donbas erupted again. Separatist groups increased their activities against Ukrainian security forces, undoubtedly coordinated by Russian forces. As the security forces reacted, and violence increased, Russia used this as a pretext to formally recognize the Donetsk People's Republic and

Luhansk People's Republic as 'independent states,' on 22 February. The very next day, it sent in troops to "protect the Russian-speaking population." The pot was reaching boiling point and erupted on 24 February when Russia launched its invasion of Ukraine.

The Offensive

When Russia launched its offensive across Ukraine in February 2022, a thrust line also headed eastwards from the Donbas, comprising the 8th Combined Arms Army with the 1st and 2nd Army Corps along with fighters of the separatist groups operating in Donbas. Surprisingly, this sector did not see any large-scale fighting till around mid-April, with the two sides largely confined along the Line of Contact. It was only after Russia withdrew from Kyiv and announced its intention to focus on the Donbas, "The original aim of the campaign", that the Donbas erupted again. Troops from Kyiv, Sumy and the north-eastern sectors were transferred here as Russia built up a force of around 60,000 men – three armies comprising over 75 battalion tactical groups – along with around 14,500 fighters of the DPR and LPR. Approximately 18,000-20,000 mercenaries from Syria, Libya, Ethiopia and the infamous Wagner Group joined the fray, as Russia prepared for a decisive battle to take over the Luhansk and Donetsk provinces.

Around a third of the Ukrainian army – most of them battle-hardened veterans, with years of combat experience in the Donbas – were deployed in the Donbas. Around six brigades, along with reservists, foreign volunteers and partisans, were build up there – a force estimated to be 40,000-50,000 men. Russia had a strong numerical superiority and had the attackers' advantage of being able to concentrate its forces at the point of decision. Most importantly, it had the firepower. They had a 10 to 1 superiority in guns, and almost 40 to 1 in ammunition, and their dreaded artillery and rocket batteries could bring down massive volumes of fire on the defenders. The Ukrainian inferiority in artillery – both in ammunition, guns and ranges – was a crippling disadvantage which would only even out in the later stages of the war, when sophisticated Western artillery like the HIMARS, with greater ranges and lethality would be made available to them.

On 18 April, Russia began an intensive bombardment of positions in Luhansk, Donetsk and Kharkiv oblasts. The impact of the concentrated fire could be felt as far as Mariupol and Kharkiv, as the front lines were churned by a continuous barrage of artillery fire. The battle of Donbas had begun.

The Russians advanced in a slow creep along the entire front in the Luhansk and Donetsk regions. They did not go in for deep grandiose manoeuvres, as they had in the initial days. Instead, they advanced slowly and steadily, in the wake of intense bombardments, that churned entire villages and defensive positions that could be mopped up by the infantry that followed. It was a slow expensive battle, but using these tactics they crept forward at 3-5 kilometres a day.

The Russians took over the major towns of Popikka, Popasna, Kremina, Rubizhne and by mid-May had reached the line of the Donets River – the line roughly separating the Donbas region from the rest of Ukraine. As the Russians attempted to force a crossing across the river they were violently attacked by Ukrainians, who destroyed the pontoon bridge they had established and virtually eliminated two complete battalion tactical groups trying to get across. Around 500 Russian soldiers were killed and the rest were eventually forced to withdraw with heavy casualties.

The Russians repaid the favour just a few days later. They had captured most of the existing bridges on the Donets River, and the Ukrainians established a pontoon bridge a few kilometres to the north to supply their forces and also enable them to withdraw. This bridge was detected and destroyed by Russian artillery fire, which cut off most of the Ukrainian forces east of the river.

Ukrainian forces still held on in towns and villages, fighting grim, isolated battles all along the front. Like the battle of Kursk in March 1943, it turned into a brutal war of attrition which could only be won by the side with greater staying power. The Russians resorted to a series of small encirclements which cut of Ukrainian units and sub-units and then pounded the trapped forces with intense fire power. The grinding tactics paid dividends as the Russians slowly but steadily extended their sway, concentrating first on Luhansk in the north and then towards Donetsk to its south.

The two major objectives that would enable the Russians to gain control over the Luhansk were the twin towns of Sievierodonetsk and Lysychansk which were astride both sides of the Donets River, with Sievierodonetsk to the east of the river, and Lysychansk to its west. The two towns formed the major

Area of Major Fighting in Donbas

administrative and communication centres of the Luhansk. Sievierodonetsk came under a major attack in mid-April from the 4th Guards tank division in early May when it was encircled and its outlying villages captured, one by one. The first direct assault came on 27 May. The Russians established a foothold, were thrown back, again, entered the town, and then continued fighting – street by street, crossing by crossing, block by block – for over a month before they could eventually take over the bombed-out town. The Ukrainians launched a violent counter-offensive to retake this vital town, which failed. By mid-July, Ukrainian troops were ordered to withdraw from Sievierodonetsk and move west across the Donets River to the twin town of Lysychansk. It was a controversial order, but the withdrawal helped save the beleaguered troops and also enabled them to occupy more defensible positions on the other side of the Donetsk River.

With the capture of Sievierodonetsk, Russia rapidly took over the communication hubs of Lysychansk and Lyman, and gained control of all of Luhansk province. They had attained one of their major objectives of the war, and now could focus on the Donetsk. The units had a much-needed operational pause in the first two weeks of July and then renewed their offensive in Donetsk province. Almost 70 per cent of Donetsk was already in their hands, and as per plans, the entire region was to be occupied by end-August to enable them to hold a referendum in the Donbas, and then annex the areas in the same way they had annexed Crimea in 2014.

Securing the Donetsk proved more difficult than the Luhansk. Over a period of six weeks from mid-July to August, the Russian war machine crept on inexorably, taking village after village and overrunning position after position. But more discerning observers would have noticed that Ukrainian resistance was reducing. Artillery firing, even in counter-bombardments, were a trickle, and no new reinforcements were being sent into the area. Not known to the Russians, the Ukrainians were building up their own strength for an offensive that would come around September and were preserving men and ammunition for it.

In August, the first Ukrainian offensive burst out of Kherson region in the South (see the Kherson Offensive). The offensive was heavily publicized, and did make some headway (but not as much as it was purported to have made); but it alarmed the Russians sufficiently to pause their own offensive and send some of their best troops to the south to help stabilize the situation.

Even now, for the Russian, things seemed to be going as per plan – as they were so fond of reporting. A little slow, but according to plan, all right. They had secured the Kherson and Zaporizhzhia regions of the south, all of Luhansk and most of Donetsk in the east – almost 20 per cent of Ukraine's area. However, their success glossed over the fact that their men had been fighting for over seven months without a pause. Their units were depleted – most had lost over 25-30 per cent of men and equipment. They held a ragged and tired front across 1,200 kilometres. It was a situation that could explode any moment now.

And, explode it did. The Russians had taken their eyes of the ball and focused in the south where the Ukrainians had launched the offensive in the Kherson sector. They had even depleted the eastern and north-eastern sectors to send reinforcements there. In the first week of September, the Ukrainians launched their counter-offensive in the northeast that burst through from the area of Kharkiv, taking the Russians completely by surprise. The offensive raced through Russian positions and retook area that the Russians had captured in months in a matter of weeks (The Ukrainian offensives are covered in detail in subsequent chapters).

The war had just changed course again – this time in Ukraine's favour.

Areas under Russian Control at the End of Phase II

REFERENCES

Adam Schrek. "Russia pours in more troops in the East," *Associated Press*, 21 April 2022.

Bellal Annyssa. "*The War Report: Armed Conflict in 2014*," Oxford University Press.

"Bloody River Battle was third in Three Days," *BBC News*, 13 May 2022.

"Inside the Frozen Trenches of Eastern Europe", *TIME*, 26 April 2022.

"Massive Bombardment signals Russia's Renewed Offensive", *Forbes*, 21 April 2022.

"New Ceasefire enters force in Donbas," *TASS*, 29 December 2019.

Parker Charlie. "Russian Battalion wiped out trying to cross River of Death," *The Times*, 14 May 2022.

"Putin announces Donetsk and Luhansk Recognition," *BBC News*, 22 February 2022.

"Putin claims Russia was forced to Defend Russian speaking Population," *The Interpreter*, 12 October 2016.

"Russia deploys 20,000 mercenaries in Battle for Ukraine's Donbas," *The Guardian*, 19 April 2022.

"Russia's Cauldron Tactics Tipping Donbas Battle in its Favour," *The Guardian*, 27 May 2022.

"The Stalingrad Cauldron," *The University Press*, https://kansaspress.ku.edu

"Ukraine says Donetsk Anti-Terror Operation underway," BBC News, 15 April 2014.

"Ukraine Struggles to Combat Russia's Artillery Superiority," *The Kyiv Independent*, 1 August 2022.

PHASE THREE: THE UKRAINIAN COUNTER-OFFENSIVE

"There is no place for them on Ukrainian soil. If they want to survive, it is time for the Russian military to surrender or flee."

—President Vladimir Zelensky, 29 August 2022

THE MATADOR'S CAPE: THE KHERSON OFFENSIVE IN THE SOUTH

The Planned Ukrainian Offensive

The Russian advance in the Donbas had taken over Luhansk province after three months of slow battle and then turned their attention towards the adjoining province of Donetsk. The war turned into a long battle of attrition, in which the Russians, with their greater resources, would eventually prevail. The Ukrainians had been beefed up with over $ 40 billion Western aid and an influx of weaponry – including the long-range HIMARS artillery system from the USA. They had also inducted over 200,000 reservists, who had been trained and amalgamated in the front lines. They were keen on breaking the stalemate and there was growing talk of a counter-offensive to recapture their lost territories.

During the southern offensive of February-May, the Russians had taken over most of the Kherson, Zaporizhzhia, and Mykolaiv oblasts and captured the important cities on the coast, including Kherson, Melitopol, Mariupol, and Mykolaiv. They advanced as far as Zaporizhzhia in the north (site of Ukraine's largest nuclear reactor) and took the area from Kherson to the Donetsk province. This was a loss of some of Ukraine's most vital territories that threatened to cut it off from the sea.

A Ukrainian counter was definitely on the cards. They had last achieved a major success in June when they managed to recapture Kharkiv and pushed Russian troops back across the border in that sector. Since then, they were on the back foot. Pushing the Russians back from the Donbas region was not feasible. The Russians were well deployed there and entrenched in fortified positions. A counter-offensive was thus planned in the south with the aim of reaching the Mykolaiv-Zaporizhzhia-Kherson line and recapturing the town of Kherson. That would provide a huge boost to morale and unbalance Russian actions in the east. Most importantly, it would keep the Russians away from Odesa – the only port still in Ukrainian hands – and divert them from their offensive in the Donbas.

Russia had captured the entire area along the coastline of the Sea of Azov during the initial days of the war and Kherson, in fact, was the first major Ukrainian city to fall. They controlled 95 per cent of the Kherson oblast and over 70 per cent of the Zaporizhzhia oblast and occupied the entire coastline. In the areas they held, the process of 'Russification' had already begun. Municipal councils were replaced with pro-Russian members; Russian passports were issued (with newly-born children being granted automatic Russian citizenship). Pay and pensions was issued in roubles instead of the Ukrainian hryvnia, and statues of Lenin had come up in the town squares. But militarily, there was a pause in the actions in the south as the Russians focused on the Donbas.

In the south, both sides had established defensive lines roughly along the line of the Inhulets and the Dnieper rivers. Raids, sniping, local action, and artillery duels continued. Partisan action in the occupied territory had also intensified which had reportedly claimed over 100 Russian soldiers. In Kherson, a bomb placed in a café frequented by Russian officers killed seven high-ranking officers. However, these were mere pinpricks. The Ukrainians had been planning a major offensive around July to divert attention from the east and also "retake all of the occupied areas of the south – including Crimea."

In early July, messages were sent to the residents of Kherson and Zaporizhzhia to evacuate their homes or stay in protective shelters for an impending offensive. Western media was agog over this great offensive which would change the war. The defence minister, Oleksii Reznikov, announced that Ukraine was amassing a million-strong force for the counter-offensive (a little exaggeration since the entire Ukrainian security forces did not have so many men) and that the entire Kherson region would be free by September. The Ukrainian offensive was to go in along a 100-kilometre long swathe from Mykolaiv in the north to Kherson in the south and simply clear the area from Russian occupation. These ambitious claims were touted, and widely publicised, – but the underlying aim was even more subtle – it aimed at drawing Russian attention towards the south and deplete their forces elsewhere.

The Counter-offensive

The Ukrainian counter-offensive began on 24 July when Ukrainian artillery began targeting Russian positions using their newly-acquired HIMARS systems. The long ranges and precision munitions of these systems allowed them to strike deep in the rear of Russian positions, an advantage they did not have earlier. In the opening salvoes, artillery attacks targeted ammunition dumps and command posts, destroying three of them in a week. Artillery fire also damaged the Antonivka Bridge and other critical bridges on the Dnieper River, cutting off the supply lines to the Russian forces west of the river and forcing them to withdraw.

The withdrawal of the Russian forces was hailed as a great success and Ukraine claimed to have retaken 44 villages in the first month of the offensive, including the vital villages of Lozove and Andrivka which overlooked the Dnieper river crossings. They followed the same tactics used by the Russians, making small creeping movements supported by artillery fire, and taking small objectives. But though the outlying villages were retaken, none of the major towns – especially Kherson – which were the aim of the offensive were severely threatened. The recapture of Kherson would have been a major morale booster, especially since Kherson was the first town to fall in Russian hands in the early days of March. But the advance forced the Russians to send in twelve battalion tactical groups from the north-eastern sector to beef up the thirteen battalion tactical groups that they had in the area. (As events would show, the sidestepping of Russian troops to this sector was one of the major aims of the Ukrainian operation). With over 25 battalion tactical groups in the area, the Ukrainian offensive slowed down and they were unable to penetrate the Russian defensive lines which were prepared along geographical lines, well dug-in, and heavily fortified. Slowly, the Ukrainian offensive began petering out and actions were more at the local level rather than coordinated activities along the entire front. But again, all this was part of an overall plan.

Area of Ukrainian Counter-Attacks in the South

The Ukrainians achieved a major success when an explosion ripped through Saki airbase in the city of Nevofedorivka, around 100 kilometres deep inside Crimea, on 9 August. The blast destroyed around eight Sukhoi ground attack fighters and some helicopters – almost half of Russia's Black Sea naval aviation resources. Ukraine did not claim responsibility for the blast, but could not resist warning the Russians of the dangers of smoking on the base. Russia claimed the blast was the result of an accident, but the Black Sea fleet commander was sacked a week later – the highest-ranking General to be removed. Another blast hit the headquarters of the Black Sea fleet killing an unspecified number of senior officers. These attacks would have definitely hurt, and the Ukrainian ability to strike target deep in the rear, coupled with an intensification of partisan activity, further divided Russian reaction.

Another crisis arose when Russian and Ukrainian troops exchanged fire near the Zaporizhzhia nuclear plant – the largest in Europe. The plant is strategically located on the Kakhovha reservoir on the south bank of the Dnieper River and thus controls the Dnieper River crossings. Heavy artillery and small arms fire set a training facility ablaze damaged the radiation sensors and shells landed dangerously close to the nuclear storage facilities. Predictably, both sides blamed the other. The fires were put out before they could cause much damage but raised fears of a radioactive leak which could easily engulf all of Europe in a Chernobyl kind of nuclear disaster.

On 20 August, the Russians launched their own southern offensive which recaptured some of the lost areas in the Mykolaiv oblast. That offensive was largely to strengthen their defensive positions and did not advance deeper into Ukrainian lines towards the west. Russia also began posturing from Belarus in the north and resumed strikes on Kyiv, thus reinforcing the threat to the Ukrainian capital. By end-August, the Ukrainian counter-offensive seemed to have run its course without achieving any of the aims it had set for itself. Then on 29 August, President Zelensky announced that the counter-offensive in the south was being reactivated and Ukrainian activities intensified in the sector. The much-touted Ukrainian aim to recapture Kherson was again announced in the Ukrainian Parliament and on the official website of Operational Command South, the military headquarters, responsible for actions in this sector.

All this was part of a grand deception plan. After all, if one is to launch an offensive, it is not advertised as broadly as the Ukrainians did, and the Russians should have smelt a rat. But they did not and allowed themselves to be diverted towards the south, and sent their best units there. The initial actions in the south were the actions of a Matador's Cape – designed to distract while the main actions took place elsewhere. As the widely publicized actions continued in the south, another grand offensive came just a week later – on 6 September. This offensive was not directed in the South. It fell 600 kilometres away in the northeast – in the area of Kharkiv. The deception tactics followed by the Ukrainians enabled it to meet rapid success, which would virtually change the course of the war.

The actions of the Kharkiv offensive will be covered in detail in the subsequent chapter. But what stood out was how well it was coordinated with the southern offensive which enabled both offensives to make impressive gains. The Ukrainian breakout in the Kharkiv sector in September re-took over 6,000 square kilometres in just a month or so. The Ukrainians used the dislocation it caused to renew their own offensive in the south, which had been halted for a while, but now gathered momentum.

In mid-September, the Ukrainians renewed their push in the south. Some Russian units had been sent back to the north-eastern sector to stem the rot there, and the Russians were divided in both sectors. At the same time, around end September, Russia held a 'referendum' in its occupied territories and formally annexed Kherson, along with Zaporizhzhia, Luhansk and Donetsk regions. Two days later, on 2 October, the Ukrainians pushed ahead with their own offensive. They advanced in a wide sweep from north to south on the west bank of the Dnipro River, that rapidly recaptured vital villages north and north-west of Kherson. The Ukrainians secured the western bank and the crucial bridges on the Dnipro River, in effect cutting off 15,000-20,000 Russian troops west of the river. The Ukrainian advance forced the Russians to blow up a dam on the Inhulets River to slow down their advance. Long-range artillery strikes also hit logistics depots, ammunition dumps, convoys, and bridges, cutting off supply and reinforcement routes. Russian commanders requested permission to withdraw to more defensible positions which was refused by President Putin, who was still smarting from the reverses in the northeast, and could not afford any further setbacks in this sector. Yet, within a month, the Ukrainians reclaimed over 2,400 square kilometres in the south.

The Ukrainian advance towards Kherson was halted as the Russians held on to the second tier of defences, which were better prepared and had secure supply lines. The long and ragged Russian front lines were also set to be beefed up by over 200,000 conscripts following Putin's declaration of 'partial mobilization.' They would be trained and ready to join the front in two or three months.

The offensive in the south slowed, as both sides took on defensive positions. The war was in a critical phase. Winter was approaching, and both sides had a window till around November or so to attain their gains. After that 'Marshal Winter' would arrive, and the entire front would become a long war of attrition.

REFERENCES

"Fighting rages near Russian held Nuclear Plant in Zaporizhzhia," *Reuters*, 8 September 2022.

"Half of Russia's Black Sea Fleet Combat Jets out of Operation," *Reuters*, 19 August 2022.

Hedenshog Jakob. "The Russian Occupation of Ukraine's Southern Region," *SCEEUS*, 2 June 2022.

"How HIMARS help Ukraine," *Al Jazeera*, 26 July 2022.

"How Russia is Imposing its Rule in Occupied Ukraine," *BBC News*, 11 May 2022.

"Putin ups the ante, to Mobilize 3 Lakh troops," *Times of India*, 22 September 2022.

"Russia annex 4 Ukrainian Territories," *Times of India*, 30 September 2022.

"Russian Offensive Campaign Assessment," Institute for the Study of War, 4 October 2022.

"Ukraine announces Offensive Operations across the South," *The New York Times*, 29 August 2022.

"Ukraine claims precise hit on Russian Military Unit in Occupied Kherson," *CNN*, 11 July 2022.

"Ukraine has One Million ready to Re-capture South," *The Times*, 10 July 2022.

"Ukraine says 2400 square kilometres liberated in the South," *CNN*, 7 October 2022.

"Ukraine strikes Antonivka Bridge, essential for Russia's Supply Lines in Occupied South," *CBS News*, 27 July 2022.

"Ukraine tells Residents to leave Occupied South due to Counter-attack Plans," *The Times*, 10 July 2022.

"Ukraine's growing 'Reserve Army' Getting Ready," https://news.sky.com, 23 May 2022.

"Ukraine's long-awaited Southern Counter-offensive Begins with a Bang in Crimea," *POLITICO*, 10 August 2022.

"Ukraine's Southern Offensive was Designed to trick Russians," *The Guardian*, 11 September 2022.

"Zelensky tells Russian forces to flee as Ukraine starts Counter Offensive in Kherson," *Reuters*, 29 August 2022.

THE UKRAINIAN COUNTER-OFFENSIVE – KHARKIV

> "*We were given our objective and told to just move. We didn't stop, we didn't sleep, we didn't eat. But we moved 90 kilometres and captured our objective in just three days.*"
>
> **—Ukrainian tankman from 92 Mechanized Brigade**

The Kharkiv sector, in the northeast of Ukraine, had seen some bitter fighting in the early days of the war. But then this area is no stranger to war. It had seen some of the bitterest battles of World War II and had been captured and recaptured thrice by both the Germans and the Soviets. Its key position – just 80 kilometres from the Russian frontier – provided the gateway to both Ukraine and Russia and it was significant to both.

Kharkiv, the second largest town of Ukraine, had been hit by the Russian offensive on the very first day of the war. It held on for over three months, till a Ukrainian counter-offensive in May reclaimed the area and pushed back the Russian forces back to the border. That victory was one of the major Ukrainian victories of the campaign and had helped stabilize the entire north-eastern sector. (see The North-eastern Front: Feb-May 2022)

For two months the sector was static as the Russians focused on the Donbas and made slow, excruciating progress in the Luhansk and Donetsk provinces.

They also made headway in the south with the capture of Mariupol and the coastal areas up to Kherson. But all this had come at a cost. Its troops were tired and depleted, and their equipment suffered from constant usage and lack of maintenance. By some Western sources Russian casualties were in the region of 65,000-90,000 soldiers. Russia maintained that it had lost just around 6,000 soldiers killed, as per their Defence Minister Sergei Shoigu. By some accounts, most units had lost almost 20-25 per cent of their strength and no new reinforcements were forthcoming. Kharkiv was a relatively dormant sector and had settled into a stalemate of artillery duels and occasional raids by both sides. But this would change abruptly, as the Ukrainians launched their decisive counter-offensive here, in conjunction with their offensive in the south.

The planning for the Ukrainian counter-offensive had been going on for months. The ideal time frame was identified as around August-September which would give a window up to November or so before winter set in. The Ukrainians had suffered heavy casualties as well, (reportedly around 14,000-16,000 till October) especially in the Donbas battles where they were losing almost 100-150 soldiers every day. Ukrainian morale, too, had suffered from the reverses in the south and the east and they needed a victory to galvanize their army and ensure that the Western allies remained committed to the war, and continued to supply them with arms and aid. An estimated 60,000-80,000 reservists had been trained and amalgamated into front line units. They had gained proficiency in the newly-acquired Western weapons, like HIMARS long-range artillery, which had a distinct qualitative edge over the earlier Soviet era weaponry. Their air defence too was beefed up with HARM anti-radiation missiles which downed one aircraft and two helicopters on the first day of the offensive, in effect, negating the Russian use of their superior air power.

Most of all, they had access to US intelligence which provided them with the exact locations and dispositions of the Russians and identified the weak spots in their deployment. Based on inputs provided by US intelligence, two broad options emerged; to strike in the south towards Kherson and the coastal areas, or to strike in the northeast towards Kharkiv. After much deliberation, it was decided to launch the offensive in both locations – first in the south, then in the northeast. The timings were deliberately staggered to disrupt Russian response and cause even further dislocation.

In early August, the Ukrainians launched their offensive in the Kherson sector, moving in a swathe from Zaporizhzhia to Kherson (see the Kherson Offensive). Over a period of a month, the offensive pushed the Russians back across the Dnipro River, along a rough line – Zaporizhzhia-Melitopol-Kherson. Though that offensive regained sizeable territory, it could not recapture Kherson or any of the major towns. But the Kherson offensive was widely publicized as part of an overall deception plan. It forced the Russians to pull out around a dozen battalion tactical groups from the north-eastern and eastern sectors – including crack units like the 1st Guards Tank Army, and sent them to reinforce the south, leaving large gaps in their defences. While Russian eyes were being diverted to the south, the offensive force was preparing for launch in the Kharkiv sector.

The Ukrainians concealed their offensive forces well. They had shifted some of their forces to the south, (to add to the impression that their focus was there) while retaining the bulk of their mechanized forces. Artillery firing and other actions in the Kharkiv sector had reduced while they built up their offensive force in great secrecy. Even their preliminary attacks were conducted with relatively little armour and heavy equipment to conceal their true strength. They did succeed in lulling the Russians into complacency in this sector.

The offensive began on the 6 September with long-range artillery strikes hitting Russian ammunition dumps, command and control centres and headquarters deep in the rear. In the wake of intense artillery barrages, the main thrust was launched in the direction of Balakliya – a vital road and rail junction which had been identified as a weak spot in the Russian front lines. Through the hole punched in the forward lines, two prongs pushed forward – one towards Kupyansk in the north and another towards Izium in the south – headed for the line of the Oskil River. This would recapture the two vital communication centres and cut off the Russians east of the river.

On the morning of 6 September, Ukrainian special forces along with tanks and combat vehicles of the 92 Mechanized Brigade moved out of their hides around the small village of Pryshyb and raced eastwards, rapidly reaching the small town of Verbibky. Mechanized columns raced through the town and special forces occupied key locations forcing the Russians to abandon their equipment and flee. Leaving a small force to mop up and hold the town, the mechanized forces continued eastwards towards their initial objective, Balakliya – a small town with a population of around 26,000 that sat astride a key river crossing and was a key rail and road junction of the critical T2110 and P78 highways.

In an overnight battle, the Ukrainians took control of Balakliya. The speed of the advance took the defenders by surprise (later identified as 18 Guards Motor Rifle Brigade) and the town was rapidly captured. Mechanized forces entered and isolated that town, while special forces seized critical buildings and junctions. Balakliya fell on the 7th itself, with many of the Russians changing into civilian clothes and trying to flee on bicycles. However, even as the mopping up was in progress, the Ukrainians raced further eastwards with their mechanized forces, seizing the key villages of Volokhiv Yar and Semenivka along the route. In most cases, the Russian defenders were taken by surprise and did not put up much of a fight. According to some Ukrainian sources, there was so much disorientation amongst the Russians that a column of Russian trucks actually came up to Ukrainian tanks asking for directions, without realizing who they were, and were rapidly disarmed and captured. The advancing 92 Mechanised Brigade linked up with troops of the 113 Ukrainian Territorial Defence Brigade advancing on a parallel axis and the combined forces now advanced towards the main objective – Kupyansk.

Kupyansk, a small town on both sides of the Oskil River,was the de facto headquarters of the Russian regional command. It was also a vital rail and road hub, through which supplies for the entire eastern front were routed. The town had been captured by the Russians in the very first few days of their offensive on 27 February, but its 195 days of occupation would soon come to an end.

The Ukrainian Offensive

The capture of Kupyansk was surprisingly swift. In most cases, the defenders were taken by surprise by the rapidity of the Ukrainian advance, and as per radio intercepts, many local commanders sent frantic messages up the chain of command, asking for directions, rather than act on their own initiative – revealing a rigidity which has been a characteristic of Russian armies. The 1st mechanized battalion captured the city centre on the afternoon of 9 September and by the end of the day, the Ukrainians had seized control of the entire western riverbank of the Oskil River and the bridges astride it. Russian soldiers trying to escape across the river were targeted with machine gun and mortar fire, causing many to leave behind their heavy equipment and try to swim across. By 10 September, Kupyansk was completely cleared and back in Ukrainian hands.

Even as Kupyansk was being addressed and captured, another prong of their offensive headed southwards towards Izium – another vital rail and road junction, which could provide the gateway to the Donbas. In a repeat of the actions at Kupyansk, Izium was addressed by mechanized forces, which bypassed the initial defences and raced deep into the rear. As per one Ukrainian tank trooper, "We did not sleep or eat for three days. We were told to just keep moving for Izium and reach there in any way possible." The tactics paid off. Izium was contacted on 9 September and captured by the 11th. It was an action reminiscent of another battle fought in Izium, way back in 1942 – The Second Battle of Kharkiv – when the Germans defeated the Soviet armies and caused over 200,000 deaths in a single battle.

With the fall of Izium, the Ukrainian defence ministry put out photographs of its soldiers in the town square with an emoji of grapes (Izium means 'raisins' in Ukraine). Just a week after the offensive had commenced, Zelensky raised the Ukrainian flag in the town square, with the promise that "it will soon come up in every town and village of the Russian occupied areas."

The Ukrainian advance was actually quite stunning. In just under a fortnight, they had retaken over 6,000 square kilometres – area which had taken the Russians months to secure. The Russians acknowledged the scale of their defeat, stating simply that their units had "redeployed to better defensive positions." The Russian forces were forced to retreat east of the Oskil River to avoid being cut off, leaving behind 338 pieces of military hardware, much of which fell intact into Ukrainian hands. By Ukrainian accounts, they captured over a brigade's worth of equipment and the hated 'Z' sign of the Russians was painted over with the white cross of the Ukrainians and their equipment pressed into service against their former owners. As per Ukraine's operational command east, which oversaw the offensive in this sector, "Russia is now the largest supplier of equipment to Ukraine."

The Ukrainians followed up their successes at Izium and Kupyansk by moving forward rapidly to the line of the Sieverski Donets River and soon established bridgeheads across it. This cut off the Russians west of the river, forcing them to withdraw, leaving behind their heavy equipment. From here, they were in a position to carry the offensive ahead to retake the Luhansk which the Russians had captured with much difficulty over the past three months. It pushed on and by 2 October captured Lyman, a transport and logistics hub which was essential for the resupply of Russian troops. The loss of Lyman was a major setback, more so since it came just a day after Putin had declared the Donbas region – where it is located – as a part of Russia. With the fall of Lyman, Russian positions in both Luhansk and Donetsk were seriously threatened.

The Russians consolidated along the line of the Oskil and Donetsk rivers, and the Ukrainian offensive lost momentum after a month or so of heavy

Areas Retaken by Ukraine

fighting. But they had made impressive gains. The north-eastern and southern offensives managed to take over 6,500 square kilometres in just around a month – area which had taken the Russians four months to occupy. The offensive weakened the Russian hold on the rest of Donbas. More than that, it also proved that Putin's declaration of Kherson, Zaporizhzhia, Luhansk and Donetsk, as Russian territory, following a 'referendum' there, was premature, and the offensive captured vast swathes of territory that were now "officially Russian". The success of the offensive, for the first time, brought about the belief that a Russian defeat was a distinct possibility, and that in many ways, raised the stakes.

The Russians still held on to 600,000 kilometres of Ukrainian territory (now Russian territory, after the referendum) which they would not give up in a hurry. The depth positions were held with better units and were well fortified and defended. Moreover, their strength would be beefed up by over 200,000 conscripts that were hastily drafted for military service following Putin's announcement of 'partial military mobilization'. Russia launched local counterattacks to stabilize the situation and halt further Ukrainian advance, as both sides dug in. Russia sharply escalated the strikes into Ukraine – even as it ramped up its nuclear rhetoric – as part of its 'escalate to de-escalate' strategy. The military reverses suffered in the Ukrainian counter-offensives only made the Russian response more violent and unpredictable.

Just like the Germans invaded Russia in May 1941 hoping for a swift victory, but got trapped in a quagmire for four years, the Russians too had miscalculated. With winter setting in after November, no large-scale campaigning was possible and both sides sought to consolidate their positions in the east and the south. Winter brought a temporary stalemate and as actions in the south slowed down, the focus shifted to an insignificant town in the Donbas – Bakhmut. This town would see the longest and most intense battle of the war.

REFERENCES

"After reclaiming key Logistics Hub, Ukraine presses on," *Times of India*, 03 October 2022.

"Crimea Saki Air Base, Seven Russian Warplanes Destroyed," https://www.cnn.com, 11 August 2022.

Henry Foy. "The 90-kilometre-long journey that changed the war in Ukraine," *Financial Times*, 28 September 2022.

"More than 14000 Casualties to date, but Number likely Higher," *United Nations News*, 09 September 2022.

Mylola Bielieskov. "Ukrainian Balakliya-Kupyansk Offensive," *Eurasiona Daily Monitor*, volume 19, issue 133.

"Over 90K 'Irrecoverable losses' in Ukraine," *The Moscow Times*, 12 October 2022.

"Putin ups the ante, to mobilize 3 Lakh troops," *Times of India*, 22 September 2022.

"Russian Offensive Campaign Assessment, 11 September, understandingwar.org

"Ukraine punches through Russian lines as surprise offensive retakes land in the East," *CNBC*, 11 September 2022.

"Ukrainian forces capture Key Town," *The Kyiv Post*, https://www.newsweek.com, 10 September 2022.

"US to supply more Missiles after Kyiv success with Anti-Radiation Weapons," *The Eurasian Times*, 17 October 2022.

"We retook 6,000 square kilometres in September, Says Zelensky," *BBC*, 12 September 2022.

Yaroslav Trofimov. "Ukraine's new Offensive is fuelled by Captured Russian Weapons," *The Wall Street Journal*, 05 October 2022.

BAKHMUT: THE STALINGRAD OF THE WAR

"Fortress Bakhmut will never fall."

—Zelensky, December 2022

The small town of Bakhmut in Eastern Ukraine has little significance, save for its salt and gypsum mines and its world-famous sparkling wines. Neatly divided by the Bakhmutka River, this small town stands astride two crucial highways which lead further west into the Donetsk region. It is just a small town with little military value, but has emerged as the site of the longest and bitterest battle of the Ukraine war.

Bakhmut was formerly known as Artyomovsk when Ukraine was part of the Soviet Union – a name which Russia chooses to call it by even today. It was in the forefront of the separatist war of 2014, when it was captured by pro-Russian forces of the Donetsk People's Republic in May 2014. The town was then counter-attacked and recaptured by the Ukrainian forces after two months of heavy fighting. This town is no stranger to war, but the scale of the fighting it saw now, was unprecedented.

The town was first shelled in mid-May 22, when the Russians launched their offensive in the Donbas. Gradually the bombardment increased as the Russians closed in on the outlying cities of Popasna, Siversk and Lysychansk. The first attack came in on 01 August – led by the Wagner Group, a collection of mercenaries under their leader Yevgeny Prigozhin. By mid-August, the group, reinforced by regular fighters from the 72 Motorised Division had captured the outlying villages and closed in to within three kilometres of the town. The fighting escalated and by November-December had degenerated into a brutal trench warfare – reminiscent of Verdun in the First World War. Constant artillery fire reduced the city to rubble and forced its inhabitants to flee. Only around 4000 or so of the original 80000 inhabitants fled – often serving as guides and spotters and delivering much needed food and water in pick-up trucks to its defenders. As the Russians closed in, fighting went on for "each bush and building." The mercenaries of the Wagner Group – many of them ex-convicts who had been promised their freedom in return for six months of fighting - made suicidal attacks on each position, often clambering over the bodies of their fallen comrades, and leaving the wounded to die. In the 'meat-grinder' of Bakhmut, the advances were just around 100-150 meters every day, and the front lines within earshot of each other.

In the mud-filled trenches – often knee deep in water, artillery shells whizzed overhead virtually non-stop. The Commanders held computers and tablets, but communicated with antiquated wind-up telephones connected by wire cables which provided the only means of secure communication. The sky above was full of drones, which each side used to detect the other, bring down artillery fire and launch attacks at crucial targets. The Russians continued intensive artillery barrages throughout the day, while the Ukrainians were hamstrung by shortage of ammunition and had to ration their fire. The Russians continued, at times up to fifty every day, which were often beaten back with heavy losses. The Ukrainians claimed that the Russians lost five men for each casualty they themselves incurred, but even then, the scale of losses to the Ukrainians too was very high. They had deployed eight brigades at Bakhmut and over fifteen brigades had been rotated in the intense fighting, two of them being almost wiped out. They were losing almost 150-200 soldiers every day, and entire units and formations were being churned in the meat-grinder of Bakhmut.

As the attacks intensified, the Ukrainian General Staff proposed a withdrawal from the battered city to more defensible positions near the high ground of Chasiv Yar to the west. But Zelensky himself forbade any withdrawal which now had acquired a symbolic significance. On 21-22 December he made an unannounced visit to the town, gave speeches and awarded medals, and declared that "fortress Bakhmut will never fall." He would repeat the visit again in March 23 – an indicator of the importance he himself placed on the town.

The Russians had a major success in January 23, when they captured Soledar – a small town 20 kilometres to the north. They now advanced from the North and cut off the T-0513 highway, which was a key artery for supplies to its beleaguered defenders. The Russians pushed forward in slow grinding attacks, and by end February had encircled Bakhmut from the North, South and East. They pushed into the town, and by 7 March, the Ukrainians were forced to withdraw west of the Bakhmutka River which now became the dividing line between the two sides. The Russians tried to cross the river, and even launched an airborne operation across it, but were pushed back suffering horrific casualties.

The fighting in the town now resembled the fighting for Stalingrad. Like Stalingrad, the town had little strategic significance and its value was largely symbolic. Like Stalingrad, the town was pounded to rubble, which made it even more difficult for the attackers to advance when they eventually closed in. Like Stalingrad, it saw casualties on a horrific scale, and eventually the cost of the capture far-outweighed its benefits.

But then, the fighting also exposed the rift between the Russians. The Wagner boss, Yevgeny Prigozhin repeatedly accused the Russian High Command of refusing to supply him with food and ammunition, and accused them of cowardice. In May, he threatened to withdraw his fighters from their hard-earned positions in the city, if they were not given ammunition. It took the intervention of the defence minister himself who assured him that the 300 tons of ammunition required per day, would be provided.

Then in early May the Ukrainians launched their own counter attacks, which followed the same pattern of the Russians, creeping forward building-by-building, block-by-block, advancing just a few hundred meters every day. The assault led by the 3rd Separate Assault Brigade and fighters from the Azov Battalion pushed the Russians back almost two kilometres along the flanks of the town. In the confused fighting, the Wagner Group accused the Russian 72 Separate Motor Rifle Brigade of fleeing and abandoning their positions.

Yet, the Ukrainian counter attacks seemed a last gasp to hold on to their positions. By then, they held on to just a small cluster of buildings in the Southwest quarter of the town called the 'Airplane.' The fighting was isolated, with units and formations slowly pulling out of the bombed-out town. All the bridges on the Bakhmutka River had been bombed and a solitary pontoon bridge was used to enable the Ukrainian defenders to withdraw – all the time under heavy artillery fire. As the Ukrainians withdrew, the Russians closed in and on 20 May, Putin announced that "Artyomovsk has been captured." Photos of Prigozhin and his fighters posing triumphantly in the ruined city with the tricolour of Russia and the Black flag of the Wagner Group were triumphantly flashed across Russian channels and newspapers. Though some Ukrainian fighters still held on, the Russians had effectively gained control of the city.

After 224 days of the hardest and bitterest fighting seen in the war, Bakhmut eventually came to Russian hands. It provided a much-needed victory to its forces that had suffered setback after setback since October 22. But there was little left of the town to capture. Not a single building remained intact, and perhaps the only thing of value was the 2 million bottles of rare Artemetis wine maturing in the caves beneath the town. Those prized, expensive wines were favored by Stalin and Putin themselves and apparently Prigozhin hoped to make a fortune through them. The fighting had claimed an estimated 15-20000 Ukrainians and around 35-45,000 Russians, most of them fighters from the Wagner Group, who had been treated as cannon fodder. Its capture now opened the gates for the subsequent advance into the Donetsk, towards the towns of Siversk, Kramatorsk and Lyshyshank, and even Dnipro on the banks of the Dnieper. But each of these towns would have to be captured using the same battering 'meat-grinder' tactics.

While at the end, the capture was more a matter of prestige than anything else, it did tie down forces of both sides there. But it were the regular formations of the Ukrainian forces that were tied down there and suffered huge losses in the attritional fighting. The Wagner Group of the Russians did the bulk of the fighting. And for them their own losses seemed expendable. As one wag put it, "The Ukrainians are losing their best soldier, the Russians are cleaning out their prison population." Perhaps Zelensky should have withdrawn from Bakhmut, around March as had been recommended by his Generals. Because, by continuing the battle, it diverted attention and resources and also delayed the much-anticipated Ukrainian Spring Counter offensive for months. That delay of almost two to three months in launching their offensive, allowed the Russians to prepare defensive lines and consolidate their positions, and is one of the reasons why the offensive could not make much headway. The impact of Bakhmut went beyond the immediate battle.

But there was more to the story of Bakhmut. The success of the Wagner Group has also raised the stature of Yevgeny Prigozhin and brought out the rift between him and the senior Generals of the Russian army – especially the Chief General Velery Gerasimov and the Defense Minister, Sergei Shoigu. The rift finally exploded when Prigozhin led his fighters out of Bakhmut on his "March to Moscow," and act of rebellion that was the first direct threat to Putin's hold on power. That rebellion was curbed and that chapter eventually ended with the fiery death of Prigozhin in an inexplicable aircraft crash two months later. That has been covered in details later.

REFERENCES

"Fighting Through Hell : Bakhmut," *A P News*, https://apnnews.com

"How the Battle for Bakhmut could Shape the War," *NBC News*, https://www.nbcnews.com

"Inside the fight for the Last Streets of Bakhmut," *BBC*, https://www.bbc.com

"Key Moments in the Battle for Bakhmut," *Reuters*, https://www.reuters.com

"Putin claims Capture of Bakhmut," *Financial Times*, https://www.ft.com

"The Battle for Bakhmut: A Timeline," *Al Jazeera*, https://www.aljazeera.com

"The Battle for Bakhmut," *New York Times*, https://www.nytimes.com

"The Bloodiest Battle of the War," *The Wall Street Journal*, https://www.ws.com

"The Kremlin's Pyrrhic Victory in Bakhmut,"Institute for the Study of War, https://understandingwar.com

"The Story of Bakhmut through the Eyes of those who Fought it," *The Telegraph*, https://www.telegraph.co.uk

"War in Europe: The Endless Battle for Bakhmut," Le Monde, https://www.lemonde.fr

"Why Russia is so determined to capture Bakhmut," *TIME*, https://time.com

THE WAGNER GROUP: MUTINY AND ITS AFTERMATH

"Blood, Honour, Justice, Homeland, Courage."

—Motto of the Wagner Group

Death of a 'National Hero'

On 23 August 2023, an Embraer Legacy private plane took off from Moscow on its way to St Petersburg. On board were Yevgeny Progozhin, the warlord who was the founder of the Wagner Group – a private army that had served the shadowy interests of Russia and Putin for years. With him were Dmitry Utkin, the co-founder of the group, and other senior leaders. Around 300 kilometres from Moscow, the aircraft crashed into a field killing all ten on board. The charred and mangled remains of their bodies were only identified through DNA testing, and little remained of the aircraft to offer any clue about the cause of the crash.

Yet, the crash was later attributed to "a massive internal explosion" i.e. a bomb on board. Russia of course, debunked that, and denied any hand in the crash. In a public eulogy, Putin himself praised Prigozhin as "a man who made some serious mistakes...but made a significant contribution to the Russia and the fighting in Ukraine." He intoned, "We remember this and will not forget."

The last words were significant. Putin never forgets. And he would have never forgotten how Prigozhin defied his authority and marched out of his positions in Bakhmut on "a march to Moscow." To redress their grievances. That mutiny was put down in just a day, without any serious harm. But Putin did not forget.

The fortunes of Putin and Prigozhin have been linked. Both came from St Petersburg and both were intensely patriotic, who were willing to go to any lengths for Mother Russia. Prigozhin, an ex-convict, started his life as a hot-dog seller. Till he moved up the ladder and opened a chain of restaurants. He became close to Putin in the late 1990s and then went on to win a series of lucrative state catering contracts that earned him the nickname, "Putin's chef."

But it did not stop there. In 2014, he went on to found his own private army – The Wagner Group, with is motto, "Blood, honour, justice, homeland, courage". Composed of a core of ex-Spetnatz commandos, ex-servicemen and convicts, the group morphed into a 35-45,000 strong force, well-armed and equipped - which was used by Putin to pursue the interests of Russia (and himself) in Syria, Mali, Central Africa, Libya, West Africa and Niger. The group helped prop up governments allied to Russia and dismantled the opponents. Many of the African rulers used them to stave off potential coups, and for their personal protection. In return, he got exclusive mining rights for gold, oil, coal and mineral and fast became a multi-billionaire.

When the war in Ukraine broke out in February 22, the Wagner Group was in the forefront of the fighting – first in Kyiv in the early days of the war, and then in the Donbas. The Group participated in the longest and bloodiest battle of the War – capturing Bakhmut and Soledar after 224 days of fighting and suffering unimaginable casualties. The expendable ex-convicts were used as cannon fodder, to charge Ukrainian positions, often over the bodies of their dead comrades. They finally got control of the town, with Prigozhin himself raising the flag of Russia and the Wagner Group in the town square on 20 May 2023.

But the glory and acclaim that came his way also earned him a lot of enemies. His harsh, abrasive criticism of senior military leadership did not make him very popular either. And as relations between him and the seniors of the Russian military declined, on 23 June, he set off on his "March to Moscow" in an act that would be the first direct threat to Putin's authority and prove to be the biggest mistake of Prigozhin's life.

The Wagner "March to Moscow"

Just two months ago, Prigozhin and his group were feted as heroes after their successful capture of Bakhmut, which gave the Russians their first victory in months. But the rift between the Wagner Group and the Russian military was growing. Prigozhin had repeatedly accused the Defense Minister Sergei Shoigu and armed forces Chief General Valery Gerasimov, of conspiring to undermine his group and denying them supplies and ammunition. He also accused the Army of vacating positions along his flanks in the battle for Bakhmut, and threatened to withdraw from there. His comments that "the Generals should be shot for their handling of the war" ruffled quite a few feathers as well. There was open antagonism between him and the defence minister and Army Chief and perhaps he was getting too big for his own boots. In June, a proposal was put up by the defense ministry to amalgamate the Wagner Group into the Russian military. This move – supported by Putin himself – implied that Prigozhin and the fighters of the Wagner Group would sign contracts that would place them under command of the Army. This would make Prigozhin directly under the defense minister and thus weaken his own position.

Prigozhin refused to sign the agreements, and instead launched an expletive laced rant, in which he told Russians that the war was a lie, and an excuse for "a small group of scumbags to promote themselves." He also accused the Army of launching a missile strike at one of their training camps and killing their fighters and demanded that the defense minister and Army Chief come to meet him. When the outrageous demand was ignored, he ordered his fighters to abandon their positions in the frontlines of Ukraine on 23 June, and march on to Moscow, in what be claimed was "not a military coup, but a march for justice."

The 35,000 strong Wagner Group in Russia-Ukraine comprised of their most battle-hardened fighters, who have been manning the frontlines for a year now. They are very well equipped, though they lack air support and have no internal logistics. In addition, around 15-20,000 fighters are protecting Russian interests in Sudan, Syria, North Africa and the Middle East. It is a formidable fighting force, more so since they swear loyalty to only one man – Prigozhin himself.

The group marched on Rostov-on-Don and Voronezh, the two centers that Russia uses as bases for their war effort in Ukraine. They quickly captured the military bases in both cities and took control. Russian air attacks on their convoys reportedly caused some casualties, but the group claimed to have even shot down three Russian helicopter and even set a fuel dump in Voronezh ablaze. The group, led by Prigozhin himself then barreled along the M4 Highway from Rostov to Moscow in T-72 tanks and BMPs and raced towards Moscow.

Even as Machine Gun posts and tanks of the Russian Army took up positions on the outskirts of Moscow, Prigozhin, abruptly halted when they were just 200 kilometers away from the city and announced that they were turning back "to avoid shedding Russian blood." In a deal, brokered by the Belarus President Alexander Lukashenko, Prigozhin agreed to halt the advance, in return for having security guarantees for his men, who would not be prosecuted or punished for their action. Prigozhin himself was sent to Belarus, and his men told to return to their positions on the front line. It was an abrupt turnaround and indicated that Putin had successfully check-mated Prigozhin and overcame the rising threat.

The Wagner mutiny – though not directed at the military leadership and not at Putin himself - was a challenge to him; more so since Prigozhin was his close friend and he himself had built him up. Criticism of the war also reflected on him directly. Putin appeared weak and defensive when he denounced the actions on television, calling it "a stab in the back." But he appeared conciliary and lacked his usual bluster. He even appealed to the fighters, offering amnesty if they surrendered.

Prigozhin's actions got the war dangerously close to Moscow He tapped on the growing anti-war sentiment, by appealing to the soldiers to join him instead, since the "Generals only want to make money at the expense of your lives." But there were no known instances of Russian troops joining him. Rather, even the Chechen warlord, Ramzan Kadyrov, vowed to help Putin and fight the Wagner Group. But though the action fizzled out, there is no doubt that it would have touched a chord in the minds of many Russian soldiers, which could reflect itself in the actions on the front lines.

A lot of theories had abounded about this action. There were speculations that Prigozhin has been bought off by US agencies, who wanted to exploit the rift between him and the Generals. A report that $6.2 Billion of funds for Ukraine was inexplicably unaccounted for also gave rise to the theory that the amount has been used to buy Prigozhin over. His abrupt halt of the march and turnaround were also attributed to his being merely brought over by Putin. But Prigozhin was known to be a quick-tempered and volatile man who often acted impetuously. It is quite likely that he moved out towards Moscow, after his latest spat with the Defense Minister and then realized that he had bitten off more than he could chew. Even Putin did manage to sideline him, by sending him to Belarus, and even got his soldiers to agree to sign the contract, bringing them under the military and sent them back to their positions on the front lines.

The Aftermath

On hindsight, Putin had handled the situation well. Western commentators had been crowing about how the mutiny was "the first nail in Putin's coffin" and how it would spark off a wave of revolt within Russia. None of this happened. There were no instances of any Russian soldier joining the revolt. And although Putin offered amnesty for all Wagner fighters who participated in the revolt, the others were made to sign a oath of allegiance to Russia and placed directly under the military – something he had wanted all along.

Prigozhin was sent to Belarus and remained low, surfacing only from time to time. He made a brief appearance at the Africa Summit in Moscow. But it was apparent that he was a marked man. Putin never forgives those who have crossed him. A former Intelligence officer who defected to UK was made to die a slow and agonizing death after being poisoned with radioactive Polonium 210. Prigozhin was literally "dead man walking" and his sudden death – exactly two months after his failed march did not surprise anyone.

But now what? Wagner Group will continue in much the same manner as before. A new Chief – hand-picked by Putin would be in charge and with the mercenaries directly under the military, there would be greater control over them. But it has brought out the perils and pitfalls of using private armies. This is becoming a growing trend now. The USA used hired contractors in Iraq and Afghanistan; Russia has a motley collection of such groups, African states like Niger, Sudan, Somalia and Yemen have often outsourced their security to the. Even in the Middle East, Hamas, Hezbollah and the Houthis are largely militia groups under the loose control of Iran. Having such fighters may be tempting, especially if a nation wants to conduct covert shadowy operations and then deny accountability for them. But as has been brought out so often, these actions often rebound. In each case, when a militia or a mercenary group gets too powerful, they go out of control and can turn against the state. There is no substitute for a strong, well-disciplined army operating for their nation. And the actions of the Wagner Group have only served to highlight that.

REFERENCES

"5 Lessons from the 24 hour Rebellion," *Le Monde,* https://www.lemonde.fr

"Band of Brothers, The Wagner Group and the Russian State," Center for Strategic and International Studies, https://csis.org

"The Ripple Effects of the Wagner Rebellion," *Foreign Policy,* https://foriegnpolicy.com

"The Wagner rebellion Timeline," *ABC News,* https://www.abcnews.go.com

"Wagner Boss, Yevgeny Prigozhin Dead," *Al Jazeera,* https://www.aljazeera.com

"Wagner Group's Revolt against Russia," *Al Jazeera,* https://www.aljazeera.com

"Wagner's Brief Rebellion Ends with a Deal," *TIME*; https://www.time.com

"What is Russia's Wagner Group," *BBC,* https://www.bbc.com

"White House suggest Kremlin behind Prigozhin's Death," *The Hindu*, https://www.thehindu.com

"Yevgeny Prigozhin confirmed dead in a plane crash," *The Guardian*, https://www.theguardian.com

"Yevgeny Prigozhin, Renegade Mercenary Chief who built an Empire," *The New York Times*, https://www.nytimes.com

"Yevgeny's death may Consolidate Putin's Power," *The Economist*, https://www.economist.com

THE UKRAINIAN 'SPRING OFFENSIVE'

"The offensive is coming. It will take time, but it will come."

—Ukraine Army Chief

The Spring Offensive

For months the world had been awaiting the Ukrainian Spring Offensive. Spring had gone and Summer arrived, with little sign of the much-anticipated offensive. Then, around 04 June the Ukrainian offensive finally began, as 'shaping operations' like probing attacks, feints, long range artillery attacks on Russian positions began all along the 1200-kilometer-long frontage of operations.

But a major Ukrainian counter-offensive had actually began eight months ago in September 22. Then, in just a little over a month, they recaptured over 7000 square kilometers of occupied territory in a swift offensive, which captured vital ground in the Northeast, and pushed the Russians behind the line of the Dnieper River in the South. They even re-took the vital town of Kherson.

That offensive in September was militarily quite brilliant, even though the gains were not as much as they were touted to be. For starters, they deceived the Russians by a series of feint attacks in the South, including well-timed tweets by Zelensky and the Ukrainian Southern Command, that the offensive was coming towards Kherson. This blatant deception worked. The Russians sent 13 battalion tactical groups from the Northeast to reinforce the South.

Even as these were on the move, the Ukrainians – aided by helpful US intelligence – attacked the gaps in the denuded Russian lines in the Northeastern sector, capturing the towns of Balakliya, Izium and Kupyansk and regained territory in three short weeks, that had taken the Russians months to capture. While Russian attention was on the offensive in the Northeast, (some units were already moving back after being redeployed in the South) the Ukrainians attacked again – this time in the South. They sent the equivalent of two mechanized brigades rolling down the Western bank of the Dnieper River, that forced the withdrawal of over 20-30000 Russian troops and enabled them to recapture Kherson virtually without a fight. These gains were a huge psychological boost, and painted as a huge Ukrainian victory that was a prelude to the final elimination of Russian presence from Ukraine. But taken in perspective, that offensive succeeded in recapturing only around 3 percent of their lost territory – over 1,70,000 square kilometres still remained in Russian hands.

With the coming of winter both sides seemed to pause to build up their tired and depleted forces. The major action actually took place in Bakhmut, a strategically insignificant town in the Donbas which sucked in over eight Ukrainian brigades and around three to four Russian divisions beefed up by 40-50,000 mercenaries of the Wagner Group. The meat-grinder of Bakhmut drew the attention of both sides for eight months, till its eventual fall in mid-May. The Battle for Bakhmut has been covered in detail, in the preceding chapter.

But though Bakhmut did not have much strategic value, it sucked in both Ukrainian and Russian troops. And Zelensky's obsession with it, meant a large portion of the available troops were engaged there. This delayed the impending Ukrainian "Spring Offensive" for months, even as Spring gave way to summer. In the intervening period, aided by western allies, the Ukrainian had built up their offensive capability to nine "combat credible," brigades freshly equipped with around 300 Leopard IIs tanks from Germany, Challenger IIs from UK, M1- Abrams and APCs from USA, and a mix of sophisticated, if disparate equipment. Around 3-6 additional brigades were pulled out from other sectors providing a force of 12-15 brigades for the offensive. Extensive bridging and mine breaching equipment – ploughs, trawls and explosive charges – also came in, along with HIMARS and Storm Shadow Missiles, Air Défense and Electronic Warfare devices.

That itself raised a question. The newly equipped brigades (many of them built around the core of brigades that were depleted in earlier battles) had a short training period of just around six months. Many of the crew members are recently inducted conscripts. The lack of training may show on the tactical battlefield – more so since the Ukrainian forces are familiar with Soviet era equipment and not Western one. Plus, there will be a host of logistical problems, like building up stockpiles of different kinds of ammunition, oils and fuel, spares and other paraphernalia required for each type of equipment.

The time gained by the delaying of the offensive by the obsession with Bakhmut and the wait for new equipment enabled the Russians to prepare their own defences. An elaborate system of defences were prepared along the frontage, described as "the most extensive defensive works in Europe since World War II." Construction of the so-called 'Surovikin Line' began as early as November 2022 and by April 2023, Russia had built an 800 km long defensive line. The defences consisted of ditches, dragon teeth – the cylindrical blocks of concrete designed to stop tanks in their tracks – trenches, artillery positions, anti-vehicle barriers, and firing positions. Russia created an extensive minefield network, and were estimated to have mined over 170,000 square kilometres of area. In the South, where the main thrust was expected, three lines of defences came up – the first with multiple counter mobility barriers and infantry trenches strongly supported by artillery. The second line was strategically located a few kilometres behind the first, enabling them to fall back, or counter-attack, if required. And the third consisted of a series of fortifications, including dams and moats around strategically important cities like Tokmak. The Russian philosophy – as seen in World War II – was to hold and break-up an enemy offensive, and then launch their own counter-offensive at an appropriate moment later. And the Russians were masters in defensive fighting. As time would show, when the Ukrainians attacked, they simply evaporated from their positions, allowing the advancing Ukrainians to move into an empty area, and then launched counterattacks on the attacking troops to simply decimate them.

The delay in the launch of the offensive was compounded by another factor. The *Rasputitsa,* the Spring thaw that follows the melting of the snow, went on much longer than expected, this year. The boggy ground would not permit large scale offensive actions till the ground hardened sufficiently and the offensive was eventually pushed till June,

Options for the Offensive

The planning for the offensive began around February 23, even as Ukraine began receiving military training and large consignments of aid from NATO. An estimated 50-60000 soldiers were built up in 12 Brigades for the offensive – nine newly raised, three built up from existing formations. There was a debate whether the new equipment would be given to new units and formations or whether it would be allotted to older, experienced units. Eventually it was decided to give it to the newly raised formations. On hindsight, perhaps the new units lacked battle experience to use the equipment optimally, and contributed to the slow pace of the offensive.

The initial plan was to conduct a lightning strike through gaps identified by US intelligence, that would pierce the Russian lines in an armored blitzkrieg and strike deep behind their positions in Eastern and Southern Ukraine. That would be in line with their earlier offensive in September 22 which had got such rapid results. The offensive was planned to be launched in May itself. But in a shocking breach of security, the US Dept of Defense classified documents were leaked and posted online. These documents give out TOP SECRET assessment of Ukraine troop levels, casualties, staying power and available weaponry. It also posted maps and charts of Ukrainian troops deployment, including the new brigades raised for the offensive. That breach caused Ukraine to revise their initial plans and led to a serious rift between USA and Ukraine. Ukraine remained understandably cagy of sharing further information with their allies thereafter.

Which were the likely areas of attack that Ukraine could have followed? The most obvious was is in the South, where they could move southwards from the direction of Zaporizhzhia towards the ports on the coastline. The Southern offensive would have two components; one from the direction of Zaporizhzhia headed in the direction of Melitopal. Another would be a deeper offensive to the East headed for Berdiansk and Mariupol. The aim of both the offensives was to reach the coast on the Sea of Azov, and thus cut off Russian troops in South Ukraine and even affect their hold on Crimea.

Another option was the Western option by which the Ukrainians would advance from the direction of Kherson and then move eastwards rolling up the Russian positions along the coast. It would involve the crossing of the Dnieper River and in all probability would be done in conjunction with the

Southern option to build up pressure from two directions. This option was handicapped by the breaching of the Nova Kakhovka dam on the Dnipro River. This inundated around 500 square kilometres on both sides of the river and effectively made the Russian western flank a 'no-go area' precluding effective operations from that direction. This enabled them to withdraw crack troops of the 49th Combined Arms Army from there, to beef up more threatened sectors. It was a heinous act that caused an ecological and humanitarian disaster of epic proportions, and though Russia denies it, the act has a parallel in history. In 1941, the Soviet Army destroyed a similar dam on the Dnipro River, that flooded the area and killed thousands of Russian civilians – but delayed the advancing Germans long enough for the Soviet forces to withdraw to safety.

The third option was in the northeast towards the Donbas to recapture vital towns and lost territory. The Ukrainians hoped to launch another offensive in the direction of Bakhmut to encircle and decimate the Russian forces there. (Just like the Soviets did in the epic battle of Stalingrad in 1942). After all many of their crack formations were already in the area and a victory would provide an immense victory and a psychological boost, and also threaten the Russian communications in the Donbas.

There is a fourth and more dangerous option. The Ukrainians could have attacked into Russian territory itself. They could hit the town of Belgorod, around 80 kilometres deep in Russia which is the logistical node for its troops in Eastern Ukraine. The Ukrainians launched raids by militia groups in April that came dangerously close to Belgorod (perhaps they were doing a reconnaissance and testing the defenses). But then, an attack into Russia meant a dangerous escalation and the US and the western allies would not permit it. But though dangerous, thus strike would have enabled the Ukrainians to be better placed on the bargaining table, for negotiations later.

As events showed later, the Ukrainians did consider all the options. But the force level that they held was enough to only follow one effectively. Other actions would have to be holding and diversionary one to tie down the Russians. When the Ukrainians attacked, they selected the most obvious Southern option and attacked from Zaporizhzhia towards Melitopol with another thrust going towards Berdiansk. At the same time, they also launched operations to regain area in Bakhmut. This in a way was a serious dissipation of their forces as the thrust lines were now 800 kilometers apart and none of the thrust lines were then strong enough to achieve their ultimate aims. The delay in the launch of the offensive and the wide dissipation of forces were the main reasons for the eventual failure of the offensive.

The Offensive

The exact date of the launch of the offensive is not clear. Shaping and diversionary actions had been taking place along the front for quite a while. But on 04 June the broad contours became clear, as Ukraine launched its main offensive in the Southern sector from Zaporizhzhia southwards towards Melitopol. Further to the east, they also attacked towards the port city of Berdiansk. It was hoped that the offensive would break through the strong Russian defensive lines and reach all the way to the coast on the Sea of Azov, thus cutting off the Russians in Southern Ukraine.

From Zaporizhzhia, the Ukrainians launched their main attack around the city of Orikhiv and contacted the first defensive line between the villages of Robotyne and Verbove. They faced stiff resistance as they encountered the first line of minefields. In one of the first engagements, a column of Leopard II tanks and Bradley AFVs were destroyed while trying to cross a minefield and Russian media enthusiastically claimed, "German Panzers again destroyed on Russian soil."

In fact, the lines of defences and minefields and the cohesive defensive battle that the Russians put up, proved stronger than anticipated. As the Ukrainians tried to storm and break through the defensive positions, they were repeatedly sighted by drones and then attacked by infantry and artillery. The tanks found it virtually impossible to breach the dense minefields which had almost five mines per meter of frontage. The Ukrainians held just 30 trawls and ploughs, but they had a limited life and were defeated using mines laid in tandem. The halted and crippled tanks were then hit by artillery and missile fire and it is estimated that Ukraine lost over twenty percent of the equipment it had received from the West in just the first two weeks of the offensive.

Faced with such losses, the Ukrainians gave up the idea of trying to breach the defences, but concentrated on breaching the minefields by hand and create safe lanes for the infantry and armor to get through. It was a dangerous role, with the sappers having to clear the mines by night to avoid being detected, and that itself claimed many casualties. Breaching in this manner was a slow tedious process, and was definitely not the Blitzkrieg hoped for. Any hope of a rapid breakthrough was lost, and advance was now at a pace of around 500 meters or so every day. Though the Ukrainians were criticized by their allies for their timid approach, they shrugged it off, stating that they were not like the Russians who considered the lives of their men as expendable and wanted to preserve lives. But by this tactic, the speed of their advance was even slower that the Russian offensive in the Donbas in the previous summer.

The Ukrainian offensive was also hampered by the lack of air cover. The tanks and infantry were repeatedly hit by Russian attack helicopters and drones. By now the Russians have obtained parity in drones and used them effectively to pass information of enemy movement and activities and then bring down strikes upon them.

Crawling forward and reclaiming small villages along the way, the Ukrainians had their first major success when they captured Robotyne. On 23 August the Ukrainian flag came up there, and though Robotyne was just a large village of around 5000 inhabitants, it was considered important enough for Zelensky to visit the frontlines and congratulate 10 Operational Corps (and its units – 46 Air Mobile Brigade, 116, 117 and 118 Mechanized Brigades) for their feat. But Robotyne was significant in that is marked the crossing of the first Russian defensive line and from here they could threaten the second. The Ukrainians moved five kilometres southwards and captured Verbone, and were poised at the edge of the second Russian defensive line. But crossing it would be as slow and as time consuming as the first. The Russians proved to be skilful in defence and adopted an 'elastic defence,' in which the forward lines delayed for as long as possible, and then withdrew just before an enemy attack. The attack would fall on thin air, as the Russians moved to prepared defences in the rear, which they then used to launch an counter attack from the flanks or rear to retake the lost position. Even the American grudgingly admitted that the Russians had learnt the lessons of the past year and adopted skilful tactics both in defence and offense.

A little further to the east of its main thrust from Zaporizhzhia the Ukrainians also launched a subsidiary thrust in the direction of Berdainsk. That thrust was to breach the Russian defensive layout, divide reaction and hoped to break through the Russian lines towards the port city of Berdiansk on the Sea of Azov.

This thrust too halted and slowed down in the face of extensive minefields and strong Russian resistance. Three small settlements were retaken in the initial days and announced with much fanfare. But as soon as they contacted the first defensive line, this thrust too slowed and stalled, unable to break through the extensive defensive layout. This thrust line too crept forward a few hundred meters a day, reaching its deepest point in the village of Novodonetshe, which was just 11 kilometres from the start line. After months of hard fighting, it had not even succeeded in breaking the first defensive line.

The Ukrainians were running out of time with winter approaching. They had to cross the second defensive line to be able to reach Tokmuk; an important town and communication hub around 17 kilometres away. This town was the intermediate objective and had to be captured to enable by August or so, to them to develop operations further southwards. But, even after capturing Tokmuk, they would have to cross a third line of defences, before they could reach the main objective – the port town of Melitopol which was still 40 kilometres beyond that. The Ukrainians had just completed the first phase of the operation, i.e the crossing the first defensive minefield over a period of five months. It is significant that as per military operational planning the crossing of the first defensive minefield is to be completed in the first night itself. The next phase would be even more difficult and involve the crossing of the second defensive minefield, the capture of Tokmuk; and then the crossing of the third defensive line and the ultimate capture of Melitopal and Berdiansk. Their aim to reach the coast seems a far cry now. They have taken five months just to cover just around 12 kilometres and cross the first line. They have to travel another 100 odd kilometres and cross two more defensive lines till they finally reach their objectives. The next two phases are even more difficult and at this rate will take them a year more to attain.

Along with the two thrusts in the Southern sector, the Ukrainians also attacked in the Northeast in the direction of Bakhmut, the town they had lost with such heavy casualties in May. This attack was almost 600 kilometers away from the main thrust and its aim seems to be more to hold down Russian troops in the sector than anything else. Some of Ukraine's most experienced Brigades were employed there. Many of them had been mauled in the earlier

fighting and had been re-equipped with older vintage equipment, with the Leopards and Challengers allotted to the Southern thrust. Bakhmut had been a prime objective for much of the past year, even though it had little strategic value. Perhaps the Ukrainians hoped to cut off and destroy the Russian forces there, and thus weaken their position in the Donbas. Two attacks were launched in a pincer move North and South of the town and the Ukrainian forces recaptured lost positions and villages reaching the Siverskys Donets – Donbas canal just 13 kilometres away from the town. Then like the Southern offensive, that too petered out as it hit the main defensive layout and crawled ahead just around 500 yards or so every day. The offensive hoped to tie down Russian forces in the sector, but it also tied down some of their best formations there. It merely dissipated their forces and made widely dispersed thrust lines, with none of them strong enough to attain a decisive breakthrough.

In fact, by the time winter came, the frontlines were almost the same as they had been at the start of the offensive. And predictably, the Russians launched their own counter attacks. On 10 October, two large mechanized columns attacked the town of Avdiivha, around 15 kilometres west of Donbas which was being seen as a prelude to a larger offensive. That would be in keeping with the Russian doctrine of exhausting an attacker, drawing him deep and then launching a counter strike to decimate the enemy.

Analysis and Aftermath

By the beginning of winter, the Ukrainian offensive had succeeded in retaking just around 500 square kilometres of territory after five months of intense fighting. It was a far cry from their stated goal of "retaking every inch of Ukrainian territory, including Crimea." Russia still held on to over 200000 square kilometres, and mathematically speaking, at this pace it would take the Ukrainians 103 years to clear the Russians from their soil.

Even though the offensive continues, most analysts grudgingly acknowledge that it has petered out and unlikely to progress much. If anything, fresh action can take place in the next spring, but it is too late. This was the last throw of the dice, and Ukraine does not have the reserves or the stamina for a fresh offensive.

The lack of success is also a turning point for its allies. Western aid is drying up and the equipment that was painstakingly gathered last year, will not be available now. The US has provided over $100 Billion in arms and aid, but now a large portion will be diverted to the Middle East to help Israel. The Middle East War has also taken attention away from Putin's actions and shifted the focus from Europe. The defeat of Russia has not come about, and it anything, Putin's position is stronger than before.

With the world diverted in the Middle East, Russia is now free to pursue its own actions. It could well be preparing for its own Spring Offensive, that could move all the way to the line of the Oskil River in the Northeast and the Dnieper River in the South. They have already taken over the provinces of Zaporizhzhia, Kherson, Luhansk and Donetsk and amalgamated them into Russia through a 'referendum.' The loss of Ukrainian territory now seems a foregone conclusion. As a war weary Europe looks away, aid dries up and Ukraine scrapes the bottom of the barrel for its own reserves, the failed offensive marks the last throw of the dice. It has tilted the war decisively and irrevocably in Russia's favour.

REFERENCES

"Explained. Is Ukraine's Counter Offensive Working?," *The Hindu*, https://www.thehindu.com

"How might Ukraine's Counter Offensive End," RAND Corporation; https://www.rand.org

"How the Ukraine Counter Offensive can still succeed?," *Time Magazine*, https://time.com/ideas/ukraine

"Major New Package in Support of Ukraine's Counter Offensive," https://www.gov.uk

"Mapping out Ukraine's Counter Offensive Strategy," *Wall Street Journal*, https://wsj.com

"Ukraine Counter Offensive Maps," *Reuters*, https://www.reuters.com

"Ukraine's Counter Offensive and what comes After," *The New Yorker*, https://newyorker.com

"Ukraine's Counter Offensive has made progress, But...," *The New York Times*, https://www.nytimes.com

"Ukraine's Counter Offensive is Speeding Up," *The Economist*, https://www.economist.com

"Ukraine's Counter Offensive moves towards Winter Phase," https://www.rte.ie

"Ukraine's Counter Offensive, what do we know so far?," *Al Jazeera*, https://aljazeera.com

"Ukraine's Counter Offensive: Will it retake Crimea?" *Council of Foreign Relations*, https://www/cfr.org

"What went wrong in Ukraine's Counter Offensive?," *VOX*, https://www.vox.com

"Winter is Coming, but Kyiv is adapting its Tactics," *CNN*, https://www.cnn.com

4

The Russian Offensives in Donbas and Kharkiv

"This is a meat-grinder."

The Third Year of the War

By February 2024, as the war entered its third year, the glimmerings of how the conflict could end were getting increasingly clear. The much touted Ukrainian 'Spring Offensive' of July 2023 had proved to be a damp squib. The offensive was too widely spread out to attain any decisive results, and eventually ground to a halt after crawling ahead around 11 kilometres. Only one breach was made in the first defensive line in the Tokmuk sector after five months of slow, painstaking advance. Those gains should have actually been done in just one night of combat.

As the Ukrainian offensive ground to a halt and the winter of 2023 set, in, the Russians sealed the breach and then launched their own offensive. They focused on Avdiivka – a large town in the Donbas of around 32,000, which was an important communication hub leading to the provincial capital of Donetsk. The fighting around Avdiivka followed the same bitter street fighting seen in Bakhmut and Mariupol, till the town finally fell. Then around May 24, they followed up with another offensive – this time in the Kharkiv sector. The Ukrainian defences, now stretched thin across a 1000 km frontage, and exhausted by over two years of continuous fighting were slowly giving way.

The Battle of Avdiivka

Avdiivka, located in the crucial Donbas region of Donetsk, had seen intense fighting since 2014. It has been attacked by pro-Russian separatists of the Donetsk People's Republic (DPR) in 2017, but managed to hold on. When Russia invaded Ukraine on 24 February 2022, it was hit by intense mortar and artillery fire right from the very first day of the war itself, and subject to repeated Russian attacks.

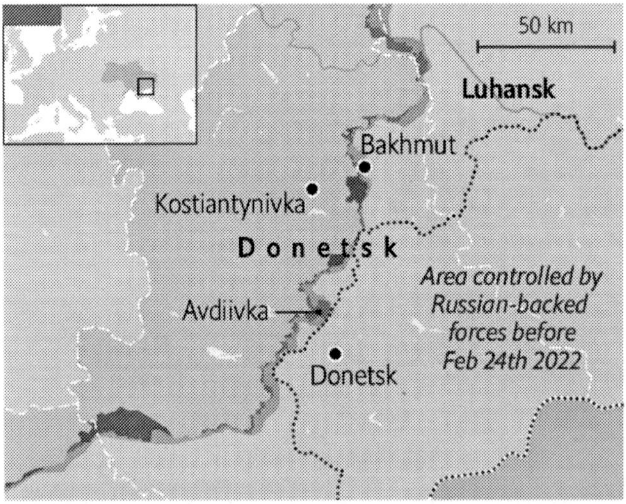

The Russian Advance (Photo Courtesy: The Economist)

Though some of the outlying villages were lost, the town held on, till a Ukrainian counter offensive in October 22, recaptured some of the lost areas and staved the threat.

There was a lull for over a year, till the Russians launched a renewed attack on 10 October 2023, using the 8th Combined Arms Army and members of the DPR. Three motorised brigades launched armoured and helicopter assaults, but were beaten back with heavy casualties. The city was attacked over 60 times over the period of the next five months, and the fighting was considered even worse than that of Bakhmut or Mariupol.

The Russians used their usual 'meat grinder tactics' – first pummelling the town with artillery fire, and then launching infantry attacks that crept forward meter by meter. They captured the outlying villages and established a foothold on the outskirts of the town. From here, they dug a 160 meter long tunnel beneath the Ukrainian defences, which they detonated causing heavy casualties amongst the defenders.

By end December 23, the Russians crept up into the town and captured the high ground of the large Coke factor the industrial areas within it. They also cut off rail and road communication, surrounding it from the north, east, and south, which left only a small corridor leading in from the West, through which the defenders could be resupplied and replenished. The Ukrainians were outnumbered by 5:1 by the Russians who also held nine times more artillery guns and ammunition. By mid-January, the Russians made a breakthrough in the Southern suburbs, by entering the town through the underground sewage system and infiltrated two kilometres deep behind the Ukrainian positions, from where they launched attacks and raids on to the defenders.

The Russian attacks came at high cost, but the Ukrainians too were taking heavy casualties – estimated at around 300 per day. 59 Motorised Brigade, 110 Mechanised Brigade and 47 Mechanised Brigade, the primary formations holding the town were exhausted after months of continual combat. Reserves was scarce and had to be pulled out from other sector. Eventually in early February the last available reserve, 3rd Assault Brigade was sent into the town. The decision to reinforce the town was a controversial one. The Army Chief, General Oleksandr Syrski, was not in favour of expending more precious life and equipment, but Zelensky insisted on holding on to the beleaguered town.

On 15 February 24, the Russians launched a pincer attack around the town which cut it off almost completely. Only one road was now open to the Ukrainians through which Ukrainian evacuation convoys finally withdrew under continuous drone and artillery fire. The heavy casualties caused during the withdrawal led to the road being named, 'The Road of Death.' On 17th February, it was announced that Ukrainian forces had withdrawn "to more favourable positions in the rear". The same day, Russia announced the capture of the town, with Putin himself issuing a congratulatory message on its success.

Aavdivka what is the first major Russian success since the capture of Bakhmut. But it came at a huge cost to both sides. Russia was estimated to have lost 30,000–35,000 men in the battle. The Ukrainian too lost around 17,000 dead and over 30,000 injured. But at the end of it, Ukraine seemed more vulnerable than before and the tide of war was going Russia's way.

Political and Global Developments

As Russia was creeping forward on the battlefield and consolidating its hold on the occupied territories, it was becoming increasingly clear that Ukraine would be unlikely to attain its slated aim of, "Removing the last Russian from occupied Ukrainian soil – including Crimea." The provinces of Kherson, Zaporizhzhia, Luhansk and Donetsk had been captured in September 2022 itself and then amalgamated into Russia by the referendum of October 2022. Yet, all of Donbas had not been completely captured by the Russians, and it continued operations to seize the remaining 15 percent of the Donetsk province.

It was also becoming clear that the status quo would be maintained and Russia would hold on to its military gains. Both sides were tired after two years of war, and looking for a face-saving exit. Yet, it was Ukraine that had suffered more. Its economy was ravaged, its infrastructure was in shambles after repeated drone and missile attacks, and it had pulled up its last reserves of manpower to beef up their weary and depleted formations. Aid continued to trickle in from the USA and the western allies, and they were completely dependent on external assistance to continue the fight. Russia, though had withstood the war surprising well, and in fact, had emerged even stronger – both politically and economically.

Putin won the Russian elections in March 2024 in a landslide victory, getting 87.4 per cent of the votes. That was no surprise. There were no contenders, and the only serious challenger Alexei Navalny, had died in jail somewhere in the Gulag, after being sentenced to 19 years of jail. His death, attributed to poisoning, was an indicator that Putin would brook no challenge to his iron rule. Putin now entered his fifth term in power, making him the longest serving Russian head of state since Stalin. He now had six more years to prosecute the war completely on his terms.

The Russian economy too was booming – sanctions or no sanctions. The economy grew at 3.4 per cent in 2023 – the fastest in Europe – and was expected to continue in the same vein. Rather than the sanctions impacting Russia, it were the western economies that had suffered by being cut off from cheap Russian gas and oil. The energy hit economies of Germany, UK, and France began slipping into recession, as inflation rose and manufacturing costs increased. US sanctions on Russia had banned the export of ship-borne crude oil (though oil continued to flow into Europe through pipelines). The flow of natural gas from Russia to Europe was impacted when the NORD STREAM I and II gas pipelines were sabotaged in a series of mysterious explosions. The exact cause is still unknown, but is largely attributed to the US. Russia however, more than made up for the loss of European markets, by simply siphoning excess oil and gas to India and China and other nations, who lapped them up at very competitive rates. Russia emerged as a largest exporter of crude oil to India in 2023. Crude oil refined in Indian refineries was then exported by India to Europe as refined oil products. This not only saved valuable foreign exchange, but perhaps even saved the European economies.

Politically too, Russia and Putin were on a much stronger footing. Putin's personal rapport with the Chinese Premier Xi Jinping, ensured that Russia-China ties had become stronger – especially since both shared the same vision of the world and had a common animosity with the US led Western order. It is significant that Putin had visited China on 10 February 2022, for the Beijing Olympics, just before the start of his invasion of Ukraine. Xi himself had followed up with a visit to Moscow in March 23, where their 'No-limits Friendship' was affirmed. In his first overseas visit after taking over for the sixth time, Putin again visited Beijing to deepen ties and the Russia-China axis seemed to be getting stronger. Putin had also successfully reached out to African and Asian nations. On 13th July, Prime Minister Modi visited Moscow (in his first bilateral visit after taking over his third term). This reaffirmed traditional Indo-Russian ties, but drew much criticism from the West, especially since it came at the same time that NATO countries were meeting in Washington to mark 75 years of the alliance.

India walked a tightrope in its ties with the USA, Russia and also Ukraine. In fact, Prime Minister Modi followed it up with a visit to Kyiv for a meeting with Zelensky. The fact that India holds strong independent relations with both Russia and Ukraine, put it in a position, where it could be the peace broker to help bring an end to the conflict.

Both sides seemed to be looking for talks – but purely on their terms. Putin had announced that he was ready for talks; but the territory occupied by Russia would be retained, and was not subject to discussion. On the other hand, Zelensky's starting demand was that Russia was to withdraw from all occupied Ukrainian territories – including Crimea. With no common point the best that could be expected was a ceasefire, or an agreement to stop targeting each other's civilian infrastructure. A much touted Ukraine Peace Summit was held on 15-16 June in Switzerland, attended by 92 nations. But Russia was not invited, making it a non-starter. The closing declaration called for a withdrawal of all Russian forces, payment of war damages, and the return of prisoners and civilians. But it was largely meaningless. Putin would never agree, and at best offer Ukraine a opportunity to cut its losses, by a cessation of hostilities.

Ukraine is even more exhausted and completely dependent on the West to continue this war. It has reached the bottom of the barrel for its manpower reserves, and has the resources to fight a war for just around 45 days. It needs western aid and equipment to continue the fight. And it is in the interest of the USA that the fight be continued, "To the last Ukrainian." To weaken Russia, the USA will continue to supply Ukraine with the resources to prolong the fight. In April 2024, the US Senate approves an additional consignment of $61 billions of aid, bringing the total aid provided to over $175 billion. It also promised fresh consignments of F-16 fighters, Abrams tanks, HIMARS weapon systems and ammunition, along with Early Warning and Air Défense resources. More importantly, USA, France, Germany, and UK finally gave permission for their weaponry to strike targets inside Russian territory. That would be a huge boost to Ukraine, as coming events would soon show.

But while political and diplomatic parleys were going on, Russia was continuing with its own offensive in the Donbas, where they had captured Avdiivka, and were closing in on the city of Pokrovsk in the Donetsk. More importantly, they had also launched a renewed offensive in the direction of Kharkiv.

The Russian Offensive in Kharkiv

Kharkiv is no stranger to war. The city was the site of some of the major battles of World War II and had changed hands five times during the Great War. Even when Russia launched their invasion of Ukraine on 24 February 2022, Kharkiv – the second largest city in Ukraine – was a prime target in the

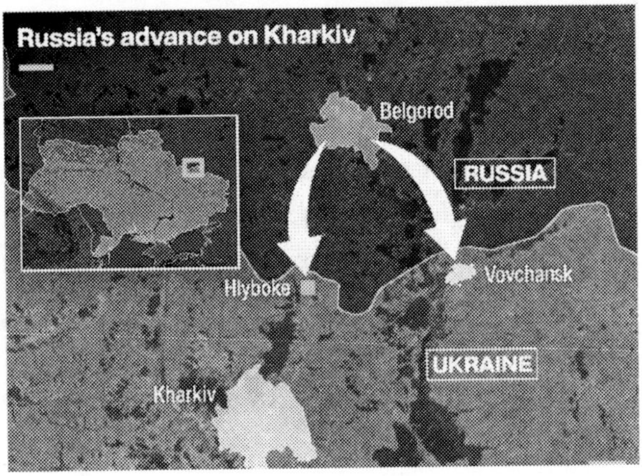

initial assaults itself. A major Russian thrust headed for the town, which was subjected to armoured and infantry assaults. Though much of the outlying villages were lost, the city held on desperately, till a Ukrainian counter offensive in September 22,eventually recaptured most of the lost areas and then advanced virtually up to the Russian border itself.

The Kharkiv sector remained relatively quiet, as the focus of Russian operations shifted to the Donbas. Like all other Ukrainian cities, it was subjected to drone and missile attacks on a regular basis, but faced no major attack as such. This relative peace was disturbed on 10 May 2024, when Russia launched a assault in that sector with around 30,000 men.

Around 4 to 5 Russian battalions, crossed the border in the Kharkiv sector at around 5 in the morning of 10 May. They moved along two axis – one towards Lyptsi, and the other further South towards Vovchansk. The area had not been fortified nor had mines been laid there. Even the cement blocks which had been sent to establish defensive fortifications were merely lying around. Zelensky apparently flew into a rage at the news, accusing his Generals of cowardice and incompetence. The Commander of 125 Territorial Defence Brigade, responsible for the area was punished for this major lapse.

The Russians had disabled the Starlink terminals, – helpfully provided by Elon Musk at the start of the war, thus blocking communications and also preventing drones from transmitting information. The Russians soon established a foothold 5 kilometres deep and 10 kilometres wide. As per Putin's pronouncements, his intention was not to capture Kharkiv, but merely to establish a 'buffer zone' in the sector against future Ukrainian attacks. The Ukrainians were forced to send in reinforcements in the form of 57 Motorised Brigade and 92 Assault Brigade along with the 'Kraken Battalion' to halt the Russian advance. But using their usual tactics of massive bombardments and creeping infantry assaults, the Russians inched forward around 500–1000 meters every day. Strangely, the Russians did not use much armour, leading to speculation is that they could be running out of mechanised vehicles. But most probably it was done to maintain surprise, as hiding the concentration of heavy vehicles would have been difficult. Instead, they used motorcycles and All-Terrain Vehicles to rush the objective during their assaults.

By end May, the Russians had captured around 13 villages, but beyond that could not make headway towards their initial objectives of Lyptsi or Vovchansk. They reached the line of the Vovcha River, and even succeeded in establishing bridgeheads across it, which were counter-attacked and destroyed. In a bid to divide reaction, the Russians launched an attack in the direction of Sumy – around 90 km to the north, on 10 June. This thrust made initial headway, but was eventually blocked by the Ukrainians.

By July, the Russian offensive in this sector has stalled they had only made moderate gains. The Russians held a large wedge of territory almost 8-10 kilometres deep. In terms of territory, these were the largest gains Russia had made since October 2022. But even though the offensive did not achieve its complete aims, it succeeded in diverting Ukrainian troops to this sector and extended them even further along the 1000 km long front. Coupled with their actions in Kharkiv, the Russians pushed ahead in the Donbas and even recaptured Robotyne in early August – one of the few positions they had lost during the Ukrainian summer offensive. They also advanced in the Donbas towards the town of Pokrovsk, an important rail and road communication center, whose loss would open the way to all of Donetsk.

So far, the Ukrainians had been merely reacting to the Russian offensive. They had launched a successful offensive in October 2022 when they recaptured much area in the Kharkiv and Kherson sector. Their 'Spring Offensive' of July 2023, had no gains to speak off. But then on 06 August 2024, the Ukrainians launched their own offensive into Russia in the Kursk sector, and the war took another turn.

REFERENCES

"After Modi's Moscow trip, where do India-Russia ties Stand?," *The Diplomat*, 19 July 2024

"Balmforth Tom, "Russian forces attack Kharkiv region, Open new Front," *Reuters*, 10 May 2024

"Despite War and Sanctions, Russia becomes a 'high-income economy'" *The Economic Times*, 6 July 2024

"Europe's Economy Risks a Recession after Output falls," *CNN*, 31 October 2023,

"F-16s arrive to help Ukraine Fight Russia," *A P News*, 01 August 2024

"F-16s: How will they impact Ukraine's War," *Centre for Strategic and International Studies*, 11 June 2024

"How much US Aid is going to Ukraine?" *Council on Foreign Relations*, 9 May 2024

"Modi's Moscow visit and Indo-Russian ties," *The Hindu*, 13 July 2024.

"Putin and Xi pledge 'New Era in Ties'," *Reuters*, 16 May 2024

"Russia advances 10 kms, halted at First Defensive Line," *The Kviv Independent*, 17 May 2024

"Russia denies Kharkiv Offensive Failing," *Al Jazeera*, 17 July 2024.

"Russia to grow faster than all European Economies, says IMF," *BBC News*, 16 April 2024

"Russian Offensive Campaign Assessment," *Institute for the Study of War*; 18 February 2024

"Russian Offensive Campaign Assessment," *Institute for the Study of War*, 12 August 2024

"Second Russian Invasion of Kharkiv caught Ukraine Unprepared," *Washington Post*, 19 May 2024

"What is in the Ukraine Aid Package?" *Centre for Strategic and International Studies*, 01 May 2024

"Why did the Ukrainian Peace Summit Fail?" *Al Jazeera*, 23 June 2024

Farrel Francis, "Surviving Avdiivka," *The Kviv Independent*, 21 February 2024

Gall Carlotta; "Avdiivka falls to Russians," *New York Times*, 17 February 2024

Keating Joshua, "Are Ukraine's Defences starting to Crumble," *VOX*, 03 March 2024

Landry Carole, "On the Front Line in the East," *The New York Times*, 22 April 2024

Rommen Rebecca; "The Colossal Cost of capturing Avdiivka," *Business Insider*, 22 February 2024

Ryan Mick, "The Fall of Avdiivka," *Futum Doctrina*, 20 February 2024

Walter Shawn; "Avdiivka: Ukrainian Troops in Embattled Town," *BBC News*, 17 February 2024

KURSK: GAMBLE OR GAME CHANGER

"Ukraine will establish a 'buffer zone' within Russia."

—President Zelensky

Kursk. The very word conjures images of the titanic battle fought here in World War II during July 1943. That battle saw over a million Germans and Soviet troops along with 3000 tanks clash in the largest tank battle in history. That six-week long battle turned the tide of the war decisively towards the Soviet Union.

The Ukrainian incursion into Kursk is nowhere on that scale, but its impact could still be quite significant. At around 8 in the morning on 06 August 2024, around 1000 Ukrainian troops, along with 20 tanks and 11 Infantry Combat Vehicles, crossed the Russian border in two thrust lines, and simply surged ahead in this lightly defended sector, held largely by second line troops and members of the National Guard. Using drones flying above the advancing columns for early warning, the Ukrainians advanced rapidly, bypassing opposition and heading for the line of the Seym River. In the initial breach made by the 80th Brigade, another brigade – the 82nd - was inducted, followed by two others a day later, to consolidate the gains. In just three days, the Ukrainians had advanced 30 kilometers deep, captured 28 villages (the Ukrainians claim 92) and occupied over 1000 kms of Russian territory. The town of Sudzhy, located 10 kms from the border, along with its natural gas processing facility, was also captured in the first two days itself. Pictures emerged of Russian flags being gleefully pulled down and replaced by Ukrainian ones, and of surrendered Russian soldiers being marched off in droves. This bold and unexpected attack was the first invasion of Russia since 1941 and for the first time brought this ground war onto to Russian soil.

This was not the first time that the Ukrainians had entered this sector. They had made limited forays earlier – once in May 2023, and again in March 2024. But these raids were by members of armed militia and not by regular troops. Perhaps they were seeking information and testing the ground for this major incursion. The Ukrainians have to be complimented for the manner in which they went about their Kursk offensive. This swift and methodically executed operation was a far cry from their 'Spring Offensive' of 2023, which crawled forward timidly and advanced around 7-11 kms in four months. This offensive was carried out in great secrecy, with only a select few involved in the planning. Elements of 103 Brigade, 22 Mechanized Brigade, and 80 and 82 Brigades got to their assembly areas just a few days before the attack. An elaborate ruse was played, wherein a likely Russian threat in this sector was built up, and that these forces were being sent as reinforcements in case of a Russian attack. The commanders were told about the exact nature of the offensive operation just two days in advance, and the crews informed when they had started their tank engines. Even their closest ally, the USA, was ostensibly kept in the dark (perhaps because the earlier Ukrainian offensive plan of 2023 was leaked from the Pentagon in the infamous Wikileaks). Though of course, the US would have been in the loop and would have provided vital intelligence and surveillance. The USA had recently given permission for Ukraine to use western provided equipment and long-range artillery like HIMARS inside Russia. That factor was vital to the success of this operation.

The Russians were undoubtedly taken by surprise, as their initial disjointed actions reveal. Over 1,20,000 civilians were evacuated from the area and an emergency declared in Kursk and its adjoining districts. As Russian reinforcements began moving towards the area, the Ukrainians interdicted advancing columns with drone and long-range artillery fire. A Russian column of around 15 trucks was hit by a HIMARS strike, which virtually wiped out an entire battalion in the largest single day loss of the war. The Ukrainians also blew up three bridges along the Seym river with air and artillery strikes to prevent move of Russian reinforcements. They also damaged a pontoon bridge laid by the Russians a few days later. This delay in the move of Russian reinforcements, has enabled the Ukrainians to consolidate their positions.

But Russia, and Putin himself, were under great pressure to seal the breach and a strong cohesive Russian response would soon follow.

The offensive, though bold, is a dangerous gamble which could go either way. But, after two years of being on the back foot, Ukraine finally got a huge psychological boost, which will be a tremendous fillip to its citizens and its soldiers fighting grimly in the South and East. As per the pronouncements of Zelensky, the main aim seems to be to capture prime Russian territory which could then be a valuable chip for negotiations. As of now, Ukraine has no card to play on the negotiating table, and this may just provide it with an ace. Also, the Russians had been pushing ahead with their own offensives in the Kharkiv and Donbas sectors. It was hoped that the Kursk offensive would divert attention and perhaps even draw resources from these Russian actions. But that is a double-edged weapon. The Ukrainians have had to thin out their own defenses in these sectors to build up the offensive force and that could provide weak spots, that can be exploited by the Russians. But its most significant achievement is that it has finally brought the war to Russia and the Russian people. That could ratchet up the pressure for a ceasefire.

The Russians have launched a 'counter-terror operation' to restore the situation, and followed up with the usual barrage of drone and rocket attacks on Ukrainian infrastructure and rear areas. But no serious counter-attacks have been launched. Perhaps their own strategic reserves were being assembled for that. Also, in spite of the pressure in Kursk, the Russians did not halt their own offensives inside Ukraine. Rather, they intensified them. In the Kharkiv sector, they pushed even deeper and captured the town of Hrodivka. In the Donbas sector, they closed in on Pokrovsk – a vital rail and road junction, that could open the way for a capture of all of Donetzk. This was a sound strategy, which could expose Ukrainian vulnerabilities and maybe even force them to recoil.

Significantly the Russians followed up with a massive strike with over 200 missiles and drones on Ukraine's power and energy grid causing intense damage. This might be done to coerce it to call off the offensive. Ukraine too responded with long range strikes inside Russia. Both sides could be seeking to "escalate to deescalate' the situation which could open the doors for negotiation.

The Ukrainians have attained a notable success but their forces were vulnerable to a Russian counter stroke and at danger of being cut off. What

Ukrainian and Russian actions along the Front
(Photo courtesy: The Economist)

were the options after this? They could advance deeper towards Kursk, and its prized nuclear reactor, or even the logistical hub of Belgorod. But that would be beyond the capabilities and they would have overextended themselves. They could consolidate along the existing positions on the line of the Seym river, which forms a good defensive line. In fact, Zelensky had taken a line out of Putin's book and stated that they intend to create a 'buffer zone' around that line. Or, they could pull back to more favorable defensive positions, 10-12 kms inside the border where logistics and fire support would be easier. The crux lies in holding on to their gains, and not overextend themselves. To convert this short-term gain into a strategic advantage, it would be prudent to restrict themselves to defensive positions – including the town of Sudzhy – which they could hold and claim as a symbol of victory.

Although Ukraine hoped to use the gains of this offensive on the bargaining table, this incursion just hardened Putin's stance. He had lost face to made up for it, by pushing even deeper into Kharkiv and Donbas and intensifying the missile and drone attacks on Ukrainian cities. There was also the fear of the war expanding in scope. Putin blamed the NATO allies for extending this war, and nuclear saber rattling is likely to increase – especially since Russian doctrine permits the use of nuclear weapons if their territorial sovereignty is impacted. So, rather than paving the way for talks, this incursion actually delayed it.

Militarily and politically, it has been a victory for Zelensky. But, it did not help in the stated aim of, "Evicting the last Russian from the last inch of Ukrainian soil – including Crimea." It did provide a tremendous boost for the defense of Ukraine, and spurred the US and their western allies to continue supplying ammunition and aid, which was also one of the underlying aims. It has also exposed Putin's and Russia's weaknesses, and hopefully it could bring some sort of pressure on him to accept a ceasefire. Modi's visit to Ukraine on 23 August 2024, coming close on his meeting with Putin at Moscow, just two months earlier, could help bring it about. Militarily, the Kursk offensive had been a well-executed action, but it would not end the war. There would be far more blood-letting before this needless war is finally concluded.

REFERENCES

"Analysis: The Battle of Kursk, 2024," *The Kyiv Post*, 10 August 2024

"How Ukraine turned the War on its Head with Surprise Attack," *CNN News*, 18 August 2024

"Intense Battles against major Ukrainian Incursion," *Reuters*, 10 August 2024

"Kursk Incursion lifts Ukrainian Hopes," *Al Jazeera*, 22 August 2024

"Kursk Incursion: Ukraine destroys important Bridges," *EH World Wire*, 15 August 2024

"Russia Offensive Campaign Assessment," *Institute for the Study of War*, 18 August 2024

"Russia strikes Ukraine power grid with over 200 Missiles and Drones," *The Indian Express*, 27 August 2024

"Russia's double punch against Ukraine's Shock raid," *The Economist*, 18 August 2024

"Ukraine Artillery blocks Russian Reinforcements," *Forbes*, 9 August 2024

"Ukraine catches Russia Off-guard," *Al Jazeera*, 12 August 2024

"Ukraine is Poking the Russian Bear," *The New York Times*, 15 August 2024

"Ukraine's Kursk Offensive: Big Stakes, big Risks," *The Institute for the Study of War*, 22 August 2024.

5

Lessons from the Ukrainian Battlefield

"Warfare has not changed. It has merely evolved."

(*Courtesy: The Economist*)

THE LESSONS FROM THE WAR

The Economist magazine ran a very interesting cover story on the Ukraine war. To illustrate it, they showed the photo of a long line of tired soldiers making their way through a muddy, trench-infested battlefield, pockmarked by artillery. It could have been a scene straight out of Ypres or Somme in World War I, except for one vital difference. In the sky above, a swarm of drones hovered overhead.

The image depicted tellingly the fact that though warfare has changed, it still remains more or less the same. The incessant shelling, the barbed wire and lines of trenches, the hand-to-hand fighting in cities and buildings, and the tanks lurking in the background are all scenes out of earlier wars. But the drones show how new technology dominates the battlefield. In other words, though warfare and its principles have remained the same, modern technology and concepts have added a new dimension to it.

The Ukraine war has changed the prevailing concepts of modern warfare. Since the break-up of the Soviet Union, theories propounded that future wars would be "short and swift and fought in restricted timelines and areas of operations." It was also believed that in an interconnected global market place, the world itself would not permit long wars. A commonly touted example was that nations with McDonald's outlets on their soil would not go to war with each other. (Ukraine incidentally had 64 McDonald's outlets, Russia 847 before the war).

The Ukraine war has debunked these theories very fast. The war, which was to be over in a week or so, has gone on for two years and will continue for some time to come. Nor has it been restricted in space. The initial Russian attacks on 24 February 2022 took place over the entire frontage of northern and western Ukraine – an area extending 2,400 kilometres. Even today, the front still extends over 1,200 kilometres. It is not a restricted war; it is the closest Europe has come to total war since World War II. And rather than the world closing ranks to halt the war, there seems to an active movement to prolong it by vested powers.

The battle degenerated into a slow attritional war, with lines of trenches and fortifications along the front lines. Here, troops hunker down as artillery rains upon them and drones peer from above. Gains by either side are measured in metres rather than in kilometres. In fact, the deep battles of manoeuvring have taken place only once or twice during this war. The first time when Russia launched an audacious airborne campaign to capture Hostomel airport, near Kyiv, which failed by a whisker – and then later by the Ukrainians during their autumn offensive when their mechanized columns blitzed their way across 90 kilometres in just three days.

All this implies that the era of long wars is back. But if we examine this closely, that era never really went away. The US war in Afghanistan lasted twenty years; the Soviet invasion took ten; the Iran-Iraq war went on for eight. Why even the stand-off with the Chinese after Galwan has gone on for over four years now. The only short, swift and conclusive war in the past fifty years have been the Arab-Israel wars of 1967 and 1973; the brilliant Indian victory over Pakistan which created a new nation in just 13 days in 1971; the Falklands War and the Russian invasion of Georgia in 2008. All others (though many have been non-conventional wars) have followed long timelines.

While the aim of any nation would be to attain a swift and decisive victory, should a long war of attrition be forced upon it, victory would go to the side with greater staying power. The importance of having adequate reserves of manpower, equipment, ammunition and an inbuilt agricultural and industrial base is essential. Seeing how easily external supply lines can be disrupted, maintaining a high level of self-sufficiency is equally important. The *Atmanirbhar* scheme is thus significant, but realistically, it will take us ten years to truly attain it.

One of the lessons that emerged from the war is that small compact groups often operated more successfully than large unwieldy formations. The large Russian divisions and armies often stalled and clogged at the start of the operation. The problem was compounded by the fact that their offensive did not have a central commander in the initial months, adding to the problems of coordination. The Ukrainians with their brigade-size battle groups often performed better and with greater flexibility. Keeping a smaller force optimally sustained for longer durations was also easier. In fact, it was the failure of logistics to sustain large offensive formations that led to the Russian offensive losing momentum after the initial days.

Both Russia and Ukraine resorted to massive conscription and mobilization to fill up their depleted manpower. But the result was mixed. While the numbers were made up, the training and motivational levels often left much to be desired. It was estimated that newly arrived conscripts lasted only around three engagements and their survival rates were abysmal compared to trained, experienced veterans who had been around for months. The Indian system of regimentation which has provided excellent, disciplined soldiers to units has stood the test of time and battle for decades, if not centuries. Diluting it with the new *Agniveer* scheme may prove counterproductive in the long run.

Both sides resorted to mercenaries to do their dirty work. However, the use of mercenaries is nothing new. The Pakistanis used hired tribal fighters in

Kashmir from 1947 to date – only for them to turn against them. The USA fought in Iraq and Afghanistan with a vast network of hired contractors. The Ukrainians used the Azov battalion and other groups, even raising a force of hired fighters from across the world that they called the 'International Legion of Defence for Ukraine'. The Russians pulled in fighters from Chechnya, Syria and motley of other groups. The most notable, of course was the Wagner Group, whose actions demonstrated both the advantages and perils of employing mercenaries. They provided a pool of expendable manpower that gained success at Bakhmut. But the manner in which they turned against the establishment and started to march towards Moscow, show the perils of using a large, well-armed force that is not fully under the control of the government. It is something that is best avoided.

The Russian and Ukrainian Manner of War Fighting

The war also revealed a great deal of the manner of war-fighting of both sides. The Western media had painted the Russians as bumbling nincompoops, but that is not true. They did make a series of errors in the initial days of the war. Their offensive was too widely dispersed, it lacked coordination, and was launched at the time of melting snow – *Raputista* – when it could not attain optimal results. The troops seemed to be unsure of what was to be done, and perhaps were primed into believing that it would be a cakewalk. Perhaps that is why there were glaring tactical errors in the battlefield – like not having all-arms teams, not following the tenets of dispersion, not using close air support, and not paying adequate attention to logistics. These factors contributed to the slow manner in which the offensive was conducted and denied the Russians the early victory they sought.

To give the Ukrainians their due, they did fight a very skilful defensive battle and launched a brilliant counter-offensive in October 2022, that recaptured over 7,000 square kilometres in just a few days. But then a shift seemed to have come over them as the war entered its second year. Their fighting capabilities actually seemed to have weakened and they were unable to attain any gains throughout the year. Perhaps it was because, their pool of available manpower was shrinking, and they were now scraping the bottom of the barrel for recruits. There also seemed to be some confusion in the doctrines they were to follow. The Ukrainian army was steeped in the old Soviet way of war-fighting, and when they received NATO equipment and were trained in Western concepts, they were unable to make the change effectively. The results translated into their actions on the battlefield.

The Russians too changed their manner of war-fighting as the war progressed. Beefed up with over 190,000 new conscripts, they strengthened their defensive layout and fought a well-coordinated defensive battle that blunted the Ukrainian Spring offensive of 2023. They followed the concept of all-arms teams, used drones very effectively, integrated attack helicopters with armour and infantry, and showed greater flexibility in operations. As a result, Russian casualties dropped significantly in the second year of the war, while the Ukrainian toll increased. The Russians seemed to be following their traditional pattern – starting slow, recovering to fight a strong defensive battle, exhausting the opponent, and then striking when the time was right.

The Drones Overhead

The lone weapon system that completely dominated the battlefield was the ubiquitous drone, around 50 to 100 drones hummed overhead during any major engagement. Both sides used drones extensively, but the Ukrainians homed on to their use as 'seeker-killers' and integrated them into "kill-chains" and "kill-webs" far more effectively. Observer drones sent images and coordinates to controllers on the ground, who passed them on to a killer drone which engaged it with missiles or homed on to a designator beam on to the target.

The optimal way of using them was to interlink them with the "shooter" – either artillery batteries, tank units, missiles or other killer drones. The Ukrainians developed a unique App called KROPYVA – which the soldiers nicknamed "Uber for Artillery" – in which the drone operator could simply mark the position of a target detected by a drone and the info would be instantly transmitted to the artillery unit best suited to engage it. This allowed fire to be delivered on to the target in just two-three minutes instead of the eight-ten minutes it earlier took and 86 per cent of all artillery target engagements were from information received from drones.

The Ukrainians also resorted to some ingenious means. In the early days of the war, they made up their shortage of drones by requisitioning commercial drones used to deliver pizza or deliver Amazon consignments. Store managers were drafted in as drone operators. These basic drone platforms were fitted with video cameras and sent to peer into the battle field, relaying real-time information. The life expectancy of the drones was not much – just around three to six flights before they were shot down. In most cases, drones were downed by high-power jammers that blocked its GPS signal or fried its electronic circuits. But the cheap cost and easy availability implied they could be easily replaced and the information they passed was invaluable.

Drones proliferated down to sub-unit level and the use of hand-held drones by both sides became a virtual norm. They were used in different ways – even in mine clearance. Drones equipped with heat sensors were flown over suspected minefields at dawn – a time when the ground would be cold, but the mines beneath still had a higher temperature. This helped identify the mines underneath which were cleared later.

The greatest problem with drones lay in relaying back massive amounts of information via video – which required immense bandwidth and power. Small artificial intelligence-enabled chips allowed the cameras to identify objects below as tanks, artillery systems, logistic dumps, troop concentrations, or any likely target and then send back only those images and their coordinates. This used just a few kilobytes of data and prevented the operator below from being swamped with a plethora of needless information.

Drones were also used in some ingenious ways. Russia formed a drone system Leer-3 RB-341V that could listen in or suppress cellular communications. Once the drone got close, the system could infiltrate the mobile network and send text messages to soldiers or make fake calls. Families in the rear also received fake news on their phones of their members being killed in action. When the panic-struck family would call their husbands/children in the field to confirm the news, the system could identify the coordinates of the phone that received the call and use it to bring down fire on it.

Drones could also strike targets deep in the rear. A drone attack on Moscow virtually reached the Kremlin undetected. Kyiv and other cities were subjected to barrages of drone attacks. Swarms of Kamikaze drones loaded with explosives penetrated the air defence and radar cover and slammed into their objectives, taking with them vital targets worth millions. It is definitely a cost-effective way of waging war.

As per most soldiers, their main aim was to avoid being seen by a drone, "If they see you, you are dead." Movement and camouflage acquired greater importance, since one had to only be seen by an enemy drone and then bear an artillery attack or a drone strike within a minute, while the unseen drone watching overhead would continue relaying info of movement and actions till one was hit.

The Russians too homed on to the benefits of drones. Although they held just around one third the number of drones the Ukrainians possessed, they procured them rapidly from allies like Iran and Turkey and they soon proliferated to company and squadron level. Drones were also the preferred method of attack for long-range strikes, and Kyiv, Zaporizhzhia and other depth locations were repeatedly hit by drone attacks. The drone was only limited by its range and bandwidth over which it could pass and receive information. Otherwise there was virtually no limit to the manner in which it could be utilized, and proved the most potent force-multiplier of the war.

Information and Cyber War

The first salvos of the war – as will be the first salvoes of any war to come – were a wave of cyber-attacks that crippled Ukraine's banking, transportation, communications and internet services. Its internet services provider, Triolan was hit by a cyber-attack, and then crippled by missile strikes on its towers and infrastructure. The national telecom operator, Uktelecom, too, was similarly hit. Denial of services attacks also hit the Viasat KA-SAT satellite, disrupting their telecommunications network.

The manner in which Ukraine's networks were targeted highlights the vulnerabilities of such an attack. Can India's railways, airports, banking and communication systems be similarly disrupted by a series of cyber-attacks? The recent train accident involving three trains has been attributed to a fault in the signalling system. What if the computerized signalling systems are hacked? leading fast-moving trains onto the paths of other trains? What if the much-vaunted UPI payment gateways are hit and banking services crippled? And if military communications systems are hacked to pass conflicting signals? Our cyber defence has to be strengthened to identify an impending attack, block it and mitigate its effects. Else it could create havoc within the country.

It is to Ukraine's credit that they maintained communications and internet services virtually throughout the war, in spite of repeated denial of services attacks. This was largely due to the SpaceX Starlink terminals helpfully provided by Elon Musk. SpaceX provided over 20,000 mobile terminals making internet services available to even the most remote commander in the field. These hand-held terminals, just 10x11 inches wide, provided commanders with access to information via hand-held tablets and laptops, and became connected to a vast information network. The mobile phone itself became a weapon of war. On it, the Ukrainians developed Apps – like KROPYVA and DELTA – for targeting, secure communications and sharing of information. Identification of mobile signals also became a vital way of targeting the enemy. Over half a dozen Russian generals were killed when they revealed their positions using mobile telephones. A missile attack on a Russian base at Makiyivka in Eastern Ukraine killed 63 soldiers in a single strike, when newly-arrived conscripts used their mobiles to speak to their homes, thus giving away the location of a large concentration of troops.

The information war also contributed towards winning the battle of perception. In that, the Ukrainians were the clear winners (if not on the actual battlefield). Every media channel and every social media platform was used to convey the Ukrainian point of view – a point of view, helpfully circulated widely by Western media. Russia was denied access to all social media platforms and it was only in the later months of the war that Russia developed its own information channels and the Russian perspective began gaining traction.

The Ukrainian success in the info warfare domain helped maintain morale on the home front. It painted a somewhat rosy picture that ensured that Western allies continued to fund and aid the war which was projected as one in which Ukraine would eventually prevail. The information campaign was also used for deception and misinformation. In August 2022, while Ukraine prepared for its autumn offensive, Zelensky announced in his nightly address to the nation that Ukrainian forces would be launching an offensive to liberate the southern areas. The Ukrainian southern command released a series of tweets from their official web site that the offensive towards the south was starting soon. Russia pulled out troops from the north-eastern sector to reinforce the south. The Ukrainian attack did follow, but it was not on the south as had been indicated. Rather it came in the depleted areas of the northeast, where it succeeded in making rapid gains. The info warfare ruse had succeeded.

Firepower – The Deciding Factor

If anything, this war has demonstrated once again that superior firepower usually carries the day. Both sides have their doctrines based on the Soviet concepts of massed fire, and used artillery extensively. The opening months of the war were characterized by long-range missile and rocket strikes on Ukrainian cities deep in the rear including Kyiv and Lyiv – the border town that received and funnelled Western aid. All along the battlefield, especially in the crucial battles of Mariupol, Bakhmut and Donbas, the issue was decided by firepower – and in that the Russians held a marked edge. Ukraine was outnumbered 12 to 1 in artillery resources of guns and ammunition. Russian artillery fired around 60,000 rounds a day in the peak of the fighting, dwarfing the Ukraine response of around 10,000-20,000 rounds per day. That extensive consumption of ammunition has far outstripped supply. Russia has scoured depots for vintage ammunition. Ukraine's situation is even direr. It already expends in a month, ammunition which its Western allies produce in over a year. Soon, even Western stocks and reserves will start running out and in this battle of attrition, the side with greater firepower resources will invariably prevail.

Precision munitions – in spite of their much higher cost – proved more cost effective and provided more bang for the buck. Excalibur-guided shells and GMLRS precision guided rockets fired by the HIMARS systems attained the same effect at the target end which required dozens of dumb munitions. It also reduced the logistics burden of moving and stocking hundreds of rounds. As the war progressed, Ukraine modified their munitions by inserting chips in the warhead to guide it to the target. However, even precision munitions have their limit. Russia used jammers to block the GPS signals to incoming shells deflecting them from their targets, which even reduced the effectiveness of the much-vaunted HIMARS ammunition. Increasingly, the use of jammers to deflect a precision-guided munitions or pre-maturely detonate an incoming missile or drone became a favoured tactic by both sides.

Eventually it was artillery that decided the day. The Russian concept of massed artillery fire enabled them to blast their way across towns and villages as they captured the southern areas and Donbas. They too paired them with drones for identification and engagement of targets and their efficacy compounded thereafter. As the war reached an impasse, the Ukrainians used their newly-acquired long-range precision artillery systems like the M114 ULH, HIMARS and Excalibur for long range interdiction, striking headquarters, communications systems, logistics nodes and troop concentrations deep in the area. In a break from its policy, the USA also provided cluster munitions to Ukraine, in spite of the dangers of their use. But the trickle of weapon systems and ammunition was not enough to keep pace with demand. The Ukrainian offensive of 2023 suffered because they could not sustain a sufficiently heavy concentration of fire to attain breakthroughs, while the Russians could respond to their actions with an seemingly inexhaustible supply of ammunition.

Both sides also used drones and missiles to strike deep into each other's cities. Kyiv, Kharkiv, Zaporizhia and a range of towns were repeatedly attacked and their infrastructure – mainly the water and electricity infrastructure, severely degraded. Ukraine responded in kind, with long-range attacks on the Kerch Bridge, the Crimea and as far as Moscow. A drone attack on Moscow in August 2023, came dangerously close to the Kremlin, leading to fears that an assassination attempt was being made on Putin himself. The long-range strikes were a statement of intent made to weaken morale, and the damage they caused was quite significant.

The superiority of Russian artillery, and the manner in which it was dovetailed into their operations – plus the enormous quantities of guns and ammunition at their disposal was one of the major reasons for their gains in the war.

Armoured and Mechanized Warfare

When the Russian invasion stalled in the initial months and images of armoured fighting vehicles being knocked out by missiles, mines and drones began making the rounds on social media channels, the 'naysayers' were quick to darkly prophesy that "the day of the tank is over." They missed a vital point. The mechanized forces – largely that of the Russians – did not perform optimally in the initial days, but both sides refined their operations considerably as the war progressed.

For starters, the timing of the operation was awry. Putin launched his offensive in February when *Rasputitsa,* the spring thaw was setting in and the melting snow turned the ground to slush. The movement of tanks and heavy armoured vehicles was thus confined to the roads. They lost their prime advantage of mobility and the road-bound columns were sucked into tank ambush after ambush. They were also forced into built-up areas and had to clear towns and large villages to open the axis. There were no manoeuvres, just a slow, creeping plod.

As the ground hardened, tanks were used in a better manner. The Ukrainians excelled in using them in a defensive role, skilfully concentrating their limited number of tanks to launch vital counter-attacks and regain lost ground. Sophisticated anti-tank weaponry like next generation light anti-tank weapons (NLAWS) and Javelins with their top attack mode, helped inflict tremendous tank casualties. Combined with drones, they could identify approaching tank columns at long ranges and then ambush them with crippling missile and artillery fire.

The Russians seem to have made the initial mistake of not using all-arms teams. That was surprising, since their concept hinges around all-arms battalion tactical groups. But their BTGs were usually short of matching infantry, reconnaissance resources, and most of all compatible logistics. As the war progressed, their armoured columns too used drones to scour the area ahead and clear suspected enemy positions by artillery fire or infantry attacks. Their own casualties diminished considerably as they refined their tactics.

Mechanized forces were increasingly sucked into towns and built-up areas. That will be the norm across the world, with its growing urbanization. Some innovative tactics were developed by the Ukrainians to clear small towns and villages. Rather than surround the town, invest it, establish a foothold and then clear it block-by-block; they raced through the town with tanks and BMPs in a 'thunder run', firing as they moved. The tanks smashed through the town and took up positions in the rear to prevent any withdrawals. The mechanized infantry dismounted, captured crossroads, communication centres, radio and TV stations and other vital objectives, with their BMPS providing intimate fire support with machine guns and cannons. From footholds inside the town, they expanded outwards towards the periphery, clearing the town much faster than could have been done through conventional means.

The war has not seen any wide sweeps of manoeuvring or classical encirclements that were seen on the same battlefields in World War II. However, one noteworthy example stands out – during the Ukrainian autumn offensive. By then it had become clear that it would not be possible to conceal large tank concentrations. Russian formations were picked up by satellites and observers even before the launch of the offensive, which allowed the Ukrainians to discern thrust lines and likely objectives. Achieving surprising in today's transparent battlefield is difficult and it is better to resort to deception instead. The Ukrainians learnt the lesson, and during their own offensive, they first deceived the Russians by depicting actions in the south instead of their true objective in the northeast. They also deliberately pruned their mechanized force to just two brigades to ensure they were not detected, sending a portion of their mechanized forces southwards to aid the deception. When they attacked, they used classical manoeuvring tactics. Their armoured columns raced 90 kilometres deep in just three days and reached the line of the Oskil River. The following infantry (largely mechanized) cleared the towns that had been bypassed en route. In most cases, the psychological dislocation caused by this deep manoeuvre made the defenders withdraw virtually without a fight.

When the Ukrainians launched their spring offensive of 2023, it was hoped that they would replicate the success of their offensive of the previous year. They had received Leopard II and Challenger tanks, Bradley and Bulldog APCs and a host of other sophisticated Western equipment. But the offensive ground to a halt after advancing just around 10 to 12 kilometres. In fact, the Ukrainians lost 20 per cent of their new equipment within just two weeks of the commencement of the offensive.

The Ukrainian mechanized brigades were expected to make break through the Russian defences and simply blitzkrieg into depth positions. But the conditions for a blitzkrieg were just not there. The force level was inadequate. There were just 12-odd brigades widely dispersed across the frontage and they were not adequate to achieve a breakthrough at a decisive point. They lacked air cover and close air support. Most of all, they lacked the means to breach the Russian defences and extensive minefields. The leading tanks were halted and crippled by mines and then the column was hammered by artillery and drones. In spite of the casualties, the tanks should have just blasted their way to cause an initial breach, which could then be exploited by the infantry. The heavy casualties imposed a sense of caution in the Ukrainians. They tried to breach the mines manually, advancing a few hundred metres every day, and the offensive ground to a halt.

The war saw contrasting use of mechanized forces. First, there was the rather clumsy handling by the Russians during their offensive. Then the classical use of rapid manoeuvres by the Ukrainians during their offensive of autumn 2022, and again, their rather inept and timid handling during the offensive of the next year. The Western media has been quick to point out how inferior the Russian equipment was by the losses they had sustained in the early days. They were conspicuously silent when equally high losses of Western equipment took place during the Ukrainian offensive. Eventually it boiled down not to the equipment, but the manner of its use, and demonstrated that when used effectively, mechanized forces could attain decisive results; if mishandled, could lead to heavy casualties.

One thing has emerged. In the race between tank and anti-tank weapons, the latter tank weaponry has come up trumps. It is pointless beefing up the tank with more armour protection; it will not be cost-effective. Instead, ensuring its situational awareness and information flow by battlefield management systems will provide better survivability. Also, smaller, all-arms teams – optimally at brigade level – seem to perform better than large unwieldy formations. Perhaps our own doctrines could keep that in mind.

Air Operations

One of the inexplicable mysteries of the war is why did the Russians not use their air force better. It was expected that with their qualitative and quantitative superiority, they would gain complete control of the skies in the first few days and that would pave the way for the ground invasion.

The Russian Air Force (RuAF) is the second-largest in the world with nearly 4,173 aircraft. Eight bomber squadrons operate Tu-22M3/MR,

Tu-95MS, and Tu-160 bombers. Thirty-seven fighter squadrons include variants of MiG-29, MiG-31, Su-27 and over 100 Su-35 aircraft. There are 27 attack squadrons operating the Su-24, Su-25 and Su-34 variants. Ten attack-cum-reconnaissance squadrons operate Su-24s and MiG-25RB. They have only around 14 fifth-generation Sukhoi Su-57 aircraft which are still under operational evaluation. Russia operates a squadron each of A-50/A50-U aircraft and FRA Il-78/Il-78M. At any given time, Russia has around 300 modern combat aircraft normally stationed in the western and southern military districts – within range of Ukraine.

Ukraine mostly has Russian and Soviet equipment and the war saw identical aircraft and systems pitted against each other. Ukraine had the world's 27th largest air force and the 7th largest in Europe. The Ukrainian Air Force (UkrAF) had 215 aircraft at the beginning of the war. As of August 2022, they were down to 175. These included nearly 100 fighters comprising MiG-29, Su-24, Su-25, Su-27, and L-39 aircraft, some of which had been recently modernized. Their aircraft had been used largely in air defence operations. They had significant AD systems including S-300 missiles with nearly 500 missiles in addition to the Western man-portable AD systems (MANPADS) that has been used to good effect to down Russian strike aircraft and helicopters.

One of the major Ukrainian aircraft losses of the war was the tragic destruction of the world's largest plane, An-225 or 'Mriya' (The Dream). Only one of this 650-ton giant transport aircraft was ever built by the Antonov Design Bureau, based at Kiev. This aircraft was destroyed in cross-fire between Russian and Ukrainian troops, in the opening week of the war, when the Russians attacked Antonov airfield at Hostomel.

Russia made limited use of their advanced air weaponry initially. The Russians reportedly were conserving assets for the eventuality of possible escalation of war involving NATO. Russia was expected to achieve air superiority, but that happened only partially and a little later in the conflict. Fighter strikes were also limited and according to the Russians they did not resort to air strikes to reduce civilian casualties.

Russia did strike military infrastructure at Ukraine's air bases and flew missions for suppression of enemy air defences (SEAD). Finally UkrAF did get grounded and thereafter Ukraine mostly concentrated on using ground-based air defence. Initially, the main targets for Russia were the political centres of Kiev, Kharkiv, Kherson, Mariupol and other towns that were subjected to air and missile attacks in the preparatory stages of their attacks.

There have been air engagements, but they were few and far in between. We heard about the "Ghost of Kiev" – a MiG-29 Fulcrum flying ace credited with shooting down six Russian planes in the Kyiv offensive on 24 February 2022. However this proved to be fictitious war propaganda, designed to boost morale and was not based on facts. The Russian defence ministry has claimed that over 100 air defence systems and over 90 Ukrainian aircraft had been disabled or destroyed. Most UkrAF losses were on the ground with a few shot in the air while most Russian aircraft losses have been to ground-based AD systems.

As the war progressed, so also the conduct of air and joint operations improved. The RuAF significantly increased the number of sorties flown in Ukraine and improved their ability to support ground operations. Russian aircraft were being committed piecemeal and often appeared in twos and threes over the battlefield. However, even during the Ukrainian counter-offensive, the Russians did not use air power to effectively blunt the Ukrainian advance – perhaps due to the effectiveness of air defence systems like MANPADS provided by the West. Their inability to control the skies in spite of having such superiority of both quality and quantity, and not completely utilise the air power at their disposal, is one of the baffling aspects of the air war.

While the Ukrainians did not record any notable victory in the air, they scored a significant success in August 2022 with their attack on the Crimean airbase at Saki. The airbase hosted the Russian Black Sea Fleet's naval attack aviation regiment and other units and was hit at ranges of nearly 200 kilometres with American M142 high mobility artillery rocket systems (HIMARS) with a maximum operational range of 480 kilometres. The Saki base was known to have around a dozen each Su-24 bombers and Su-30 fighters. They also had some Mi-8 helicopters and the Il-76 medium-transport aircraft. At least one Su-24, several ground support vehicles and possibly one of the base's munitions dumps were reportedly destroyed. This attack was morale boosting for Ukraine and temporarily impacted Russian air operations in the south.

As the war progressed, the Ukrainian Air Force virtually disappeared from the skies. Russia did succeed in attaining domination, even though they never used the full weight of air power. During the Ukrainian offensive, their air force was not able to provide effective support, not could it stop Russian attack helicopters and SU-25 ground attack aircraft from striking Ukrainian columns at will. The lack of effective air defence played a major role in the inability of the Ukrainians to attain the aims of the offensive.

Naval Operations

When Russia attacked Ukraine on 24 February 2022, most (including this writer) expected a short, brief conflict. Most of the attention has been focused on the land battles (which have been covered in detail in the earlier chapters) but the effective utilization of air and naval power has also influenced the course of the conflict. There were no widespread naval actions, but maritime security and control of the Black Sea and the Sea of Azov – along with the Baltics and North Atlantic – forms a major reason for the war.

The Black Sea is the only maritime outlet for Ukrainian trade from Odessa in its south-west directly into the Black Sea, and primarily through Mariupol in its the east via the Sea of Azov and the Kerch Strait. Thereafter, this passes through the narrow Strait of Bosporus which runs through Turkey and onwards into the eastern Mediterranean and to different parts of the world. The war at sea – in conjunction with land actions – helped Russia gain control over the Black Sea and the Sea of Azov and strangulate the Ukrainian economy.

The Black Sea is important to Russia as it is its only access to the warmer waters of the Mediterranean and the shortest approach to the Red Sea and the Indian Ocean. This conflict actually began with the annexation of the Crimean Peninsula by Russia in 2014. In the maritime domain, it gave the Russians complete control over the port town of Sevastopol and effectively neutralized the Ukrainian navy in those waters.

Russia had begun shaping operations to assert its control over the Black Sea and on 25 November 2018, a Ukrainian tug and two gunboats, were fired upon and rammed while transiting through the Kerch Strait from the Black Sea to the Sea of Azov and aircraft and the vessels were detained. The obvious reason for this provocative action was Russia's intention to choke Ukraine economically and subdue it politically. The Kerch Strait had become a bone of contention between the two countries when Russia constructed the 19-kilometre long bridge connecting Crimea and Russia across the Kerch Strait as the height of the bridge precludes large vessels from transiting under it, thus affecting the movement of Ukrainian trade. The bridge was a major project for President Putin and provided the only road connectivity from the Russian mainland to the Crimean Peninsula. The land operations in coastal areas and ports in conjunction with naval actions, are all part of Russian strategy to gain control of the Black Sea.

The movement of Russian naval ships towards the Black Sea began prior to the outbreak of the conflict, with units from its other fleets in the Mediterranean. On 8 February 2022, six ships of the Baltic and Northern fleets entered the Black Sea to participate in naval drills. The Black Sea fleet then went on to carry out naval exercises with 30 or so ships, which also included live-fire drills from 13 to 19 February. By the time Russian forces commenced their action on land, they had already established sea control around Ukraine. The Russian Navy had also closed the Kerch Strait thus establishing complete control of the Sea of Azov, and had deployed its ships off Odessa and other Ukrainian ports.

The Russian navy had a formidable presence in the Black Sea comprising the Slava-class cruiser 'Moskva' which was the flagship of the Black Sea Fleet, two Admiral Grigorovich-class frigates, three Buyan-M-class corvettes and a Kilo-class diesel-electric submarine (SSK), all of which were armed with the Kalibr family of cruise missiles. In addition, at least ten amphibious landing craft were also present in the Black Sea. The Russian presence in the Black Sea was overwhelmingly superior to the Ukrainian Navy's, 'mosquito fleet' of small vessels for near-shore operations to primarily protect Ukraine's territorial waters and shorelines. To add to Ukraine's woes, the initial gains made by Russia on the maritime front led to the Ukrainian Navy scuttling its own flagship and its only frigate, the Krivak III-class 'HETMAN SAHAIDACHNY', lest it fall into Russian hands.

When the land operations commenced, Russia made an amphibious landing to take control of Mariupol. The amphibious assault coupled with the land attack from Donbas eventually led to the isolation and eventual capture of Mariupol. The Russian Navy also supported the land effort by firing a large number of Kalibr land attack missiles from seawards at targets well inland as well as along the coast. With the blockading of the Sea of Azov and effective neutralization of the Ukrainian navy, Russia was able to intensify its assault on Mariupol and the other coastal towns with large scale bombardment.

A major loss for Russia was the sinking of the flagship of its Black Sea Fleet, the MOSKVA. On 13 April 2022, the ship was hit by two R-360, Ukrainian 'Neptune' cruise missiles successfully while it was patrolling off Zmiinyi Islands over 200 kilometres away. The damage ignited the warship's ammunition and set it on fire. While the ship was being towed back to harbour, it sank en route due to internal damage. This was a remarkable success, since the 12,500-ton warship was the pride of the fleet and the largest Russian ship sunk since World War II. More than the loss of the ship, it was the loss of face and the inherent weaknesses in the Russian Navy which stood exposed. The loss of the MOSKVA forced the navy to keep a safe distance and out of range of long-range anti-ship missiles fired from the coast. It also put paid to any plans of launching an amphibious operation thereafter.

Ukraine also sank the Russian Alligator-class amphibious ship SARATOV in Berdyansk. It also used the Turkish-supplied Bayraktar TB-2 drones to attack various targets including the headquarters of the Black Sea fleet. As on land, drones were used effectively in the maritime domain as well. Ukraine's crew-less surface vessels (USVs) – essentially drone boats – entered Russian waters undetected. Paired with aerial drones that passed back information, they attacked Sevastopol, hit an oil depot in Novorossiysk, and a ship harboured in Bosporus. On 22 September 2023, the HQ of the Russian Black Sea Fleet was hit by a Ukrainian Storm Shadow missile killing 34 senior officers and injuring 105 servicemen. It was reported that the Commander-in-Chief of the fleet was also killed, but he had escaped unhurt. The Ukrainian raids did hurt, but could not remove the stranglehold that had been established around its coast.

In fact, one of the major roles performed by the navy was imposing a complete sea blockade over Ukraine that denied it access to the Black Sea. They were thus able to prevent Ukraine from exporting any of their produce overseas. The Black Sea grain deal did allow Ukraine to tranship its grain under Russian supervision, but that deal too was not renewed by Putin in July 2023. With the control of the sea that Russia attained, Ukraine had become virtually a land-locked nation, unable to export or import goods from sea. That would have a crippling effect on its economy, and eventually decide the course of the war.

Nuclear Shadows: The Doomsday Clock moves Closer to Midnight

The Nuclear Threat

The Doomsday Clock is a symbolic clock maintained by the Bulletin of Atomic Scientists, since 1947 to depict how close the world is to a global man-made catastrophe. In the aftermath of the Russian invasion of Ukraine the time on the clock was moved up to 90 seconds to midnight. Never before – not even during the Cold War, or even during the Cuban Crisis, when the clock stood at two minutes to midnight – has the world stood so close to a likely nuclear disaster. And though the threat of nuclear war has receded considerably, during some of the earlier days of the war, the danger of nuclear weapons was a very real one.

When Putin readied for the invasion of Ukraine, amongst his final actions was an exercise of Russia's nuclear forces which tested the readiness of its nuclear arsenal and the delivery systems of ships, submarines, aircraft and missiles that would carry them across the globe. It was a clear statement that he would consider using nuclear weapons if the need arose, and a veiled threat.

The nuclear threat came up repeatedly during the war, was mainly voiced by the Foreign Minister, Sergei Lavrov, who warned that "World War III will be a nuclear war." Nuclear rhetoric did arise, especially when Russia faced reverses in the battlefield after the Ukrainian offensive of 2022, when there were calls to use tactical nukes on the battlefield. Many Russian commanders feel that a tactical nuclear device is just another weapon and feel they could get away with its use, without a climb up the escalatory ladder.

But that is self-delusionary. The use of a nuclear device, no matter how small, is the crossing of the red line, and will lead to rapid escalation. There are other weapons of mass destruction that Russia could use. The Russians are suspected to have used chemical weapons in Grozny to suppress the Chechen uprising; and against Syrian rebels, in support of their ally, Assad. But, using them in Ukraine will be a different proposition all together. It seems that much of Russia's nuclear rhetoric was just rhetoric to prevent NATO from entering the war. They used their nuclear forces as a deterrent – and their nuclear bluff worked.

Nuclear Capabilities

Putin has the wherewithal to call his bluff. Russia is the world's largest nuclear power with 5,977 nuclear warheads, which includes 1,458 strategic warheads that are deployed and ready to fire. They also hold the complete array of delivery means including intercontinental ballistic missiles, submarines and strategic bombers to strike virtually anywhere in the world.

In comparison the USA holds 5,428 nuclear weapons of which 1,389 are operationally deployed on a similar array of delivery means. NATO, in totality holds 5,943, (the bulk with the USA, with France accounting for 290 and the UK for 225). The USA has around 100 B 61-3 nuclear gravity bombs of variable yields, ranging from .3 KT to 170 KT deployed in six airbases in Europe (Belgium, Germany, The Netherlands, Turkey and Italy (two).

However, it is in terms of tactical nuclear weapons that Russia has a clear edge. It holds almost 2,000 warheads of different yields and capabilities which can be fired from Kalibr SS-N-30 ship launched missiles, or the shorter range Iskandar-M missiles (SS-26 'Stone') which can hit targets 400-500 kilometres away – sufficient for the tactical battlefield. Incidentally, Russia moved 200 of these mobile launchers to the Ukrainian border just before the start of hostilities.

They can even be fired from conventional artillery guns like the 155-mm Malka self-propelled guns or the more deadly 2S7, 203 millimetre gun (also called the Soviet atomic cannon) which can fire up to four nuclear-tipped warheads across the battlefield.

Russia also has a massive complement of 286 ICBMs, which can carry up to 958 warheads. Its recently developed RS-28 Sarmat ICBMs can fly at over seven times the speed of sound, penetrate anti-missile defences, and deliver 15 nuclear warheads 35,000 kilometres away. Its ability to strike as far as mainland USA gives it a deterrence that will hold NATO's hand considerably. It is significant that Russia has already used Kinzhal hypersonic missiles to destroy ammunition and supply dumps in Lyiv, where Western aid was collected and distributed, in a veiled threat that it could use these weapons (with deadlier warheads) should the need arise.

Ukraine of course, has no nuclear weapons of its own. It possessed the world's third largest nuclear arsenal as part of the USSR and held 1,900 nuclear warheads,176 ICBMs and 44 strategic bombers on its soil. After the Soviet Union disintegrated, it willingly surrendered its entire nuclear arsenal under the Budapest Agreement of 1994, in return for security guarantees from the USA, Russia and the UK. Most of them were purchased by Russia for the paltry sum of $ 1 billion. The guarantees that Ukraine received, were ultimately not worth the paper they were written on.

As per Russia's nuclear doctrine, nuclear weapons can be used if similar weapons are used against it; if Russia faces an existentialist threat; or by an attack on its own territory. What this implies is that if Russia faces reverses on the battlefield, it could resort to the use of these weapons. After taking over the provinces of Luhansk, Donetsk, Kherson and Zaporizhzhia and amalgamating them into Russia after a 'referendum', these captured territories are now formally Russian. Should Ukraine succeed in recapturing large tracts of lost land, Russia could well consider it an attack on their own territory and use nuclear weapons to defend what they call their own land.

In spite of the rhetoric, it is unlikely that nuclear weapons will be used. The nuclear posturing was part of the 'escalate to de-escalate' strategy, in which Putin has raised the stakes counting on the West to back down. It also ensures that Russia does not suffer a complete defeat, since that too could provoke a nuclear response. In other words, he has used nuclear weapons, just as they should be used – as a deterrent to stay the opponent's hand.

Arms Control Treaties

It is significant that there was some control on the deployment of tactical nuclear weapons till around 2019. Then the USA – following Trump's policies – withdrew from the Intermediate Nuclear Forces Treaty, which regulated the move and deployment of ground-launched nuclear weapons with ranges up to 500-5,500 kilometres. Hence, even the treaty restrictions, which could have been leveraged to a small extent cannot be applied now.

In response, Putin raised the stakes by suspending participation in the New START Treaty. The treaty is due to expire in February 2026, and is the only surviving nuclear control treaty between the USA and Russia. It implies that Russia no longer had to inform the USA of the movement of its strategic missiles, nor was it obliged to open its strategic assets for verification – under the conditions of the treaty. A very vital confidence-building measure was lost at a time when the world needed it the most.

Simultaneously, Russia also announced that it would be deploying tactical nuclear missiles – the Iskander II, on the soil of their ally, Belarus. It was the first time that Russia had deployed nuclear weapons beyond its own borders since 1990. It would provide additional range to strike westwards, but more than that, it was posturing to demonstrate the nuclear power which Putin still held at his disposal.

Putin further upped the ante by withdrawing from Russia's ratification of the Comprehensive Test Ban Treaty – a treaty banning all forms of nuclear testing – less computer simulation. The world has been fortunate that in this century, only six nuclear tests have been conducted – all by North Korea. Should Russia go back to nuclear testing, the USA will feel compelled to follow suit, as would China. Other nations could commence testing as well, and it would be a dangerous return to nuclear proliferation.

The withdrawal from these nuclear treaties had another even more dangerous spin-off. In November 2023, Russia formally withdrew from the Treaty on Conventional Armed Forces in Europe – an agreement signed in 1990 that laid limits on five key categories of conventional military equipment; tanks, armoured vehicles, artillery, helicopters and combat aircraft. They claimed that NATO's expansion circumvented the restrictions imposed by the treaty and it would not be in Russia's interests to continue with it. With this, another major restraining treaty is now gone, and Europe is getting closer to the dangerous days of the Cold War.

In Ukraine, a large number of people feel that giving up nuclear weapons in 1994 was a mistake. The ongoing war would never have happened if Ukraine possessed nuclear weapons. This has sent wrong signals to other nations. Iran, Saudi Arabia, South Africa, perhaps even Syria and Turkey amongst others, may decide to seek nuclear weapons as a guarantor of security. With the situation in the Middle East also deteriorating, Iran will intensify its nuclear program. It will be loathe to re-enter a nuclear deal which will require it to abandon its nuclear program (especially after being betrayed by Trump earlier) and could go ahead with developing its own nuclear weapons as a hedge against a future attack by the USA or Israel. This could set off a nuclear race in the Middle East. And of course, Pakistan and North Korea will be similarly emboldened. So, nuclear proliferation, which the world tried so hard to contain over the past few decades, is back, and the Doomsday Clock inches closer to midnight.

REFERENCES

"Fact Sheet – US nuclear weapons in Europe," Centre for Arms Control and Non-Proliferation.

"Army Incorporates Lessons from Russia-Ukraine War," *Indian Express*, https://indianexpress.com

"Artillery Duels in Ukraine," *Forbes*, https://www.forbes.com

"Does the Tank have a Future?," *The Economist*, https://www.economist.com, 15 June 2022.

"Drones in Ukraine and Beyond," ecfr.eu, https://www.ecfr.eu

"Getting to Know Russian Battalion Tactical Groups," *RUSI*, https://rusi.org dt 14 April 2022.

"Information Warfare in Russia's war in Ukraine," *Foreign Policy*, https://foriegnpolicy.com

"Inside Ukraine's War", *The Economist*, https://economist.com

"Lean on the Barrage: The Role of Artillery in Ukraine," Royal United Services Institute, https://www.rusi.org

"Military Aircraft Strength (2022)," *Global Fire Power*, https://www.globalfirepower.com/aircraft-total.php

"Moskva's sinking, the rise of anti-ship cruise missiles and what that means for the US Navy," *Defence News*, 3 May 2022, https://www.defensenews.com/opinion/commentary/2022/05/03/moskvas-sinking-the-rise-of-anti-ship-cruise-missiles-and-what-that-means-for-the-us-navy/

"NATO bolsters arms supply to Ukraine with Anti-Tank Weapons," *Al Jazeera*, 26 February 2022.

"NATO entry could lead to World War III: Russia," *Times Global, The Times of India*, 14 October 2022.

"Near Donetsk Front lines," *Reuters*, https://www.reuters.com

"Nuclear Armageddon risk worst since 1962," *Times Global, Times of India*, 8 October 2022..

"Number of nuclear weapons Worldwide, 2022," *Statista*, https://www.statista.com, 5 August 2022.

"Putin leads sweeping Nuclear exercises as Tensions soar," *Reuters*, 19 February 2022.

"Putin: Russia suspends participation in last remaining Nuclear Treaty," *Reuters*, https://www.reuters.com, 21 February 2023.

"Putin: Russia to station Nuclear Weapons in Belarus," *BBC*, https://www.bbd.com, 26 March 2023.

"Putin's Threats: How many Nuclear weapons does Russia have?," https://www.bbc.com , 7 October 2022.

"Russia's Nuclear Weapons: Doctrine, Forces and Modernization," https://sgp.fas.org, 21 April 2022.

"Russia's War in Ukraine: Insights from RAND," Rand Corporation, https://rand.org

"Russian warship destroyed in occupied port of Berdyansk," *BBC*, https://www.bbc.com/news/world-europe-60859337

"The Air and Missile War in Nagorno-Karabakh," https://www.csis.org, 8 December 2020.

"The Presence of Russian Warships in the Black Sea and the Mediterranean Sea" in January 2022, *Black Sea News*, 1 February 2022, https://www.blackseanews.net/en/read/184301 Accessed on 17 October 2022.

"The role of naval forces in Russia's war against Ukraine and its implications," 25 March 2022, https://behorizon.org/the-role-of-naval-forces-in-russias-war-against-ukraine-and-its-implications/

"Ukraine once claimed 3rd largest Nuclear Arsenal in the World," https://www.republicworld.com, 24 February 2022.

"Ukraine punches through Russian lines as surprise offensive retakes land in the East," *CNBC*, 11 September 2022.

"Ukraine War: Could Russia use Tactical Nuclear Weapons?," *BBC*, https://www.bbc.com , 25 September 2022.

"War in Ukraine," Global Conflict Tracker, https://www.gct.com

"Western Tanks arrive in Ukraine: Will it turn the War in Kyiv's favour?" https://www.voanews.com

"What are Himars missiles and are they changing the war?," *BBC*, 30 August 2022, https://www.bbc.com/news/world-62512681

"What we know about Drone attacks in Russia," *BBC*, https://www.bbc.com

A. Aliaksandrov. "The Information War between Russia and Ukraine," *Sage Journal*, https://www.sagejournal.com

Barbara Starr. "NATO and Russia hold Exercises of Nuclear Forces as Tensions over Ukraine remain high," *CNN Politics*, 16 October 2022.

David Axe. "The Ukrainians Hammered A Russian Air Base 120 Miles From The Front," *Forbes*, 9 August 2022, https://www.forbes.com/sites/davidaxe/2022/08/09/the-ukrainians-blew-up-a-russian-air-base-120-miles-from-the-front/?sh=561c4f0e772e

Indian Maritime Doctrine 2009, https://www.indiannavy.nic.in/sites/default/files/Indian-Maritime-Doctrine-2009-Updated-12Feb16.pdf

Laurence Peter. "How Ukraine's 'Ghost of Kyiv' legendary pilot was born," *BBC*, 1 May 2022, https://www.bbc.com/news/world-europe-61285833

Lt-Col Johnny R. Jones. "Air Power", USAF Air University, https://www.airuniversity.af.edu/Portals/10/ASPJ/journals/Chronicles/jjones.pdf

Murphy. "Troops and Military Vehicles enter Ukraine from Belarus, *CNN*, 23 February 2022.

Ukrainian Air Force (2022), *World Directory of Modern Military Aircraft (2022)* , 18 August 2022, https://www.wdmma.org/ukrainian-air-force.php

6

Endgame in Ukraine

"The war will not end till Russia attains its complete military goals."

—Vladimir Putin

The War so Far

A war that was expected to be over in a fortnight or so has gone on for over two years. It has seen its shares of twists and turns. No one expected the determined resistance of the Ukrainians after the invasion on 24 February 2022, which halted each of the Russian thrust lines, and checkmated them virtually at the gates of Kyiv. Most also expected a Russian blitzkrieg that would simply sweep through Ukraine – but the attempt took much longer and proved far more difficult than anticipated. Russia did eventually succeed in occupying most of the south and the Donbas, but it was a slow and expensive grind. The Ukrainian counter-offensive in the northeast and the south in the autumn of 2022 was brilliantly executed, but in the end only recaptured around

3 per cent of its lost areas – 17 per cent of its territory was still held by Russia. It was expected that 2023 would be the year of decision when Ukraine would launch its offensive to reclaim "all of the occupied territories, including Crimea." But, that much delayed 'Spring Offensive' proved quite a squib. At the end of five months of slow grind, Ukraine managed to just penetrate the first defensive line in only one location, in the area of Robotyne, and advanced to a maximum depth of around 17 kilometres. If the Ukrainians continue advancing at the present rate, it will take them another 103 years to recapture their lost areas. So, even though there is talk of the offensive continuing in the next year, it has lost all momentum and the tide has turned against them.

The global climate too seems to have turned against Ukraine. With the horrific October attacks on Israel and the eruption of the Gaza war, global attention has shifted away from Europe towards the even more dangerous tinder box of the Middle East. The USA, Ukraine's staunchest partner (in aid and moral support, if nothing else), is now focused on Israel and has diverted aid and diplomatic capital towards it. It is significant that in the latest tranche of US aid earmarked for Ukraine, 20 per cent of the amount was shifted towards Israel. Much needed hardware, like 155 mm artillery shells, AD resources, and long-range precision missiles have also moved away towards Israel. Slowly, the Ukraine war seems to be losing its importance.

There is also a sense of war-weariness. In the USA, there is a growing divide about continual support for Ukraine, with the Republicans questioning President Biden's policy of aiding and funding the Ukraine war – to the sum of $ 126 billion already. In a divided Congress, with the Presidential elections looming, Biden may find it difficult to continue support for Ukraine in the face of growing domestic disenchantment with the war. It is very telling that in the USA, leaks of secret documents were put up on Wikipedia, in which the Pentagon provided a dismal view of Ukraine's ability to win the war or attain anything tangible with its offensive. That itself leads to many questioning the rationale for aid towards a losing cause.

The US presidential elections of November 2024 could well prove to be the game-changer. Should Donald Trump return to the White House, he will definitely not propagate Biden's 'blank cheque policy', and will focus inwards, rather than on an unwinnable war in Europe. It would not be too surprising if the USA takes a diametrically opposite stance towards the war thereafter.

There is also growing lack of support amongst Ukraine's other allies as well. Poland, one of its most steadfast supporters announced that they would no longer be providing arms and support to Ukraine, but would focus on developing their own defensive strength. Slovakia too announced the same. And we have to only hear the silence in European capitals to realize, that more and more nations are rapidly veering away from the earlier concept of "Russia must be defeated at all costs" and adopting a more balanced approach of sacrificing Ukrainian "land for peace."

This sentiment seems to be growing in Ukraine as well. There is growing discontent with Zelensky's handling of the war. Some of his recent actions, like the insistence on holding on to Bakhmut and suffering needless casualties against the advice of his Generals have not gone well. In a recent interview, the Ukrainian Army Chief, Valery Zaluzhny, seemed to imply that the war had reached a deadlock and could not be won any longer – a realistic appraisal of the situation. Ukraine is now scraping the bottom of the barrel. Most of the young motivated crop of young people have enlisted and many have already been wasted in the war. The new recruits are not so motivated and Ukraine finds it increasingly difficult to make up its losses and raise new formations for future action. Its own industry and faltering economy will only be able to sustain the war for 45 days on its own, and if Western support dwindles it will be impossible for it to continue the war. The signals emanating from Ukraine indicate that their offensive has run its course and at best, Ukraine can now just hold on.

At the end of the second year of fighting, it is Russia that seems better placed. They can sustain the long war of attrition with their vast reserves of manpower, ammunition, and resources. The infusion of 190,000 reservists in December 2022, has helped them replenish units and formations and beef up the frontlines. With the successful blunting of the Ukrainian offensive – both in the Zaporizhzhia and in the Bakhmut sectors – they now hold an unbroken frontline extending from Kherson to Kharkiv. Their defensive layout is strong and well-coordinated and will be further strengthened to repel another Ukrainian offensive, should it come. Militarily, Russia seems better poised than Ukraine, and will be able to sustain a long war better.

There has been a pause in winter, which will continue till the Spring thaw of March-April. And then what? Western media seems to imply that Ukraine will continue its offensive in the coming year, till they eventually attain their military aims. But that seems far-fetched. The Russians are silent about their intentions, but history shows that Russian military policy usually entails absorbing an enemy offensive, imposing heavy losses on them, and then launching their own counter-offensive deep into enemy territory. They had done the same in the battles of Moscow, Stalingrad, and Kursk, and it is quite likely they would follow a similar pattern, by launching their own counter-offensive to consolidate their gains. The coming year will tell how the war could go, but the glimmerings of a likely end state are slowly appearing. We could evaluate some of the possibilities, one by one.

A Negotiated Peace

A fair and equitable negotiated peace that looks after the interests of both sides would actually be the most desired end state. But with both sides having such diametrically opposed interests, this may not be possible.

Both sides claim that they want to commence discussions, but the start point differs. Zelensky has clearly outlined his 10-point peace plan based on the reinstatement of Ukraine's territorial integrity to its pre-2014 boundaries – which includes Crimea. It also includes security guarantees to preclude further aggression, criminal consequences for Russia's war crimes, reparation of war damages (estimated at $ 700 billion so far) and the return of refugees and prisoners.

"Nyet," says Russia. They too want a negotiated peace, but their start point for any discussion is that territories liberated by them – including Crimea, Kherson, Zaporizhzhia, Luhansk and Donetsk are already part of Russia and no discussion on that can be entertained.

That means the underlying cause of the problem – a restoration of Ukraine's territorial integrity – is out of the window. Ukraine had hoped to improve its position at the negotiating table through battlefield successes in its Spring Offensive of 2023. That has not happened and if anything, Ukraine is in a worse position than before. It is unlikely to enter into negotiations from a position of weakness. Neither will Russia negotiate now, except to reinforce its own demands. So, in the immediate future, a negotiated solution seems improbable.

Should the war go on inconclusively for some time to come, there may be added pressure on Ukraine to accept a negotiated peace, on a line of a "land-for-peace" solution, in which they concede their lost territories in return for a cessation of hostilities. They could be faced with this, especially if Western aid declines, and there is a change in the political leadership. But the fear is that this kind of enforced peace will actually embolden Russia, give it time to further build up its strength and then maybe try another similar action later. It could actually be far more dangerous on the long run.

Russian Military Success

When Russia set out on its war, it had three broad aims for itself. To quickly capture Kyiv; to occupy the eastern and southern part of Ukraine right up to the Dnieper River; and bring about political change with the ouster of Zelensky and his 'neo-Nazi government' and the installation of a favourably disposed regime in Kyiv.

They came very close to achieving the first objective and almost captured Kyiv in the first week of the war itself, by an audacious air assault on Hostomel airfield near the capital. That assault failed by a whisker. The land offensive too was called off after a month or so, and the threat to Kyiv has receded. The second objective – capture of all of Eastern Ukraine has not materialized, but the Russians have managed to take over the provinces of Kherson, Zaporizhzhia, Luhansk and Donetsk – 17 per cent of Ukraine's richest and most fertile lands. Besides capturing the Donbas in the east, they have also taken over 70 per cent of the Ukrainian coastline leaving it with just the port of Odessa and two minor ports. With the Russian navy controlling the Black Sea and the Sea of Azov, Ukraine's access to the sea is effectively gone.

With the Ukrainian offensive having fizzled out, with just minor penetrations, the Russian defensive lines are stronger and more compact than before. Will the Russians now follow up their defensive successes by launching their own offensive? It seems quite likely. winter has given them time to consolidate and they have reserves to launch an offensive in the widely-dispersed Ukrainian lines. They could attack again from the south and the east to strike out towards the line of the Dnieper River, which would carve Ukraine neatly into two. They could even restart offensive action in the Kharkiv sector, or even threaten Kyiv once again. This would depend on the residual Ukrainian strength now, and the amount of aid it receives from the West. But it is a viable option, and one that could be followed by Russia to consolidate their already impressive military gains.

The long war of attrition suits Russia better and they can use their present position of strength to carry the war into the next year, and then attain the military objectives they had set for themselves.

A Ukrainian Success

In the Western media, much has been made of the small successes of Ukraine's offensive, but even that is slowly giving way to a grudging acknowledgement that Ukraine cannot win the war – irrespective of the amount of aid and arms that the West pours into it. Realistically now, Ukraine's possibilities of attaining its military goals – that is, the removal of Russian presence from all its occupied territories – seems increasingly remote.

The only saving grace is that Ukraine has committed only five of the twelve brigades it had built up for the offensive (the others presumably are held in reserve in the hope of exploiting a breakthrough that never came). There is still talk of how a Ukrainian offensive in the coming year can follow up its limited success and eventually reach the coastline on the Sea of Azov. But in that time, even the Russians will have built up their formidable defences further. Even a renewed Ukrainian offensive is unlikely to make any tangible gains. In fact, if they are halted again, it may merely weaken them further and make them vulnerable to a likely Russian offensive.

A Ukrainian victory thus seems a little unlikely. More so since Western aid is dwindling and they are now unable to build up reserves or military capabilities. At best, they would be able to merely bolster their own defensive capability to halt a Russian offensive – should it come– and prevent any further loss of territory.

A 'Forever War' along the LOC

In April 2014, Russia simply annexed Crimea. They marched into it on the pretext of saving the Russian-speaking population there, occupied it, conducted a referendum and in a *fait accompli* made Crimea a part of Russia.

In the Donbas, the separatist movement by the militia of the Luhansk

People's Republic and Donetsk People's Republic, which began in 2014, went on for eight long years. The LPR and DPR aided by Russian soldiers in civilian clothing succeeded in taking over 40 per cent of the Donbas. The line dividing the area controlled by the Russian-sponsored forces and the Ukrainian forces saw intense trench warfare, raids, skirmishes and artillery duels almost on a daily basis and became known as the Line of Contact. A small-scale war has been going along this line for over eight years, with occasional periods of calm, during pauses and ceasefires. The Minsk II Agreement of 2019 enabled some measure of peace along the LOC. Then the Russia-Ukraine war broke out in February 2022 and the entire front erupted again.

The LOC has been in force for eight years now. With the Russian territorial gains in this war, it has merely shifted around 200 kilometres inwards all along the frontline from Kherson to Kharkiv. Along this new Line of Contact, trenches, mines and fortifications have come up and brutal trench fighting goes on almost on a daily basis. With the failure of their offensive, Ukraine will not be able to evict Russia from its occupied territories, nor will they be able to push the LOC backwards. Russia too, may not be able to make tangible gains along the line (unless they launch a major offensive). It is quite likely that this war could slip into a stalemate and become a 'frozen conflict' that goes on interminably, with the fighting raging along the new LOC as it has since 2014 onwards. Even if a ceasefire, a truce or even an armistice is implemented, the line dividing the positions held by Russian and Ukrainian troops will still be in place. It could be very much like the Line of Control between India and Pakistan, and that LOC too will keep festering, see firing, artillery duels, raids and skirmishes, and even small wars erupting from time to time.

The most likely outcome of this war will be the Russian occupation of its captured areas and a long stalemate that could lead to the establishment of a LOC. This line could well become the permanent dividing line between Russia and Ukraine and *ipso facto* the rest of Europe.

What will the Next Year Bring?

The year 2023 was expected to be one when the much-awaited Ukrainian offensive would push the Russians out and make decisive gains to change the course of the war. The offensive has come and gone with intangible results, and in spite of the Western media proclaiming that the offensive will continue next year till it finally attains its aims, it seems unlikely.

War-weariness is already showing. The world has shifted attention to the even more dangerous situation in the Middle East. Much of US aid and arms are being diverted there. Europe too seems to be tiring of the continue drain which is not showing much results.

Left to itself, Ukraine will be able to fight the war for just 45 days before it runs out of ammunition and reserves. Russia with its vast stocks can continue this war of attrition, much longer with Putin banking on Russia's staying power to eventually attain the country's military and political aims. There is also Putin's personal staying power. Contrary to expectations, he has emerged stronger and enjoys an unprecedented approval rating of over 80 per cent. He has also announced his decision to run for the presidential elections in March 2024, and there is no doubt of the results. So, Putin will be in power till at least 2030, and will continue the war till its aims are achieved. The political change that was hoped for in Russia has not materialized.

Ukraine too faces a presidential election in March 2024, which Zelensky is likely to conduct in spite of war-time restrictions. His own position is less secure, and should the next incumbent be less inclined to continue a pointless war, they could decide to cut their losses, and accept a 'land-for-peace' truce, and the war could end on Russia's terms. And, of course, we have the much-anticipated US presidential elections in November 2024, which may prove to be Putin's 'Trump Card.'

The ideal state for the war to end would be, of course, through a negotiated solution with Russia withdrawing from Ukrainian territory, (but being allowed to keep Crimea); Ukraine abjuring its intention to join NATO, but offered security guarantees instead; NATO moving back from Russia's borders in deference to its genuine security concerns; and the West removing the sanctions on Russia and also chipping in for rehabilitation of war-torn Ukraine. That may be an ideal situation that caters for all sides. Unfortunately, we are not in an ideal situation. The West will not abandon Ukraine, but keep supplying it with enough aid and arms to continue the war without capitulation (after all, it suits them to continue to weaken Russia, as well). That will keep the war going for some time to come. A Russian offensive may come later; perhaps even another local Ukrainian offensive could take place, but they may not prove decisive. In all probability, the Russia-Ukraine war will continue in a long stalemate and the *status quo* will lead to the formation of a LOC between the two nations. Along that LOC, a long slow war could continue interminably in a state of frozen conflict.

REFERENCES

"A Plausible Endgame to the War in Ukraine," *TIME*, https://www.time.com

"An Unwinnable War: Washington needs an Endgame in Ukraine," The RAND Corporation, https://www.rand.org

"In Ukraine War, neither side is Winning: Is it Time to Negotiate?," *CBC News*, https://www.cbc,org

"Russia's War in Ukraine: Insights from RAND," The RAND Corporation, https://www.rand.org

"Russia-Ukraine War at a Glance," *The Guardian*, https://www.guardian.com

"Russia-Ukraine War," *The New York Times*, https://www.nytimes.com

"Russia-Ukraine war: Insights and Analysis", Harvard Kennedy School, https://www.khs.harvard.edu

"The Russia Ukraine War and its Ramifications for Russia," Brookings, https://www.brookings.edu

"Tracking the War with Russia," *BBC News*, https://www.bbc.com

"Ukraine at War," *The Economist*, https://www/economist.com

"War in Ukraine," Global Conflict Tracker, https://www.cfr.org

"War in Ukraine," *NBC News*, https://www.nbcnews.com

"What is Russia's Endgame in Ukraine?," Atlantic Council, https://www.atlanticcouncil.org

GAZA

Major Characters

Benjamin 'Bibi' Netanyahu

Has served as Prime Minister of Israel for three terms from 1996-99, 2009-21 and since 2022 onwards. The chairman of the Likud Party, his hard-line views have alienated many, and his controversial reforms have led to internal divisions within Israel itself. He is held responsible for allowing Hamas to rise and not detecting its actions in time; his political future is at stake in this war.

Yahya Sinwar

The head of Hamas in Gaza, Sinwar is a brutal hardliner who planned and executed the deadly 7 October attacks. He has spent 21 years in Israeli prisons (where his life was saved when Israeli surgeons operated and removed a tumour from his brain) till he was released in a prisoner swap in 2011. He successfully deceived Israel in the conduct of the attacks and brought the Palestinian issue back on the world stage.

Mohammed Deif

The shadowy head of the al-Qassam Brigade – the military arm of Hamas. He is one of Israel's most wanted men and has survived seven assassination attempts. He built up al-Qassam into a formidable force of over 20 to 30 thousand well-armed and motivated fighters that launched repeated strikes in Israel, and even managed to keep the Israeli army at bay in the initial days of their offensive.

Yoav Gallant

A retired IDF General and the present Defence Minister of Israel, overseeing the operations. Known to be hard-line in his views, he has vowed to eliminate Hamas. But his excessively harsh actions during the conduct of the war have invited adverse world reaction.

General Herzi Halevi

The Chief of the Israeli General Staff, overseeing the planning and conduct of Israeli operations. He has faced flak for the intelligence lapses of 7 October and also his conduct of operations.

Joe Biden

The US President who has stood by Israel and even sent two carrier groups into the region as a sign of US support. He has a delicate task of preserving US influence in the region, maintain support and aid for both Ukraine and Israel, and still stave off growing Chinese belligerence. His task is complicated by the presidential elections due in 2024.

Mahmoud Abbas

The head of the Palestinian Authority in the West Bank. He proposes a more moderate approach towards Israel and recognizes its existence, with the aim of eventually attaining "a two-state solution." His position as the representative of the Palestinian people is under threat by Hamas, whose hard-line approach seems to be gaining traction.

Chronology of Major Events

Early times: The area of modern day Israel and Palestine is part of the Canaanite empire where the ancient kingdoms of Israel and Judea flourished. The area was under repeated invasions and conquered by different kingdoms till it finally came under the Ottoman Empire in 1517.

1917: The Ottoman Empire defeated. The area of Palestine came under a British mandate.

2 November 1917: The Balfour Declaration promises the international Jewish community with "the establishment in Palestine of a national home for the Jewish people." This 67 word letter sets the foundation for the State of Israel.

1917 onwards: Influx of Jews towards Palestine to avoid persecution and anti-semiticm in USA and Europe. This intensifies in the wake of World War II and the Holocaust.

29 November 1947: The United Nations passes Resolution 181 to partition Palestine into Arab and Jewish states with Jerusalem as the common capital. The resolution is welcomed by Jews, but rejected by the Arabs who fear being displaced in their own land. Fighting and civil war breaks out between Jews and Arab militia.

14 May 1948: The British mandate in Palestine ends, and they withdraw. The same day. David Ben-Gurion announces the declaration of the state of Israel in Tel Aviv. It is recognised by the USA, and three days later by USSR.

15 May 1948: Five Arab states attack Israel and the first Arab-Israel war breaks out. The war goes on for a year, but at the end of it, Israel manages to hold on to its allotted territories, and even captures additional land allotted to the Arabs.

1956: The Suez crisis. President Nasser of Egypt nationalises the Suez Canal. Israel, France and Britain attack the canal and take it over, but are forced to withdraw under international pressure. This is seen as a victory for Nasser.

05-10 June 1967: The Six-Day War. Israel comprehensively defeats the combined armies of five Arab states in a daring pre-emptive attack. It takes over the Sinai Peninsula from Egypt, the West Bank from Jordan, and the Golan Heights from Syria.

1969: Yasser Arafat takes over as the chairman of the PLO. Palestinian actions intensified against Israel.

1972: Palestinian militants attack the Israeli Olympic contingent at the Munich Olympics, killing 11. This sparks a wave of revulsion across the world.

06-26 October 1973: The Yom Kippur war. Egypt and Syria attack Israel on two fronts, bringing it very close to defeat. However, Israel retrieves the situation by pushing back the Syrian in the Golan Heights and by crossing the Suez Canal to cut off Egyptian forces.

June 1976: The Israeli raid on Entebbe. Israeli commandos launch a daring mission to rescue Jewish passengers taken hostage by a militant Palestinian organisation on a plane hijacked to Entebbe. The passengers are got safely home.

1978: Egypt and Israel, enter into the Camp David Accord, brokered by the USA. Israel agrees to give back all its captured territory to Egypt. Egypt recognises Israel. It brings peace between the nations but does not address the Palestinian issue.

June 1982: Israel invades Lebanon to halt rocket strikes and raids by the PLO from South Lebanon. It evicts the PLO from Lebanon and destroys its bases but starts a civil war there which continues for years thereafter.

December 1987-1992: The First Intifada – or 'the great shake-up' is launched in the occupied territory. Palestinians come out in the streets in stone-throwing and violence against Israelis in a low level violence that goes on for five years.

1993: The Oslo Accords signed between the PLO and Israel. Both sides agree to recognise the other. Transfer of power in the Occupied territories of the West Bank and Gaza Strip is to take place to the Palestinian authority with the eventual aim of creating a Palestinian state. However, that is not implemented and accord breaks down.

2001 to 2005: The Second Intifada breaks out in the occupied territories. This is even more violent than the first.

2004: Mehmoud Abbas takes over as the President of the Palestinian Authority after the death of Yasser Arafat. They adopt a slightly more moderate stance thereafter.

2005: Israel withdraws from Gaza Strip, in what is seen as a major success for the Palestinians following their Second Intifada.

2006: Hamas comes into power in Gaza by defeating Fatah in the legislative assembly elections. However, this sets off in-fighting between Palestinians themselves. Eventually Hamas takes over Gaza, and Fatah retains power in the West Bank.

2007: Israel places Gaza under a land, sea and air blockade which continues to till this day.

December 2008 to January 2009: The first Israel-Hamas war takes place. Operation CAST LEAD. Israel launches a limited ground and air offensive in Gaza.

November 2012: Second Israel- Hamas War. Operation PILLAR OF DEFENSE. Israel launches air strikes on Gaza in retaliation for rocket attacks but no ground invasion is launched.

June 2014: Third Israel-Hamas War. Operation PROTECTIVE EDGE. In 50 days of fighting Israel launches a ground invasion that reaches up to Gaza city, but withdraws its forces thereafter.

10-21 May 2021: Fourth Israel Hamas war. It is caused by Israeli police entering the Al-Aqsa mosque in Jerusalem. Both Israelis and Hamas exchange rockets and missiles strikes, but there is no land invasion.

7 October 2023: Hamas launches Operation AL-AQSA FLOOD, a violent land, air and ground raid into Israel that kills over 1200 persons and takes over 240 hostages. It is the largest single day loss of life that Israel has suffered in its history. Operation SWORDS OF IRON is launched and Israel goes to war declares war against the Hamas.

THE WAR

7 October 2023: Hamas attacks Israel on Simchat Torah Day in the worst single day attack on the country. Over 1400 are killed and around 250 are taken hostage:-

- 0530h – Over 5000 rockets fired into Israel. Most intercepted by the Iron Dome, but over 2-300 get through and cause damage
- 0630h – Hamas terrorist enter Israel by land, air and sea and attack settlements and army camps.
- 0700h – Terrorists enter the Supernova Music Festival – site of the greatest carnage. The shooting and kidnapping goes on till almost 1200h
- 0823h – Israel declares a state of emergency and activates its reserves
- 0834h – Israel security forces launch operations to evict terrorists on Israeli soil
- 1047 – Israeli Air Force launches air strikes on Gaza City targeting Hamas HQs
- 1800h – Israel officially declares a state of war for the first time in 50 years.

7 October onwards: Israeli air and missile attacks inside Gaza. Air campaign lasts for three weeks.

17 October 2023: Explosion at al-Ahli hospital in Gaza City causes almost 500 casualties. Hamas says it is the result of a IAF strike, Israel submits evidence to prove it was the result of a malfunctioning Hamas rocket

18 October 2023: US President Joe Biden visits the Middle East to meet Arab and Israeli leaders. Arab leaders cancel meeting with him in protest of the hospital deaths.

27 October 2023: Israel launches its ground offensive into North Gaza, after giving warning to all residents to evacuate North Gaza. Move towards Gaza City in three prongs.

31 October 2023: Israeli air strike at Jabalia refugee camp kills over 50 people. Israel claims Hamas terrorists were hiding there.

13 November 2023: Israeli tanks surround Gaza City from three directions. Troops enter al Shifa hospital which they claim conceals a tunnel leading to Hamas Headquarters.

24-30 November 2023: Truce brokered by Egypt and Qatar for four days that calls for a halt in fighting, permits aid to enter Gaza. Hamas agrees to release 50 hostages in exchange for 150 Palestinians. Truce is extended by 2 more days and then an additional day.

01 December 2023: Truce ends. Israel air strikes launched 8 minutes after truce expires. Israel warn residents to vacate South Gaza as operations move towards the cities of the south.

05 December 2023: Israel closes in towards the main cities of the South including Khan Younis where most of the Hamas leadership has reportedly fled to from Gaza City.

09 December 2023: U N Secretary General Antonio Gueterres invokes Article 99 of the UN Charter to call for a ceasefire on humanitarian grounds Vetoed by USA.

11 December 2023: Israeli tanks enter the heart of Khan Younis after intense combat. They surround the house of Yahya Sinwar. Fighting near Jabalia camp, the largest refugee camp.

13 December 2023: Houthis step up attacks on shipping bound for Israel in the Red Sea. Hezbollah too intensify attacks against Israel from Lebanon.

18 December 2023: USA proposes 'Operation Prosperity Guardian' an international maritime coalition to enable safe passage of shipping through the Red Sea against Houthi missile and drone attacks on international shipping.

23 December 2023: UNSC adopts resolution calling for 'urgent suspension of hostilities." India votes for the resolution. USA abstains. USA had earlier vetoes two resolutions calling for ceasefire.

25 December 2023: A quiet sombre Christmas in Jerusalem.

29 December 2023: Israel moves towards Central Gaza in the Nusseirat, Bureji and Magazhi area forcing people already displaced from the North further away. Israeli Premier Benyamin Netanyahu says operations will continue till all aims met, including destruction of Hamas. Refuses ceasefire.

First Week Jan 2024: Israeli operations shift to Central Gaza. Khan Younis, the second largest city in Gaza is surrounded and pummeled. The operation causes casualties and widespread destruction, but little military gains.

23 Jan 2024: 24 Israeli soldiers killed in Gaza in the largest single day loss of Israeli life in the war.

February–March 2024: Israeli operations continue inside Gaza. At the same time actions against Hezbollah also increase. Peace talks in Cairo between Hamas, Israeli, Egyptian and Qatar representatives reach no conclusion.

10 March 2024: Holy month of Ramadhan begins. However, the hoped-for ceasefire does not materialize.

17 March 2024: Marwan Issa, the Number 3 in the Hamas hierarchy reportedly killed by an Israeli airstrike on a Hamas tunnel complex in Nuseirat refugee camp. The strike also kills around 70 others.

13 April 2024: Iran fires over 320 drones and missiles into Israel in retaliation for an Israeli attack on its consulate in Damascus that killed 7 senior Republican Guard officers. The strikes were ineffective as most of the projectiles were shot down and few actually hit Israeli soil.

16 April 2024: Israeli missiles reportedly hit the Iranian cities of Isfahan and Tabriz in retaliation. No damage was done in these tit-for-tat strikes, which were largely seen as messaging by both sides.

Mid-April 2024: Israel winds up operations in North and Central Gaza. It claims that the Hamas cadres and leadership have shifted to Rafah in the south and announce plans to intensify operations there.

06 May 2024: Peace deal proposed in which all hostages would be released in a phased manner in return for a 'complete ceasefire' and 'eventual long-term solution for the Palestinian problem.' Hamas accepts the proposal, but Israel refuses a complete ceasefire, offering only a temporary cessation of hostilities. Peace talks break down.

06 May 2024: Israel launches its military operation in Rafah, in spite of international condemnation. It raises fears of a humanitarian catastrophe, since 1.4 million Gazans had sought refuge in Rafah after being displaced from the fighting in the north. Israel also launches a renewed assault on Gaza City, claiming that Hamas cadres had shifted back there.

June–July 2024: Israeli operations continue in South Gaza and Gaza City. At the same time cross border attacks and raids with the Hezbollah in Lebanon intensify, raising fears of a larger war.

13 July 2024: Mohammed Deif, the head of the Hamas military wing – the Al Qassim Brigade, killed in an Israeli airstrike in Gaza. This leaves only Yahya Sinwar, the head of Hamas, who is still holed up in Gaza.

30 July 2024: Israeli jets hit a Hezbollah building in Beirut, killing Faud Shukr, a top Hezbollah commander. This was in retaliation for a Hezbollah rocket attack into an Israeli settlement three days earlier that killed 12 children.

31 July 2024: Ismail Haniyeh, the Chief of Hamas and their chief negotiator, assassinated in Teheran where he was come to attend the swearing-in of the new President. The attack was attributed to Israel and predictably Iran vowed revenge.

25 August 2024: Hezbollah targeted Israel with over 320 rockets and drones in their largest attack. Israel launched over 100 jets to attack Hezbollah targets in Southern Lebanon and what they called "Self-defense pre-emptive strikes." This marked a major escalation of the war.

7

The Creation of Israel and its Fight for Survival

"We have returned to our Promised Land."

—Israeli Slogan

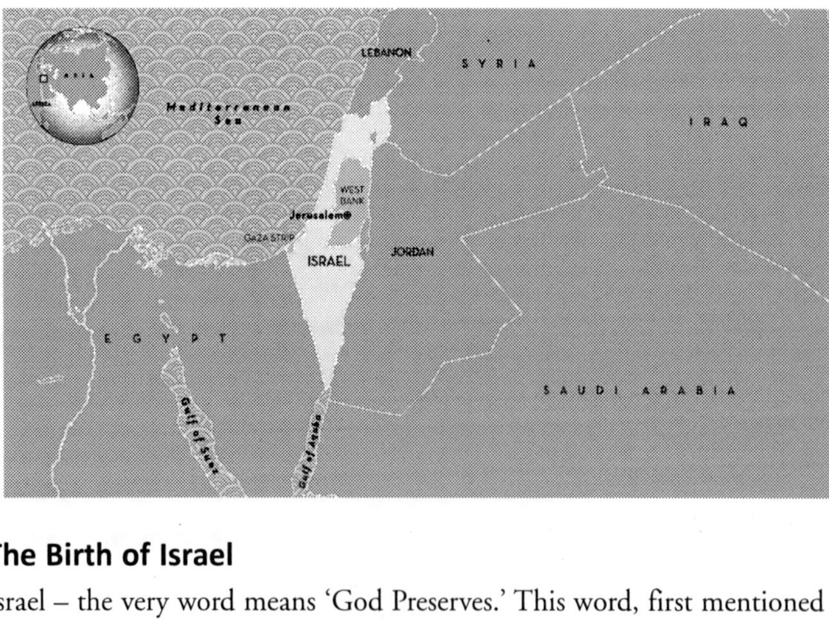

The Birth of Israel

Israel – the very word means 'God Preserves.' This word, first mentioned in the Old Testament, has its origins over ten millennia ago when the Biblical figure, Jacob, was renamed Israel after wrestling with an angel of God. His descendants were called 'Israelites', or 'Children of Israel' and the land they lived in was called 'The land of Israel'.

The swathe of land on the banks of the Mediterranean Sea, with the fertile plains of Lebanon and Syria to its north, Jordan and the Dead Sea to its east, and the arid deserts of Negev and Sinai to its south, has a long and troubled history. This land has given birth to Judaism, Christianity, and Islam and as the cockpit of the world's major religions, has seen much strife and bloodshed which religious differences often bring in their wake. Even now, it is one of the major flashpoints of the world.

Israel's origins can be traced back to Abraham, who is considered to be the father of both Judaism (through his son, Isaac) and Islam (through his son Ishmael). The Jews were enslaved by the Egyptians for centuries till they broke free of their shackles and were led away by Moses into the Sinai desert, where they wandered for 40 years till they settled in the area of Canaan – a land promised by God himself to the Jews – in the area of modern-day Israel.

In their Promised Land, the Jews prospered and thrived under wise and learned kings. Around the 11th Century BC, the Israelites established their own kingdom with Jerusalem as its capital. For over millennia they lived in relative peace and prosperity. Yet, the area which formed the hub of Europe, Africa and Asia saw repeated invasions over the centuries by the Assyrians, the Babylonians and then by the Persians, Greeks, Romans and Arabs. The Romans took it over around the second century BC and many of the local Jews were killed, displaced or simply sold into slavery. In the first century, Christianity arose in the area, and then Islam came up in the sixth century. This land became the site of some of the great battle of the Crusades for the control of Jerusalem, considered sacred by Jews, Christians and Muslims alike. Even today the holy city of Jerusalem is bitterly disputed, claimed and contested by all three religions.

With the defeat of the Crusaders, the area became part of the Mamluk Sultanate and then under the great Ottoman Empire which ruled it for four centuries from 1517 to 1917. The continuous invasion by foreign powers pushed the local Jews away from the area and they sought refuge in different parts of the world. But even though the hard-working, intelligent community thrived and contributed greatly to local society and the nations which harboured them, the Jews still faced anti-Semitism. Jews were increasingly discriminated against in America, Europe, Russia, and virtually across the world. As persecution increased, the idea of returning to their own homeland and establishing a Jewish nation there began gaining strength. This idea was given shape by the Zionist movement, under Theodore Herzl in 1897, which believed that Jews could not survive unless they had a nation of their own, and began pressing for a Jewish homeland in the area of the origin –the same area which had now been named Palestine.

In 1914, World War I broke out. The four-year-long war saw the defeat of the Axis powers and also marked the end of the Turkish Ottoman Empire. The area of Palestine now came under a British mandate which was entrusted by the newly-created League of Nations with the task of administering it. By this time, the Zionist movement for the creation of a Jewish homeland had also picked up momentum. It comprised some of the most influential Jews, who were leading members of industry and business. They now pressed Britain for a Jewish Homeland. The efforts of the influential community bore fruit. On 2 November 1917, Britain's' then foreign secretary, Arthur Balfour, wrote a letter to Lionel Rothschild, one of the leading figures of the Jewish community, which expressed the commitment of the British government, "to the establishment in Palestine of a national home for the Jewish people and felicitating the achievement of this objective."

This 67-word letter, henceforth known as the Balfour Declaration became the foundation on which the future Jewish state would be built. In effect, it promised the creation of a Jewish state in the area of Palestine. It however overlooked the fact that local Arabs made up over 90 per cent of the population there and no thought seemed to have been given to where they would go – as it still is. Following the Balfour Declaration, a massive influx of Jews flowed into Palestine in the period between 1923 and 1948 – the years of the British mandate over Palestine. These years were also marked by increased persecution of Jews in Europe and the USA and other parts of the world. Perhaps the worst moment came when six million Jews were killed in the gas chambers and by the firing squads of Nazi Germany and millions more were hounded and displaced, not only in Germany, but virtually all over Europe. This heightened the fears of the Jews, and the influx of Jews towards their promised homeland in the area of Palestine increased dramatically. In the process, they changed the demographic balance and uprooted the local Arabs who were the traditional holders of the land. As more and more Jewish settlements came up, clashes began between the local Palestinian Arabs and the Jewish migrants. The clashes soon went out of control and began to engulf both communities.

The Arabs rose to the defence of the Palestinian brethren and created the Arab League to evict the Jewish settlers. In response, the Jews created a self-defence force called Haganah. Aided by arms and aid from influential Jews across the world, the Haganah battled the Arab League and a virtual civil war broke out in mid 1947.

As the situation went out of control, the newly-created United Nations was called on to resolve the issue. In a historic (though ill-considered) decision, the UN passed Resolution 181 on 29 November 1947. This Resolution was in effect a plan to partition Palestine into Arab and Jewish states with Jerusalem as the common capital. A map of the area given to Arabs and Jews was drafted with 55 per cent of the land given to the Jewish settlers and 42 per cent of non-contiguous areas given to the Arabs. The plan was predictably rejected by the Arabs and could never be implemented but it identified the borders of the to-be-newly created state and gave it shape. The civil war that had already been raging between Arabs and Jews, now intensified and soon swept out of control.

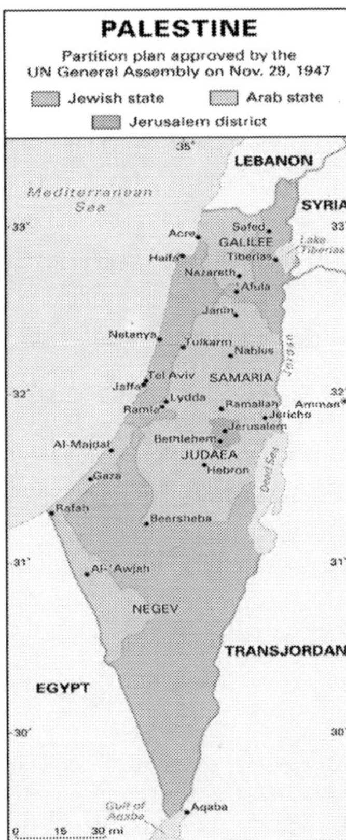

Unable to control the situation, the British did what they usually do. They withdrew and left the Arabs and Jews to sort out the mess that they themselves had created. On 14 May 1948, the mandate over Palestine expired and they withdrew on the same day. Even as the British forces began their withdrawal, the Jewish People's Council gathered at the Tel Aviv Museum, and under the chairmanship of David Ben-Gurion, declared the announcement of the State of Israel. Even as the declaration was being read out, the sounds of firing and mortars could be heard as Jewish and Arab fighters, continued battling each other. However, in the turmoil came a bit of good news. The USA announced its recognition of the new nation and at midnight on the night of 14/15 May the state of Israel officially came into being. Three days later, the USSR too recognised Israel.

The text of the Declaration of the establishment of the State of Israel is at the attached Appendix.

Of course, that was a situation that could never be accepted by the Arabs. The very next day, the Arab armies of Egypt, Transjordan (now Jordan) Syria, Lebanon and Iraq attacked the newly-created state as Israel faced its first battle of survival, virtually on the day of its birth.

Appendix

The Declaration of the State of Israel

David Ben Gurion reading the Declaration of Independence of the State of Israel

On 14 May 1948, on the day in which the British Mandate over Palestine expired, the Jewish People's Council gathered at the Tel Aviv Museum, and approved the following proclamation, declaring the establishment of the State of Israel.

ERETZ-ISRAEL [(Hebrew) - the Land of Israel, Palestine] was the birthplace of the Jewish people. Here their spiritual, religious and political identity was shaped. Here they first attained statehood, created cultural values of national and universal significance and gave to the world the eternal Book of Books.

After being forcibly exiled from their land, the people kept faith with it throughout their Dispersion and never ceased to pray and hope for their return to it and for the restoration in it of their political freedom. Impelled by this historic and traditional attachment, Jews strove in every successive generation to re-establish themselves in their ancient homeland. In recent decades they returned in their masses. Pioneers, ma'pilim [(Hebrew) – immigrants coming to Eretz-Israel in defiance of restrictive legislation] and defenders, they made deserts bloom, revived the Hebrew language, built villages and towns, and created a thriving community controlling its own economy and culture, loving peace but knowing how to defend itself, bringing the blessings of progress to all the country's inhabitants, and aspiring towards independent nationhood.

In the year 5657 (1897), at the summons of the spiritual father of the Jewish State, Theodore Herzl, the First Zionist Congress convened and proclaimed the right of the Jewish people to national rebirth in its own country.

This right was recognized in the Balfour Declaration of the 2nd November, 1917, and re-affirmed in the Mandate of the League of Nations which, in particular, gave international sanction to the historic connection between the Jewish people and Eretz-Israel and to the right of the Jewish people to rebuild their National Home.

The catastrophe which recently befell the Jewish people – the massacre of millions of Jews in Europe – was another clear demonstration of the urgency of solving the problem of its homelessness by re-establishing in Eretz-Israel the Jewish State, which would open the gates of the homeland wide to every Jew and confer upon the Jewish people the status of a fully privileged member of the comity of nations.

On 29 November, 1947, the United Nations General Assembly passed a resolution calling for the establishment of a Jewish State in Eretz-Israel; the General Assembly required the inhabitants of Eretz-Israel to take such steps as were necessary on their part for the implementation of that resolution. This recognition by the United Nations of the right of the Jewish people to establish their State is irrevocable.

This right is the natural right of the Jewish people to be masters of their own fate, like all other nations, in their own sovereign State.

ACCORDINGLY WE, MEMBERS OF THE PEOPLE'S COUNCIL, REPRESENTATIVES OF THE JEWISH COMMUNITY OF ERETZ-ISRAEL AND OF THE ZIONIST MOVEMENT, ARE HERE ASSEMBLED ON THE DAY OF THE TERMINATION OF THE BRITISH MANDATE OVER ERETZ-ISRAEL AND, BY VIRTUE OF OUR NATURAL AND HISTORIC RIGHT AND ON THE STRENGTH OF THE RESOLUTION OF THE UNITED NATIONS GENERAL ASSEMBLY, HEREBY DECLARE THE ESTABLISHMENT OF A JEWISH STATE IN ERETZ-ISRAEL, TO BE KNOWN AS THE STATE OF ISRAEL.

WE DECLARE that, with effect from the moment of the termination of the Mandate, being tonight, the eve of Sabbath, the 6th Iyar, 5708 (15 May 1948), until the establishment of the elected, regular authorities of the State in accordance with the Constitution which shall be adopted by the Elected Constituent Assembly not later than the 1st of October 1948, the People's Council shall act as a Provisional Council of State, and its executive organ, the People's Administration, shall be the Provisional Government of the Jewish State, to be called 'Israel'.

THE STATE OF ISRAEL will be open for Jewish immigration and for the Ingathering of the Exiles; it will foster the development of the country for the benefit of all its inhabitants; it will be based on freedom, justice and peace as envisaged by the prophets of Israel; it will ensure complete equality of social and political rights to all its inhabitants irrespective of religion, race or sex; it will guarantee freedom of religion, conscience, language, education and culture; it will safeguard the Holy Places of all religions; and it will be faithful to the principles of the Charter of the United Nations.

PLACING OUR TRUST IN THE 'ROCK OF ISRAEL', WE AFFIX OUR SIGNATURES TO THIS PROCLAMATION AT THIS SESSION OF THE PROVISIONAL COUNCIL OF STATE, ON THE SOIL OF THE HOMELAND, IN THE CITY OF TEL-AVIV, ON THIS SABBATH EVE, THE 5TH DAY OF IYAR, 5708 (14 MAY 1948).

REFERENCES

'Balfour Declaration – History and Impact', *Britannica*, https://www.britannica.com

'Balfour Declaration: The Divisive Legacy of 67 Words', *BBC*, https://www.bbc.com

Ben-Sasson, *A History of the Jewish People*, Harvard University Press.

'How Israel was Founded', WION, https://www.wion.com

'Israel's Declaration of Independence', The Jewish Virtual Library, https://www.jewishvirtuallibrary.com

'Jews – History, Beliefs and Facts', *Britannica*, www.britanicca.com

Kramer Gudrun. *A History of Palestine from the Ottoman Conquest to the Founding of Israel*, Princeton Press.

Raymond Scheindlin, *A Short History of the Jewish People*, Oxford University Press.

'State of Israel Proclaimed – May 14, 1948', History Channel, https://www.history.com

'Text of the Balfour Declaration', The Jewish Virtual Library, https://www.jewishvirtuallibrary.org

'The Nakba in 1948', *Al Jazeera*, https://www.aljazeera.com

8

Israel's Wars with its Neighbours

"*We are back. And we will never leave.*"

—Israeli soldiers in Jerusalem – 1967 War

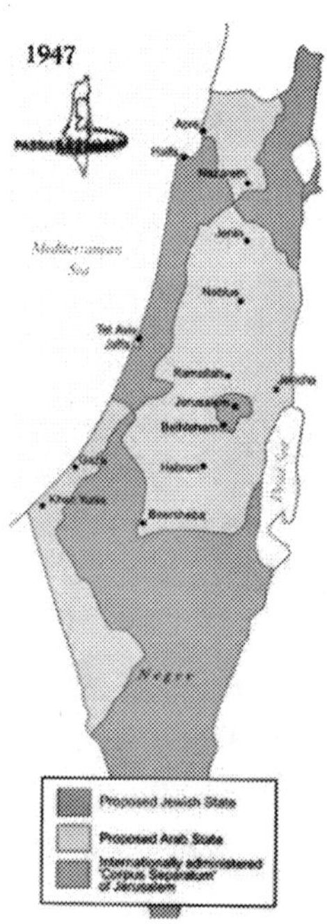

Area allotted to Israel by the UN Plan

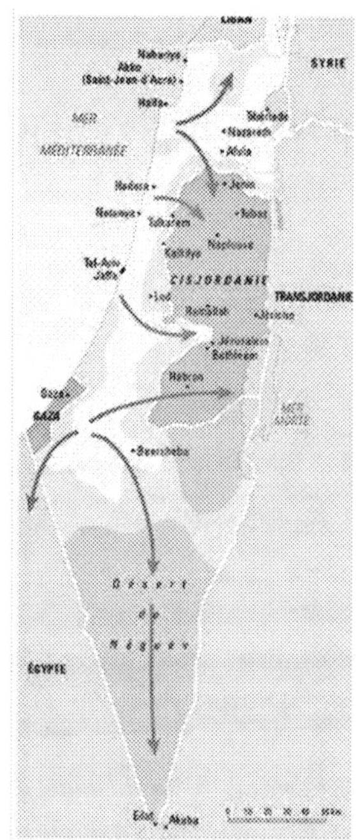

Area held by Israel after 1948 War

The Battle for Creation – 1947-48 War

The creation of the new nation was bound to meet with a very violent response from the Arab nations. After all, they had never accepted the United Nations

Plan for the partitioning of Palestine into Arab and Jewish states (with most of the area going to the Jews) and a violent civil war had been raging ever since it was announced in November 1947. In fact, both sides seemed to be waiting for the end of the British mandate on 14 May 1948, when the British forces would withdraw and the last semblance of control would be over. Almost as soon as David Ben-Gurion had completed making his historic announcement declaring the creation of the State of Israel on the afternoon of 14 May 1948, the Arabs launched an air attack on Tel Aviv, striking the Museum from where the announcement had been made. At the same time, the Palestinian and Arab militia, which, in any case, had been in a state of civil war with the Jewish self-defence group called Haganah, intensified their actions and began a series of attacks on Jewish settlements.

The very next day, the Arab armies of Jordan, Egypt, Syria, Lebanon and Iraq invaded and crossed the boundaries of the newly-created state. This force initially pushed back the Jewish self-defence militia on all fronts, evicting the newly-arrived settlers and burning the Jewish settlements. The civil war had already been raging since November 1947 and now merely intensified with Arab armies entering the fray to help their Palestinian brethren. The 1947-48 War of Creation was the longest and bloodiest war Israel has ever fought and claimed over 6,000 lives and left over 15,000 maimed and wounded – a casualty figure of over 1 per cent of its population at that time. The Arab armies arrayed along the entire borders of the newly-created state of Israel, with Lebanon and Syria in the north; Transjordan, (which was renamed Jordan during the war) in the east; Egypt, along with contingents from Sudan and Saudi Arabia in the south; and Palestinian and Arab volunteers operating in the interior of the country. It seemed that the new state would be wiped out before it was even created by the very scale of the attack.

In the initial phase, the Arab armies simply poured through as the newly-formed nation and its ill-organised self-defence militia tried desperately to stem the multi-pronged attacks. By 29 May, the Egyptian army was just 30 kilometres from Tel Aviv, and the Jordanians had closed in on Jerusalem. However the Jewish fighters held on grimly, and even maintained their tenuous hold on West Jerusalem. The Jewish settlements under attack were grimly defended against repeated attacks. Jews from across the world began pouring into Israel to help defend their newly-created state. Vast amounts of arms and aid were also sent, many of which had to be done clandestinely to avoid detection. With their usual ingenuity, they set up their own arms industry which manufactured weapons and ammunition in hidden underground foundries. Two British Cromwell tanks were stolen from a depot at Aqaba; three US Shermans were recovered and then reconstituted from scrap. These tanks were the nucleus of what would go on to become one of the most formidable armoured forces in the world. The Israelis also developed their fledging Air Force, using reconnaissance aircraft to fire Bren guns and drop grenades to support Jewish fighters on ground and provide relief to isolated settlements. As a full-scale war broke out, the Israelis began procuring fighter aircraft from all over the world; Avia S-199 from Czechoslovakia, Spitfires, Hurricanes and Messerschmidt – ME 109s from different depots and even three B-17 bombers as scrap from the USA. These bombers were refurbished and flown to Israel in July 1948, one of them even dropping a bomb on Cairo en route to Tel Aviv in an attack that caused little damage but much confusion. Even their navy was built up by procuring three ships from scrap, which were then refurbished by engineers, working at night to avoid detection, fitted with cannons and then used to shell Arab positions in a surprise attack from the sea.

By end June 1948, the Israel had halted the Arab offensive and stabilised the front. By July, they moved on to the offensive and not only recaptured their lost territories, but took over vast tracts of area which had been allotted to the Arabs in the partition plan. By the end of the year, the Israelis had pushed back the Arab armies, regained control of all the area allotted to it by the United Nations Plan and even captured 60 per cent of the area allotted to the Palestinian Arabs, including Jaffa, Ramle, Upper Galilee, Negev, and a wide strip along the Tel Aviv-Jerusalem Road which provided access to East Jerusalem. That success laid the seeds for perpetual warfare. The local Palestinian Arabs, who were displaced from the area, now became refugees. Over 1 million Palestinians were uprooted and forced to move away from their homeland and Jewish settlements came up there. Even today, the Palestinians refer to this event as the Naqba – the Great Catastrophe – and refer to 15 May as Naqba Day.

The major success of the Arab armies was the capture of the West Bank and East Jerusalem by Jordan. They occupied the area west of the Jordan

River – including East Jerusalem – when they then held till 1967, when it was captured by the Israelis. In the south, Egypt, took over the Gaza Strip, which it retained till 1967. Barring these two successes, the Arab armies were pushed back. Israel not only retained the land allotted to it, but captured sizeable territory all around which would act as a buffer for it.

The fighting and skirmishing went on for almost a year till July 1949. Then, one by one, the Arab nations entered into agreements with Israel and signed an Armistice. The guns fell silent, temporarily at least, because the Palestinians, whose legitimate grievances had not been addressed, continued the attacks against Israeli troops and settlements. Over 1 million Palestinians had been displaced from their homeland to make way for a Jewish homeland. They were left with nowhere to go, and the Palestinian state which was promised to them showed no signs of materialising.

The 1947-48 war was just the beginning. It helped create Israel and expanded its original borders, but Israel remained alone and isolated in the region. No Arab nation accepted its existence, leave alone recognise it. The Palestinian issue was still unresolved, and the influx of Palestinian refugees into neighbouring countries would create their own problems, as events would show later. The Palestinian issue would go on for decades thereafter, but for the time being, Israel had been created and held its own in their first battle for survival. There would be many more battles in the future at the next round that was coming soon.

The 1956 Suez Crisis and the Six Day War of 1967

The armistice of 1948 was only a temporary cessation of hostilities. In fact, it wasn't even a complete cessation of hostilities because armed actions by the Palestinian Arabs continued. Moreover, the Arab states had not yet recognised Israel's right to exist. Nor had the Palestinian issue been addressed, leaving them with nowhere to go. But Israel developed its own military, economic and technological prowess, using the pool of talented, motivated manpower that flowed into its shores. The young nation grew and prospered, even as it prepared for the next round which was sure to follow.

The next crisis came in 1956 – the Suez Crisis. In July 1956, President Gamal Abdel Nasser of Egypt nationalised the Suez Canal – the 120-mile long canal linking the Mediterranean Sea to the Indian Ocean via the Red Sea. It

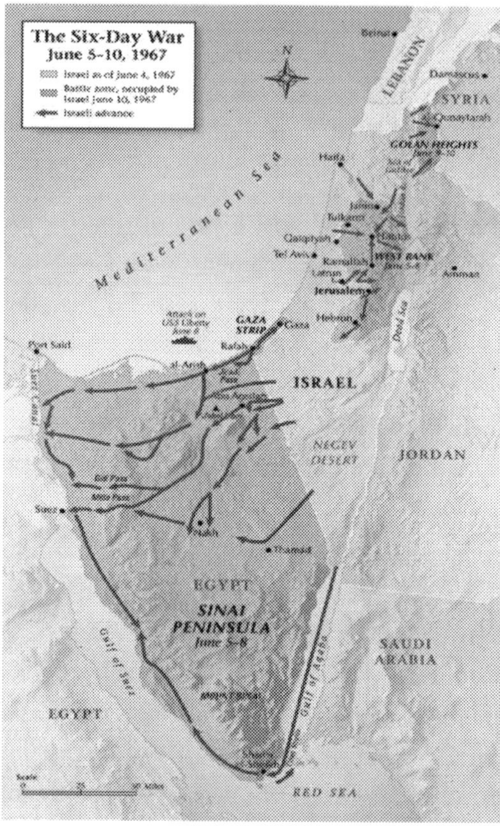

Israeli Advances

had been built and run by a British-French organisation that controlled it to that day, even though it was on Egyptian land. The nationalisation of the canal was widely welcomed in Egypt and boosted Nasser's popularity tremendously. It gave Egypt control of the Suez Canal and its vast revenues. More importantly, it provided control over one of the most important shipping routes of the world. Egypt also blocked the Straits of Tiran to Israel, which was its only sea route to the Red Sea and the Indian Ocean. The loss of the Suez Canal deprived France and Britain of one of its most vital geo-strategic locations in the world. At the same time, the blocking of the Suez Canal and the Straits of Tiran would have serious economic consequences for Israel.

When Nasser refused to back down, Israel, France and Egypt got together for a military action to regain control of the canal. Israel used the pretext of the blocking of the Straits to attack Egypt on 29 October 1956, striking through the Sinai Peninsula towards the Suez Canal. Its tanks reached the 110-kilometre long canal in three prongs. Britain and France also joined the fray as they dropped paratroopers at Port Said –– the vital port town at the mouth of the canal where it joined the Mediterranean Sea. It was apparent that it was a joint Israel, UK, French ploy that had been planned much earlier.

Rather than give up the canal, Nasser sank 40 ships into the channel, blocking it and declaring it inoperable. The situation in one of the world's major waterways was fast getting out of hand, and the USA, USSR and the United Nations eventually pressurised Israel, France and the UK to withdraw their forces from the canal. In return, Egypt eventually re-opened the canal to traffic, and permitted Israel shipping to use it and provided access through the Straits of Tiran. Nasser emerged as a hero in the Arab world for standing up to the Western powers, and in a way, it set the tone for the next conflict.

Tensions between Israel and its Arab neighbours heightened considerably after this crisis. Attacks on Israel settlements by Palestinians increased. Cross-border raids into Israel from Jordan, Syria and Lebanon also intensified. Air clashes began and in April 1967, the Israeli Air Force shot down six Syrian MiGs. The Arab armies were being built up by a generous influx of arms and equipment from the Soviet Union. Syria, Jordan and Egypt signed a defence pact, and the die was being cast for another war which would perhaps eliminate Israel once and for all.

In May 1967, President Nasser received information from the Soviets (later proved wrong) that the Israelis were planning an attack. In preparations for his own attack, he ordered the United Nations Emergency Force (UNEF) to withdraw from the area and began sending his troops into the Sinai Peninsula close to Israel's borders. More significantly, Egyptian troops occupied positions on the vital Sharm-al-Sheikh heights from where they could dominate the Straits of Tiran and prevent movement of Israeli shipping through it. The blocking of the Straits of Tiran could cripple Israel economically, and Prime Minister Golda Meir warned that it would be seen as an act of war. Jordan too began deploying troops along the borders and in the West Bank. In the north, Lebanon and Syria concentrated forces along the Golan Heights – the vital heights separating Israel from Syria. Arab nations such as Iraq, Sudan, and Morocco sent contingents to help them overcome Israel in the coming war. Once again, Israel was faced with an existential threat as five Arab nations – Egypt, Jordan, Syria, Lebanon and Iraq – poised to attack it from all directions.

But rather than waiting passively for the coming attack, the Israelis launched their own pre-emptive strike with OPERATION FOCUS (Moked). Using all but 12 of its 196 of its operational fighter aircraft, they launched a surprise attack on Egyptian airfields at 7:45 a.m. on the morning of 5 June 1967. Flying low to avoid radar, Israeli Mirages and Mysteres flew in a wide circuitous route across the Mediterranean Sea to strike at Egyptian airfields. They had been aided by the fact that Egyptian radars were switched off and did not detect the Israeli Mirages till they were virtually over them. It first eliminated the SAM and radar sites and then swooped on the airfields. The runways were disabled with special tarmac shredding penetration bombs which prevented any aircraft from taking off. Their aircraft, lined up on the tarmac, were simply decimated on the ground in a series of day-long strikes. Israeli pilots had been training for this attack for three years, and knew each aspect of the operation in fine detail. The location and layout of each of the airfields had been memorised by the pilots. Nearly 338 Egyptian aircraft and over 100 pilots were killed in that devastating strike while Israel lost just 19 planes in the attack, which is widely considered to be one of the most successful air strikes of all time.

This attack was planned in fine detail by the IAF Chief, Major General Mordechia Hod. The ground crew had practised preparing an incoming aircraft for the next strike in just eight minutes. Pilots would return from an attack, grab a quick sandwich and coffee and then take off again for the next attack in 10 to 15 minutes, often flying up to four sorties in a day and ensuring that the targets were under continuous attack. Even the time was precisely selected. At 7.45 in the morning, most of the senior officers were travelling from their homes to the offices and there was no one to take decisions at the most critical moments. Years after the war, when General Mordechai was asked the reason for the spectacular Israel success, he put it down to just one thing. "It was not that we had better planes or better pilots or any such thing. It was just that we knew we had 'no alternative.' Had the attack not succeeded, Israel's survival would be at stake."

With air supremacy assured, Israel attacked in the Sinai Peninsula to encircle and destroy the Egyptian forces deployed there. Moving along three thrust lines, their tanks penetrated deep into the desert. Paratroopers landed in the rear to seize key features like the Mitla Pass and the Gidi Pass and cut off the Egyptians from their withdrawal routes. The speed of the offensive took the Egyptians by surprise and fearful of having their army cut off, the Egyptian High Command ordered a general withdrawal from the Sinai. In the confusion that followed, the disorganised retreat turned into a rout and the Egyptian columns were attacked repeatedly by Israeli aircraft and artillery, losing over 10,000 soldiers in a day. Three Israeli divisions raced westwards towards the Suez Canal. Cut off from their routes of withdrawal, the Egyptians began surrendering in droves, so much so that the Israelis were unable to cope with the mass surrender and retained only the officers, sending the soldiers across. It was a complete defeat of an army that had started the war with much optimism and gung-ho.

For a while, Jordan seemed to be undecided about joining the war, but as Israel attacked Egypt, they were fed with false reports stating that Egypt had shot down 80 Israeli aircraft and were winning and going on the offensive. This encouraged them to launch their own strike from the east. As Jordanian troops attacked from the West Bank (which they had captured in the 1947-48 War), the Israeli AF launched a massive air strike on both of Jordan's air bases, destroying all 21 of their Hunters on the ground. Israeli paratroopers pushed into the West Bank and by 7 June, entered Jerusalem. Images of Israeli soldiers, praying at the Wailing Wall in the Old City of Jerusalem were flashed across Israel and the world. "We are back," defence minister Moshe Dayan proclaimed, as he walked through Jerusalem in combat fatigues, helmets, and his signature eye-patch, "And we will never leave."

As had been the case with the Egyptians, the speed of the Israeli advance caught the Jordanians by surprise. Fearing a cut-off of their troops on the West Bank, the Jordanians ordered a withdrawal across the Jordan River into Jordan, to prevent the Israelis from advancing deeper into Jordan territory itself. By some accounts, Israel had no intention of capturing or holding on to the West Bank, but seeing the Jordanian forces dissipate so fast, they simply moved on right till the Jordan River itself and consolidated their positions. In just three nights of fighting, the entire West Bank and the prized city of Jerusalem was in Israeli hands.

Israeli Soldiers entering Jerusalem: In the Centre is Defence Minister Moshe Dayan

With the Egyptians and the Jordanians destroyed in the south and in the East, Israel now focused its attention towards the north – in the Golan Heights, opposite Syria. Israeli tanks, led by the famed Golani Brigade, climbed the treacherous heights and secured Mount Hermon – the highest feature in the area which provided observation right into Israel itself. In two days of fighting, the Israelis seized all of Golan Heights – something they occupy even today.

A United Nations ceasefire finally brought an end to the fighting on 10 June 1967. In just 132 hours of fighting, Israel had defeated five Arab armies, and virtually tripled its territory. Over 20,000 Arab soldiers died, at the cost of 800 Israelis. It had taken over the Sinai Peninsula and the Gaza Strip in the south; the West Bank in the east; and the Golan Heights in the north, creating a buffer between its three major adversaries. The West Bank and the Gaza Strip – henceforth known as the occupied territories – came into their hands along with 1.5 million Palestinians who lived there. It was a success beyond their wildest imagination and seemed that it would ensure security for the future. It was undoubtedly a great victory, but as events would show later, it would not bring permanent peace or security. Rather, it lulled Israel into a sense of overconfidence – something akin to what it had before the Hamas attacks of October 2023 – and set the tone for another, even bloodier conflict six years down the line, that would bring Israel dangerously close to defeat.

'The War of Atonement' – Yom Kippur War, 1973

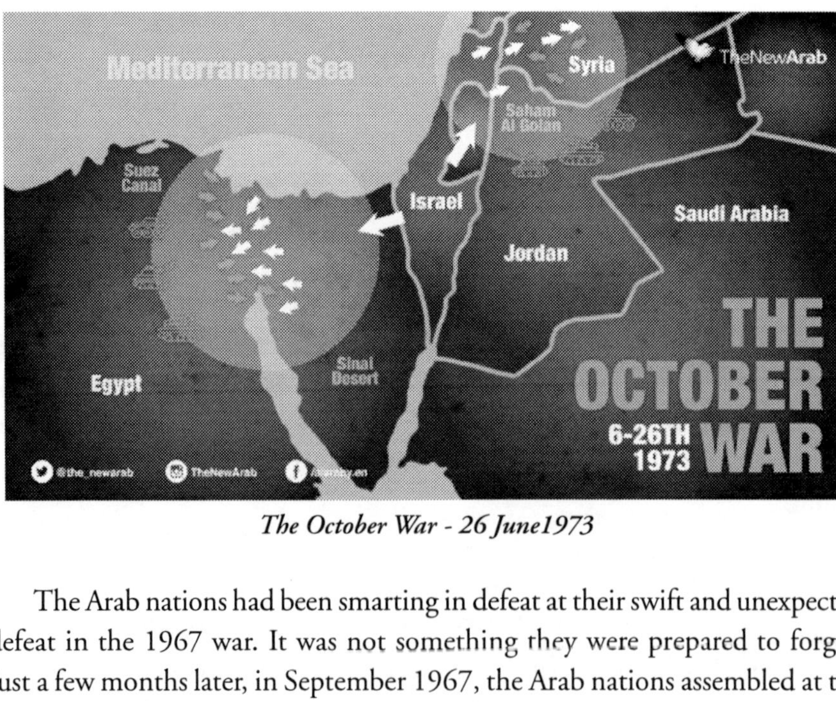

The October War - 26 June1973

The Arab nations had been smarting in defeat at their swift and unexpected defeat in the 1967 war. It was not something they were prepared to forget. Just a few months later, in September 1967, the Arab nations assembled at the

Khartoum Arab Summit and passed a resolution that said: "No peace, no recognition, no negotiations with Israel." Israel's right to exist was not recognised even now. In fact, preparations to eliminate the state were beginning in earnest once again.

In Egypt, a change had come about. President Abdel Nasser was forced to resign in disgrace after the debacle of 1967, and Anwar Sadat, a suave, articulate person, slightly more liberal in his outlook, came in his place. He seemed more grounded in reality and was willing to recognise Israel in return for the territories they captured from Egypt in the war. The offer was even conveyed to the Israeli premier, Mrs. Golda Meir but, smug in victory, no action was taken. Anwar Sadat's aim seemed more to recover Egypt's lost territories, rather than fight for the Palestinian cause.

Sadat knew that this could only be done from a position of strength. Egypt built up its armed forces once again. MiG 21 fighter jets, anti-tank missiles and surface-to-air missiles were helpfully provided by the USSR to make good the losses of the '67 war. In fact, the 1967 war had not really stopped. Continuous firing, raids and cross-border exchanges continued on a regular basis, and a 'War of Attrition' continued. Egypt built up its forces along the Suez Canal, and conducted regular exercises on crossing it. The signs of the Egyptian build-up were noticeable, but surprisingly ignored by Israeli intelligence, who were convinced that the formidable Bar Lev Line – the long line of defence fortifications they had developed on the Suez Canal – would suffice to halt any Egyptian misadventure.

The Egyptians had planned it well. They continued exercising along the canal for months, moving forward and then withdrawing, till they had lulled the Israelis into thinking that these actions were just routine moves. Then on 6 October 1973, Yom Kippur Day, the holiest day of the Jewish calendar (which also coincided with the Muslim holiday of Ramadan), which the Jews traditionally spent in prayer and reflection – at 2 in the afternoon, the Egyptians launched a coordinated attack across the Suez. Facing them was the depleted 'Jerusalem brigade' deployed in 16 forts along the 110-kilometre long canal. Many of the officers and men were away on leave and Israel had just around 290, tanks in the area which were widely dispersed in three armoured brigades in the Sinai desert.

'OPERATION BADR', the crossing of the Suez Canal by the Egyptians, was a major feat of arms. The Egyptians used water cannons to simply blast the sand walls on which the enormous defence fortifications were made, sending them tumbling into the waters of the canal. The Egyptian Air Force had learnt from the mistakes of 1967, and with new equipment and tactics, got mastery of the skies over the area. Engineers rapidly established pontoon bridges across the 200 metre wide canal, and tanks, artillery and trucks of the Second and Third armies moved across it. Around five divisions crossed in 12 waves in five different locations to establish a series of bridgeheads. The Israeli fortifications on the Bar Lev Line were simply swamped. Fifteen of the fortifications fell in the first six hours itself, with only one, the northern most one called 'Fort Budapest' which held on throughout the war.

The Israelis seemed to have woken up to the threat too late. They had received a warning from one of their major sources – Ashraf Marwan, who was codenamed 'Angel' and was also the son-in-law of former Egyptian President Abdel Nasser who had passed on to Israeli intelligence, "There is a 99 per cent chance that the war will start tomorrow. It will start simultaneously on both fronts, the Egyptian and the Syrian." The warning was passed to Israeli Prime Minister Golda Meir, who disregarded it and did not call for mobilisation of reservists even when all signs pointed to a looming offensive. They would make the same mistake 50 years later when they discounted intelligence reports of the Hamas attacks of 7 October 2023.

The Israelis were slow to react on the first day. They had few mobile troops in the Sinai desert and by the time they responded, the Egyptians had already established their bridgeheads across the canal. Israeli air strikes were launched at the bridgeheads, but were effectively countered by handheld surface-to-air missiles and the effective Air Defence screen that the Egyptians had set up. Their armoured counter-attacks were initially launched piecemeal and without coordination and simply beaten back by SAGGER missiles, small, portable anti-tank missiles carried in suitcases that were held by Egyptian infantrymen in their foxholes.

Yet the Israelis had one success in the air on the first day. The Egyptians had launched a massive air strike with over 200 aircraft on Israeli targets and the Israeli air base, Ofir, at Sharm-el-Sheikh came under attack by a flight of MiG-17s and their MiG-21 escorts. These were countered by a pair of Phantom

F4E fighters that took off even as the runway was under attack. In an eight-minute long aerial duel, seven Egyptian MiGS were shot down, without any loss to the Israelis. One of the Egyptian pilots killed in the battle was Atef Sadat – the younger brother of President Anwar Sadat.

Over the next two days, the Egyptians gradually widened their bridgehead till it was almost 10 km deep and consolidated their positions around it. Two full armies, the 2nd and the 3rd Egyptian Armies were now across the canal. Five full divisions were still on the Egyptian side of the canal waiting to be inducted for a thrust into Israel itself.

Even graver was the situation in the north. The Syrians had launched a coordinated attack, with the Egyptians, and now advanced into the Golan Heights to retake the area they had lost in the 1967 war. Syrian troopers recaptured Mount Hermon, the highest point in that area, which provided observation deep into Israel and Syria and was strategically vital to both. Israel had only its 7 Armoured Brigade in the area at that time. In an attempt to stop the tide, the brigade moved its few tanks from position to position to give the impression of being an even larger force. Even though the brigade was almost wiped out as it faced overwhelming odds, their action gave time for reinforcements to move up and halt any further Syrian advance into Israel.

Tel Aviv was now within striking distance of both Egypt and Syria. Golda Meir, the Israeli premier who reportedly lasted out the war smoking 40 cigarettes a day and drinking innumerable cups of coffee, contemplated the use of nuclear weapons to halt the tide. It was perhaps the world's most widely known secret that Israel was in possession of the bomb and a nuclear strike on the Egyptian bridgehead was seriously considered. Israel Phantoms and Skyhawks began practising toss-bombing techniques – the preferred mode of attack when delivering a nuclear warhead. The possibility of the use of nuclear weapons was revealed to the USA, and alarmed at the situation going completely out of control, Henry Kissinger, the US Secretary of State, and President Richard Nixon decided to provide emergency supplies of weaponry and aid to enable the Israelis to stem the breach without resorting to nuclear weapons.

By then the Israel had mobilised its reservists. Their superbly efficient call-up system, ensured that over 300,000 reservists reported for duty and were available within 18 hours itself, instead of the 24 it normally took. With its army up to full strength and buoyed by shipments of arms and ammunition from the USA, Israel was in a position to launch its own counteroffensive. The priority was in the northern sector, since the Syrian incursion was even closer to Tel Aviv. In a series of attacks, the Israelis retook all the area that had been captured by the Syrians in the preceding week and recaptured all of the Golan Heights. They then pushed deeper till they were in Syrian territory itself and poised to launch a thrust towards Damascus, just a hundred kilometres away.

In the southern sector, Israel managed to contain the Egyptian armies in their bridgehead and prevented any further advance. Initially, the Egyptians had merely concentrated on widening the bridgehead, but seeing the reverses on the Syrian front were urged to attack to relieve pressure on the north. The five divisions which had been waiting on their side of the canal for a deep thrust into Israel were now launched for an attack through the Sinai desert into Israel itself.

The Egyptian attack to break out of its bridgehead was a disaster. They moved out of the protective cover of their Air Defence umbrella and were pounded by the Israeli Air Force, which had now regained mastery of the air. The Israeli Southern Command had been completely mobilised and their tanks were in skilfully sited positions to block the Egyptian advance. In just a day's fighting, the Israelis destroyed over 90 Egyptian tanks, and forced the rest to withdraw to the safety of their own bridgehead. The Egyptian advance was successfully countered and they were now confined within their bridgeheads.

It was then that the Israelis launched what is possibly the greatest armoured manoeuvre in the post-World War II era. Having detected a gap between the Egyptian 2nd and 3rd armies in the area of Dervosoir, (which was helpful with information provided by US satellites). The Israelis established bridges across the Suez Canal and moved three armoured brigades across it, getting behind the Egyptian positions and effectively cutting off the Egyptian 3rdArmy on the other side of the canal.

This operation, 'OPERATION STOUT-HEARTED MEN' masterminded by General Ariel Sharon, completely reversed the situation. The Israelis had identified crossing places on the canal where they themselves could cross over, and had prepared them in the preceding years itself. A

The Israeli Crossing of the Suez

reconnaissance battalion was first pushed across on rafts and boats, which revealed that the Egyptians had no forces on the opposite side. (They had pumped across the five divisions waiting behind in an ill-conceived attempt to break out of the bridgehead two days earlier and now held no reserves.) A tank battalion was then ferried across on rafts to establish a bridgehead and then their own bridges on the canal. A 100-metre pre-fabricated bridge was dragged to the shore and laid across the canal, over which their tanks began inducting. The bridge was under repeated attack by air, artillery and even Egyptian commandoes and frogmen, and had to be continually repaired, but it held on. Three divisions were pushed across over the next few days which then fanned out along the Egyptian side of the canal striking the logistic units there. They even cut off the roads leading into the Egyptian bridgeheads, in effect blocking the 2nd and 3rd Egyptian armies from their supplies and replenishments. The tables had now been turned.

Israel still maintains that had it been allowed to continue the war, it could have decimated the entire Egyptian 3rdArmy. But imposing another complete defeat on Egypt was something which neither the USA nor the world community was prepared to allow. The United Nations passed a resolution calling for a ceasefire which was proposed by both the USA and the USSR and on 22 October; the guns finally fell silent after 21 days. Israel had not only recovered the area it had lost in the early days of the war, but had also made significant gains both on the northern and southern fronts. But it was a close thing, and it had come dangerously close to losing it all.

The war is touted as a victory by both nations. Even today, Egypt celebrates 5 October – the day of the crossing of the canal – as a major victory. But actually, both Egypt and Syria were in a more precarious position at the end of it. Though to some measure the war and the initial gains helped President Anwar Sadat to attain his original aims. He had started the war hoping to pressurise Israel into returning the areas of the Gaza Strip and the Sinai Peninsula which it had captured in 1967. He was unable to do so militarily but could attain it politically. The 1973 war convinced the Arab nations that Israel could not be defeated militarily. It also demonstrated to Israel that it too could face the possibility of a military defeat. It was this realisation on both sides that enabled the beginning of a peace process that culminated in the Camp David Accords of 1978.

Five years after the war, Egyptian President Anwar Sadat and Israeli Prime Minister Menachem Begin, met for two weeks of secret negotiations at Camp David, the country resort of US President Jimmy Carter. Here they hammered out a series of agreements that could bring peace to the troubled region. Israel agreed to return all the territory it had captured in 1967 and 1973 wars back to Egypt – this included all of the Sinai Peninsula and the Gaza Strip. Egypt promised to establish normal diplomatic relations with Israel, and acknowledged its right to exist as an independent nation. But though it normalised relations between Israel and its major adversary, the aspirations of the Palestinian people and their own demand for an independent state were pushed back to be resolved at a future date – as it has always been since then.

Both Menachem Begin and Anwar Sadat went on to receive the Nobel Peace Prize in 1978 for their role in securing a historic peace. But both would be vilified in their own nations. Egypt was charged with betrayal by the Arab nations and even removed from the Arab League. Anwar Sadat himself would be assassinated three years later, ironically on 6 October 1981 while he presided over a victory parade held in Cairo to commemorate the eighth anniversary of the Suez crossing by the Egyptian forces. His assassin was an Egyptian army officer who had felt that Sadat had betrayed the Army and the nation by the peace agreement with Israel. He carried concealed hand grenades and live ammunition while participating in the parade and then, as he approached the dais, fired and hurled grenades at President Sadat as he was taking the salute, killing him on the spot. Peace always comes at a tremendous cost.

The 1973 War was the last that Israel fought with Egypt. In a way it bought peace between the two nations. But it did not bring the permanent peace or security that Israel hoped for. The core issue of the Palestinian people remained unaddressed, and it would continue to erupt over the decades. Israel would be faced with continual uprisings of the 2.3 million Palestinians who demanded their own state. It would face two Intifadas for over 10 years. It would be forced to fight the Lebanon wars of 1982 and 2006, and battle the PLO, Hezbollah, Hamas and other terrorist organisations for decades. This unresolved issue of the Palestinian people would finally reach a flashpoint with the horrific Hamas attacks on 7 October that brought the horrors of terrorism right into Israel.

REFERENCES

'1967 War: Six Days that Changed the Middle East', *BBC*, https://www.bbc.com
Anita Shapira, *Ben-Gurion – Father of Modern Israel*, Yale University Press.
'Anwar Sadat – Biography, History and Assassination', History Channel, https://www.history.com
'Camp David Accords and the Arab-Israel Peace Process', US Dept. of State, https://history.state.gov
'Camp David Accords: Summary, History and Facts', *Britannica*, https://www.britannica.com
Colly Elbridge, 'The Israeli Nuclear Alert of 1973', CAN.
Edgar O'Ballance, *No Victor, No Vanquished: The Yom Kippur War*, Barrie and Jenkins.
Herzog Chaim, *The War of Atonement*', Skyhouse Publishing.
'How the Yom Kippur War Changed Israel', *TIME Magazine*, https://time.com
'Israel Air Force's Scrappy Beginnings', Jewish Telegraphic Agency.
'Israel's War of Independence: Background and Overview', Jewish Virtual Library: https://www.jewishvirtuallibrary.org
Joseph Dor, *The Siege of Jerusalem – 1948*, Simon and Schuster.
Lapierre Dominique and Collins Larry, *O Jerusalem*, Harper Collins.
Martin Van Crevald, 'Lessons of the Yom Kippur War,' Wayback Machine.
Simon Dunsten, *The Yom Kippur War of 1973*, Bloomsbury Press.
Morris Benny, *1948 – The First Arab-Israel War*, Yale University Press.
'Six-Day War – Definition, Causes, History, Summary', Britannica, https://www.britannica.com
'The Crossing of the Suez Canal', Defence Tech Info Centre, https://apps.dtic.mil
'The Yom Kippur War: Background and Overview, The Jewish Virtual Library, https://www.jewishvirtualibrary.com
'Timeline: The Arab-Israeli Conflict', *Financial Times*, https://www.ft.com
Uri Kaufman, *18 Days in October*, Books Inc.

9

War and Peace with the PLO and Hezbollah

"*The Two-State Solution – That is the only way to lasting peace in the Middle East.*"

— Yasser Arafat

The Palestinian Issue

Israel had succeeded in creating its own state and even preserving it. However, as per the United Nations partition plan, Palestine was to have been divided between the Jew and Arab nations. The Jews did get their territory and their own land of Israel, but, the Palestinians – the local inhabitants of the land were forced away from the areas allotted to Israel. When Israel captured even more territory in the 1947-48 War, the Palestinians were forced to flee from that area as well. This mass displacement of over 1 million Palestinians from their homeland is referred to as Nakba or the great catastrophe and is something that has affected the Palestinian psyche for generations since then.

The basic issue of providing a separate homeland for the Palestinian people was not addressed even after that. The Palestinian state never materialised, not even in the small sliver of land left to them after the UN plan. After the 1948 War, when Israel captured even more area of the land allotted to the Arabs, the Palestinians became pawns in a bigger game. The Arab nations entered the war claiming to fight for the rights of the Palestinians, but they had their own vested interests. Jordan took over the West Bank, where about 1 million Palestinians lived, and simply held on to the area as their own. Similarly, Egypt held on to the Gaza Strip. Over 1.5 million Palestinians were now confined in these areas divided by over 115 kilometres of Israeli territory between them. And, of course, their own homeland was nowhere in the offing.

In the 1967 War, Israel captured both the West Bank and the Gaza Strip and took over the territories. These areas came under it and would be called the 'Occupied Territories' thereafter. Palestinians were confined to the 41-kilometre long sliver of land along the Mediterranean in the Gaza Strip and an irregular projection of land with Jerusalem as its centre, in the West Bank of the Jordan River. Angry and resentful, the Palestinians erupted from time to time against Israel, whom they saw as an occupier.

In many ways, their demands were justified. They demanded that while Israel would continue to exist in its present boundaries, a state of Palestine be allotted to them in the Occupied Territories of the West Bank and Gaza Strip. Jerusalem, the historical city held sacred by Jews, Christians and Muslims alike, would be an international territory common to all. That was at the heart of 'The Two-State Solution' – which is seen by many as the only just and fair solution to this seven-decade long problem.

However, as Israel prospered and strengthened with the complete backing of the USA, the Palestinian people became gradually forgotten. Most Arab nations realised the futility of the cause and abandoned it. Egypt signed a treaty with Israel in 1978, and Jordan and Syria followed suit. Lebanon fell into civil war in the early Eighties and Iraq was too far to really pose a threat. The Palestinians were promised "An eventual homeland for the Palestinian people," by a series of peace agreements and accords, but it was never implemented. Three generations of Palestinians grew up in the occupied territories, living in abject conditions and surviving on aid – angry, resentful and vengeful. And the anger erupted in violent terrorist strikes, attacks on its kibbutzes, rocket and missile strikes into Israel and violence against Israelis.

These attacks have been going on for over 70 years and the horrific Hamas attacks on 7 October 2023 were just a culmination of these – an eruption of anger, designed to draw attention to the Palestinian people and bring the 'Two-State Solution' back on the table.

PLO and Yasser Arafat

The PLO came about at an Arab summit meeting in 1964, under its founding chairman, a former diplomat named Ahmad Shugayri, to bring the different Palestinian groups under one umbrella. Till then, the disparate Palestinian groups operated largely under the flag of Egypt, Jordan, Syria and other neighbouring states. It was only after the defeat of the Arabs in 1967 war that the PLO actually came into its own and began being seen as the representative of the Palestinian people. Even then, it was divided from within, with hardliners, advocating perpetual enmity and the eradication of Israel, and moderates who were willing to accept a negotiated settlement with Israel that would give them a Palestinian state. The differing views have led to violence and infighting which was often utilised by Israel itself to weaken the organisation.

In 1969, Yasser Arafat, took over as chairman of the PLO. Under his watch, the PLO became even more hard-line and launched a series of attacks and terrorist strikes against Israel. The PLO had its bases in neighbouring Jordon from where it could launch repeated attacks into Israel. Invariably, the attacks led to Israeli retaliation into Jordan itself and clashes with Jordanian armed forces. The PLO was emerging as a strong organisation and creating instability within Jordan. Fed up with their activities, Prince Hussain finally expelled the PLO from his country and it shifted base to Lebanon. From there, it continued its actions against Israel, bringing Lebanon into the fray. They also began to get embroiled in the sectarian strife between Christians and Muslims in Lebanon – a situation that precipitated Lebanon into a civil war. It was this propensity of the PLO to get unduly involved in the internal affairs of the nations that gave it refuge and that led it to be gradually shunned with time.

Palestinian Terrorist Attacks

At the early Seventies, the PLO began shifting strategy. Instead of merely attacking targets inside Israel, they began launching high-profile terrorist attacks against Israeli targets around the world, to draw attention to the Palestinian cause. These actions rebounded. It drew attention in the wrong way. The horrific attacks of the PLO and its affiliated organisations led to a sense of revulsion that lost them sympathy and turned world opinion squarely against them.

The Popular Front for the Liberation of Palestine (PFLP) launched a spectacular strike in September 1970 when three planes were hijacked, the hostages removed, and the planes blown up in front of television cameras "to pay special attention to the Palestinian problem." Yet, perhaps their most spectacular and most dastardly attack was in the 1972 Summer Olympics Games at Munich. Eight members of the Palestinian organisation, Black September, infiltrated the Olympic village, killed two members of the Israeli Olympic contingent and took nine others hostage. In a botched operation to rescue the captured athletes, West German commandos stormed the hideout, resulting in the death of all nine hostages. The killing of innocent Israeli sportspersons at an event as sacred as the Olympic Games, caused revulsion around the world. Israel retaliated through air strikes and attacks on PFLF bases, which killed an estimated 200 militants. More significantly, they launched a covert operation to track down the terrorists involved in the attacks. Each one was systematically hunted down and eliminated by Israeli intelligence agencies over the next two years.

Equally dramatic was the hijacking and rescue of Flight 139 in June 1976. This Air France Airbus 300 was carrying 246 Jewish and Israeli passengers from Tel Aviv to Paris when it was hijacked by Palestinian terrorists and taken to Entebbe in Uganda. Here, the terrorists were feted and given shelter and support by the maniacal Ugandan dictator, Idi Amin.

In what is considered to be one of the most audacious rescue operations anywhere in the world, Israeli commandos flew 3,000 kilometres from Israel to Entebbe. Flying in two C-130 Hercules transport aircraft, they flew at heights of just 30 metres or so above sea level to avoid detection by radar. They reached Entebbe airfield around midnight and landed in pitch dark conditions. Around 30 commandoes of the assault team disembarked from the aircraft and raced from the runway to the terminal building where the hostages were kept using a black Mercedes Benz – the car used by President Idi Amin himself in his visits to the airport. The Israeli commandoes were dressed in Ugandan army uniforms complete with formation badges sewed on the lapels to confuse the guards. In a 53-minute operation, the commandos entered the terminal building, killed all four of the terrorists, and got 102 of the 106 hostages back into the waiting Hercules aircraft. In a pitched battle with Ugandan forces, they also destroyed 11 MiGs waiting on the tarmac to prevent them from giving chase, and damaged the control tower. The two aircraft, now loaded with the rescued hostages, made the return journey back in relative safety, stopping only to refuel in Kenya, and were welcomed in Israel as national heroes. Incidentally, the only fatality was the commander of the operation – Yonathan Netanyahu – brother of the present Prime Minister, Benjamin Netanyahu – who has often used his link to a national war hero to further his political career.

The successful rescue at Entebbe was one of the highlights of Israeli history and had as much impact on their psyche as the victory in 1967. It strengthened the feeling that terrorists should not be negotiated with; rather the nation could fight back and prevail over them. It is an admirable sentiment and the Israelis have proved it repeatedly, fighting against all odds and ever so often, even attaining the unthinkable. In fact, the confidence the nation received after this amazing feat gave it the boost to launch a raid on a nuclear reactor in far-away Baghdad and destroy Iraq's fledging nuclear program even before it got off the ground. That has been covered in detail in the Appendix attached.

Though the PLO had been admitted in the Arab League and recognised as a representative of the Palestinian people – sympathy to the cause was slowly drying up, even within the Arab world. In 1978, Egypt and Israel entered into the historic Camp David Accord, in which Egypt recognised Israel and its right to exist and Israel gave back all the Egyptian territories it had captured in the 1967 War – including the Sinai Peninsula and the Gaza Strip. It got peace between Israel and Egypt that has lasted ever since. But the accord did not address the core issue of the creation of a Palestinian state, something that most peace agreements would conveniently shrug aside even in the coming years.

In the early Eighties, Palestinian attacks into Israel from Lebanon intensified. Their continual attacks reached a point of no return, and Israel launched a full-fledged invasion of Lebanon to crush the PLO and eliminate its bases. Lebanon – as would happen so often even after that – was caught in the crossfire as the Israeli invasion advanced virtually up to Beirut itself.

Invasion of Lebanon 1982

OPERATION 'PEACE FOR GALILEE': The Israeli invasion of Lebanon began in June 1982 after a series of terrorist attacks on Israel from Lebanese soil. The telling moment came when PLO activists attacked the Israeli Ambassador to the UK in London, which was seen as the final straw. However, there was more to it than that. By then, Lebanon was in the throes of a civil war, with the PLO allied to the Muslim Lebanese forces against the Christian Moronite Party. Israel hoped that the invasion would not only expel the PLO, but also destroy the Syrian and Lebanese Army-aided Muslim militia which could then help bring the Moronite Party into power – thus securing a favourable government in Damascus.

Around 60,000 Israeli troops and over 800 tanks attacked Southern Lebanon in three prongs destroying the PLO bases in Rashidiya, Burj ash-Shamoli and al-Bass. The battle sucked in both the Lebanese and the Syrian Army and PLO fighters took up positions along with them. Syria had its SAM batteries and radar stations in the Bekaa valley in South Lebanon which had taken an initial toll of Israeli fighters. These were overcome with the usual Israeli innovation. Drones were flown over the missile sites which caused the radars to open up and give away their locations, where they could be destroyed by Israeli fighters that followed them. Israel destroyed 17 Syrian SAM batteries and shot down 29 fighters losing just a UAV in the action which was the first time drones had been used in battle. It would be the forerunner of many more.

The Israeli advance fought off the Syrian, Lebanese and PLO forces – even destroying a Syrian armoured brigade in a day-long action. They reached Beirut by mid-June and reached the last PLO stronghold near Beirut Airport. Beirut was surrounded by Israeli tanks, and the airport was bombed to prevent any air activity. After almost three months of siege, an agreement was hammered out in which more than 14,000 PLO fighters – including Yasser Arafat himself – were forced to leave the country. No neighbouring country was willing to take them and they eventually found refuge in far-off Tunisia, where they set up base in Tunis.

However, the Israeli operation was only partially successful. They succeeded in removing the PLO from Lebanon, but the country fell into chaos. With the Lebanese army weak and disunited, another party – the Hezbollah, a Lebanese Islamist party and militant group, began emerging in South Lebanon,

The Hezbollah, literally meaning 'party of God', was a Shia militia that was liberally funded and supplied by Iran. It proved to be an even more intractable adversary. Over the years, as the Hezbollah built up its power, it began firing rockets and missiles into Israel, launched raids, attacked Israeli settlements and kidnapped soldiers, becoming even more vehemently anti-Israel. This war did not bring Israel the peace it had hoped for. Rather, it created a long-term threat in the form of the Hezbollah.

The Intifadas

Expelled from Lebanon to far away Tunisia, the PLO changed tactics once again. Rather than resort to high-octane terrorist attacks, which were making them lose world sympathy, they decided to launch a local home-grown movement in the occupied territories. This movement called Intifada – or the great shake up – tapped the latent anger and the pent-up frustration of the Palestinian people and got them out in the streets, pelting stones, burning vehicles, destroying government buildings, attacking Israeli policeman and soldiers in a low level of violence that extended across all over the occupied territories of the West Bank and Gaza Strip.

The pot had been boiling for years and needed just a small trigger to unleash itself. That trigger came in December 1987 when an Israeli military vehicle struck two vans carrying Palestinian workers, killing four of them in an unfortunate accident. This act was seen by the Palestinians as a deliberate one in retaliation for the stabbing of an Israeli soldier a day earlier.

Palestinians came out in the streets in protest. Rioting began, then intense stone-throwing, which soon graduated to Molotov cocktails and bombs. Israeli soldiers and security forces were attacked with rifles, hand grenades and explosives. Israeli settlements too came under attack. In any case, the growing Israeli settlements that were sprouting in the occupied territories were a sore point which caused much resentment amongst Palestinians. In fact, Pakistan had tried vainly to arouse the Kashmiris into a similar Intifada in the valley and had pumped in millions to bring the locals out in the streets in similar stone-throwing and arson. That situation was very delicately handled by the Indian security forces and got under control. However, India used a combination of both soft and hard power to resolve the issue. Israel almost invariably resorted to heavy-handed measures that would further inflame sentiments.

That low level of violence of the First Intifada continued for almost five years. However, fatigue was setting in on both parties. The PLO was nowhere near attaining its aim by armed revolt or terrorism, and nor could Israel get the peace it hoped for, even though the Arab nations were no longer openly hostile to it. Finally, both sides agreed to meet and talk. Israeli Prime Minister Yitzhak Rabin and the PLO Chairman, Yasser Arafat, met in a series of talks facilitated by Norway that culminated in the historic Oslo Accords. Two such accords were signed – the first was called Oslo I in Washington in 1993; and the second, Oslo II, in Egypt in 1994. In essence, the accords implied that PLO recognised Israel's right to exist and Israel recognised the PLO as the sole representative of the Palestinian people. The PLO promised to halt terrorism and violence against Israel, while Israel promised to halt settlements in the occupied territories. The Gaza Strip and the West Bank would gradually be handed over to the Palestinian Authority so as "to facilitate conditions for the creation of a separate state of Palestine."

The historic accords were hailed across the world and Israeli Prime Minister Yitzhak Rabin, Foreign Minister Shimon Peres, and PLO Chairman Yasser Arafat, received the Nobel Peace Prize in 1994 "for their efforts to bring peace in the Middle East". But the Accords never really created the peace it hoped for. On the contrary, right-wing groups in Israel opposed it bitterly. The more militant factions of the PLO called it a sell-out of the Palestinian cause. Yitzhak Rabin would eventually be assassinated by a right-wing extremist in 1995 and Arafat himself would be side-lined within the PLO and gradually eased out by more extremist forces.

The terms of the Accords were actually never implemented. Barring the fact that both sides agreed to recognise each other, no progress was made in subsequent talks of the taking over of the West Bank and Gaza Strip by the Palestinian Authority; leave alone any talk of the eventual creation of a Palestinian state. The 'Two-State Solution' was being gradually pushed under the carpet and continually deflected. Conditions in the West Bank and Gaza Strip were as bad as ever, and the Palestinians still felt a sense of repression. This angst finally erupted in the Second Intifada of 2000.

The Second Intifada – also known as the al-Aqsa Intifada – was even more violent than the first. It erupted in September 2000, when the Israeli opposition leader, Ariel Sharon (the hero of the 1973 War), made a visit to the al-Aqsa mosque compound in East Jerusalem. Al Aqsa is held sacred and visits by non-believers are forbidden. The West Bank erupted in angry protest by the Palestinians against his visit. Stone-throwing began, violence erupted and the situation slowly went out of control.

This was the trigger for the many years of protest that followed thereafter. The hard-line Likud party under Ariel Sharon took over in 2001, but rather than apply a healing touch, they clamped down harshly. Attacks took place on Jewish and Palestinian settlements, buses were bombed, suicide attacks intensified, and riots between Jewish and Palestinians broke out. The state of low-level violence continued for five years claiming over 1,000 Jewish and 3,000 Palestinian lives, till it petered out in 2005. Though inconclusive in most ways, it had one interesting outcome. Israel agreed to withdraw from the Gaza Strip and leave it to the administration of the Palestinians.

As events would prove later, this contributed to the rise of the Hamas in the Gaza Strip – the first link in the chain of events that led to the 7 October attacks of 2023.

2006 Invasion of Lebanon

Even as the Intifada was winding down in 2005, Israel would soon get embroiled in war with Lebanon again, this time with the Hezbollah, the same organisation whose rise they had indirectly contributed to when they invaded Lebanon in 1982. In the chaos following that invasion, Lebanon plunged into civil war which allowed the Hezbollah, an Islamist militant group armed and supported by Iran, to gradually take over Southern Lebanon.

The Hezbollah followed a hard-line policy. It did not recognise Israel as an independent state and sought its destruction. Iran had armed, financed and supplied it with a liberal stock of rockets and modern weaponry to enable it to combat Israel – its sworn enemy. In many ways, the Hezbollah was Iran's proxy which they used effectively to wound Israel and keep it engaged in continual low-level war.

Israel withdrew from South Lebanon only in 2000 and vacated the area it had been occupying there since 1982. The Hezbollah quickly took over the area and used it as bases for attacks into Israel itself. In the period 2000 to 2005, they conducted around 200 attacks into Israel. They received large stockpiles of rockets and missiles from Iran, which were hidden in caves and hills in South Lebanon and fired into Israel with increasing frequency. The simmering situation exploded on 12 July 2006, when Hezbollah fighters infiltrated into Israeli territory and attacked a patrol, killing three soldiers and capturing two others whom they carried away into Lebanon. A tank and an APC sent to rescue them were ambushed and damaged, killing five others.

This blatant action was seen by Israel as an act of war. Israel responded with air strikes on Hezbollah positions in South Lebanon, which hit as far as Beirut itself. Beirut airport was bombed and the runway damaged to prevent its use in taking away the captured soldiers. Hezbollah HQs, communication centres, rocket sites and armouries were attacked in a week-long series of air and missile attacks and then Israeli tanks and troops moved into South Lebanon in a ground offensive to completely destroy the Hezbollah. Three divisions – almost 60,000 men – advanced in three prongs right up to the Litani River. The Hezbollah, however, proved to be a stronger force than anticipated. The fighters were a trained and motivated force and well-equipped with flak jackets, NVDs, communication equipment, and anti-tank missiles. They fought off the advancing Israelis, damaging 52 of their prized Merkava tanks – though most were recovered subsequently. The Israelis managed to capture most of the Hezbollah strongholds and destroy their rocket sites, but, as is the case with most terrorist organisations, they could not completely defeat them.

The Hezbollah continued its rocket attacks and raids into Israel, each attack being projected as a victory for it. Israeli attacks had caused huge damage to infrastructure and caused much civilian damage, and the Hezbollah repeatedly broadcast footage of civilian casualties, gaining world sympathy and bringing on pressure to stop the war. Eventually, on 14 August, a ceasefire was negotiated and Israel withdrew from Lebanon and UN peacekeepers moved into the area. The Hezbollah won the war of perception. It had not been defeated and with time its strength would only grow. With the help of Iran, it rebuilt its arsenal to an impressive 130,000 rockets and missiles, most of them hidden underground. It is strongly linked to Hamas and the Houthis – two groups similarly affiliated to Iran. And now as the war in the Gaza Strip unfolds, they are at the forefront to provide moral and material aid to Hamas, fire rockets and missiles into Israel and tie them down with diversionary attacks. Their presence increases the dangers of a regional war.

Israel has followed the same tactics against the Hamas that it did with the Hezbollah in 2006 – only on a far wider scale. And the consequences could be even more horrific and long-lasting.

Appendix

OPERATION OPERA: The Raid on the Nuclear Reactor

In 1976, Iraq purchased a nuclear reactor from France. This reactor, the Osirak reactor, 12 kilometres southeast of Baghdad, was ostensibly used only for research, but it could be used to produce nuclear fuel for their atomic bombs. Iraq's fledgling nuclear program was nipped in the bud, when it was attacked by Israeli fighters on 7 June 1981, and declared non-operational. That strike pushed back Iraq's nuclear program indefinitely.

Israel has always had the fear that should any of their enemies get hold of a nuclear bomb, they would be able to virtually obliterate the small nation. They themselves are known to possess nuclear warheads and have both the means and the will to deliver it (Though it is a fact that is never acknowledged). They contemplated using a nuclear warhead when their backs were to the wall in the early days of the Yom Kippur War and were restrained by the USA. However, the likelihood of Iraq – or any of the Arab nations – possessing a bomb would virtually be an existentialist threat to them.

The planning for the strike began in 1977, virtually as soon as the development of the Iraqi reactor had begun. In 1979, Mossad agents planted a bomb that destroyed the first set of core structures for the reactor just as they were awaiting shipment to Iraq. Top Iraqi nuclear scientists were also mysteriously killed, and others abducted. But in spite of setbacks, the reactor was on its way to become operational and could become critical by end June 1981. After that, it would not be possible to attack it, since the radioactivity would spread across the region, and that would not be condoned.

As is their norm, Israel had begun preparations for OPERATION OPERA, the code name for the operation, almost two years before the actual attack. Israeli began practicing on F-4 Phantoms and A4 Skyhawks, and rehearsed the strike on mock-ups of the reactor built in the Negev Desert. Then, in 1980, they received their first batch of advanced F16s and F15 fighters, which, with their greater ranges and payloads, were ideally suited for the role.

Striking the target 900 kilometres away involved overflying the territory of other nations, especially Saudi Arabia, and reaching the target undetected by radar. Then, they had to overcome Iraqi air defence and aircraft, launch a precise strike and get back. On 7 June at 3.55 p.m., an attack team of eight F16s, each armed with two M-24 penetration bombs with delayed action fuses, took off from Israel and flew in at very low levels along the Saudi Arabian border keeping to a blind spot they had discovered in Iraqi radars. The reactors were at the extreme edge of their range, and the Israelis had to resort to the very dangerous practice of hot refuelling. That is filling up the aircraft while it was still starting on the runway to get the maximum amount of fuel into it.

Disaster struck almost as soon as the mission began. As the strike package was over the Gulf of Aqaba, at low altitudes, the aircraft overflew the yacht of King Hussein of Jordan. Being a pilot himself, he recognised the Israeli aircraft and the armaments they carried and from the direction they were headed, he discerned their intention immediately. He called up his headquarters from the radio on his yacht, telling them to inform the Iraqis that an attack was coming. However, surprisingly that message was never received by the Iraqis and the F16s and their fighter escort entered Iraqi airspace undetected.

The attack squadron of eight F16s, split into four groups of two aircraft each. They had been flying just 30 metres above ground level to avoid radar detection and now climbed up to a height of 2,100 metres to begin their dive. The F15 escorts climbed up to 25,000 feet to be able to intercept any approaching enemy aircraft and provide cover. The F16s reached their attack path and dived towards the reactor in pairs, releasing the 2,000-pound bombs at five-second intervals. Surprisingly, no Iraqi air defence guns opened up, nor did Iraqi radar detect them. Iraqi radar was switched off and the air defence crew were having tea when the attack was made. In a strike lasting just 80 seconds, 14 of the 16 bombs released struck the dome of the reactor and penetrated it. The delayed action fuse meant that the bombs exploded inside, near the core, destroying it completely. By the time the Iraqi had opened up with anti-aircraft fire, the pilots had climbed up and started their return to Israel, where they landed virtually on their last drops of fuel. The strike had lasted just around two minutes and the aircraft had been in the air for just three hours and ten minutes – three hours that changed the complexion of Israeli security.

The destruction of the reactor drew initial world condemnation, but was privately welcomed by most nations. The US President, Ronald Reagan, when informed of the strike, reportedly shrugged his shoulders and said, "Well, boys will be boys." When the USA attacked Iraq ten years later in the First Gulf War, US generals thanked their Israeli counterparts for scuttling Saddam's nuclear program; else that invasion would not have been possible.

The Iraqis would follow with a similar attack in 2007 when they attacked a Syrian nuclear reactor and damaged it. With Iran close to possessing nuclear weapons, there was a very strong possibility of an Israeli strike on its reactors at Natanz and Qom. Fortunately or unfortunately, that strike never came about and perhaps the Middle East is safer or more unsafe because of it.

REFERENCES

'Air Strike at Osirak', *Air and Space Forces Magazine*, https://www.airandspaceforces.com

'Entebbe Raid – Summary and Facts', *Britannica*, https://www.britannica.com

'Fifty Years Ago: Black September for PLO', *France 24*, 15 September 2020, https://www.france24.com

'First Lebanon War', War and Operations, https://www.idf.il

'Hamas, Fatah, Islamic Jihad, PLO and the Palestinian Authority,' *Indian Express*, 12 October 2023, https://indianexpress.com

'Lebanon War – 10 Years later,' *Time Magazine*, 12 July 2016, https://time.com

'Lebanon War – 40 Years on,' *Haaretz*, 3 June 2022, https://www.haaretz.com

'Munich Massacre: Facts, Victims, Terrorism, Olympics,' *Britannica*, https://www.britannica.com

'My Life in the PLO', Pluto Press, https://www.plutobooks.com

'Operation Entebbe, 1976: When Israeli Army undertook its most dangerous mission,' *Zee News*, 12 October 2023, https://zeenews.india.com

'OPERATION OPERA', Wikipedia https://en.wikipidea.com

'Operation Thunderbolt – The Raid on Entebbe', Wars and Operations, https://www.idf.il

'PLO Strategy: From Total Liberation to Co-existence', PIJ Organisation, https://pij.org

'The bombing of the Osirak Reactor,' *JSTOR*, https://www.lstor.org

'The Divided PLO: Future of the Palestinian National Movement,' *The New Arab*, 9 February 2022, https://www.newarab.com

'The Ghosts of Lebanon,' *Foreign Affairs*, https://foreignaffairs.com

'The Lebanon Civil War: History and Significance,' *Britannica*, https://www.britannica.com

'The Munich Massacre', *The New York Times*, 5 September 2023, https://www.nytimes.com

'The Oslo Accords and the Arab-Israeli Peace Process', US Dept of State, https://history.state.gov

'The PLO and the Palestinian Armed Struggle', Gale, https://www.gale.com

'The True Story behind Entebbe', *Time Magazine*, 16 March 2018, https://time.com

'What is Hezbollah – Meaning, History and Ideology,' *Britannica*, https://www.britannica.com

10

Hamas, the Gaza Strip and the Israel-Hamas Wars

"Gone is the time when Hamas discussed recognition of Israel. The only discussion now is about when we will wipe out Israel."

—Yahya Sinwar

The Gaza Strip

Gaza. A swathe of land on the banks of the Mediterranean Sea, just 41 kilometres long and around 11 kilometres wide. To its south lies Egypt; Israel surrounds it from the east and north. For centuries, this land was part of Palestine – as was all the area around it. When the United Nations Partition Plan of 1948, divided this land between the Palestinian Arabs and the Jews,

Gaza was allotted to the Palestinians. But this troubled land could never become part of the promised Palestinian state. In the 1948 War, Egyptian forces moved into Gaza City and it became their headquarters from where they waged a year-long war against Israel. It remained under Egyptian control till it was captured by Israel in the 1967 War and remained under it till the Israelis finally vacated the enclave in 2005.

The Gaza Strip can be divided into North and South Gaza by the Wadi Gaza – a dried-up river bed of the Gaza River that cuts horizontally across the strip on its way to the Mediterranean. In the northern part lies Gaza City – the capital and its largest city. In the south is Khan Younis – its second largest town. It has no port to speak of, and though it has a long coastline, the fishing area is restricted. Its only airport – the Yasser Arafat Airport in Gaza City – opened briefly in 1998, and then was forced to shut down in 2002, after Israeli attacks declared it inoperable in the Second Intifada.

Like the West Bank – another Palestinian enclave, which is part of the Occupied Territories – it hoped to be part of a Palestinian state. But that has never come about, in spite of all the talk and promises. It is one of the most-densely populated areas of the world, with around 2.3 million Palestinians staying in a 363 square kilometre swathe of land. Most of them are descendants of Palestinian refugees who were displaced from the land in 1948, and three generations have lived here in conditions of squalor and deprivation, largely subsisting on aid. Over 48 per cent of the population are unemployed, and more than half live in poverty, in makeshift refugee camps without basic amenities. This has given rise to anger and frustration that can be easily exploited by militant organisations.

The Rise of Hamas

Hamas, the Islamic militant organisation that has ruled Gaza since 2006, tapped into just this sentiment when they launched their horrific attacks of 7 October into Israel. The word 'Hamas' is an acronym of its official name – *Harkat-al-Muqawamah-al-Islamiyyah*, which means the Islamic Resistance Movement. Hamas has its roots in the Muslim Brotherhood, which had been operating in Gaza and the West Bank since the late

Seventies. The Muslim Brotherhood's activities were initially nonviolent – largely devoted to reconstruction work, education and aid. But even then, a number of a hardliners were advocating a holy war against Israel to retake the occupied territories. In December 1987, the First Intifada erupted against Israeli occupation in both Gaza and the West Bank. Hamas (which also is an Arabic word meaning 'zeal') was established by members of the Muslim Brotherhood and factions of the PLO in 1987, with a charter to regain Palestine from Israel and establish a Palestinian state in its place. Unlike the PLO that has accepted the existence of Israel, Hamas has never recognised Israel and was committed to its destruction and the establishment of a Palestinian state 'from the River to the Sea' – the area between the River Jordan and the Mediterranean Sea – in its place.

Hamas proved itself to be one of the most violent organisations, and its actions even led to a fallout with the more secular and moderate Palestinian factions. In 1996, Hamas established its military wing – *Izz-al-Din al-Qassam* – or the al-Qassam Brigade – which morphed into a well-armed and organised force of around 20,000 fighters and launched some of its most violent attacks. Their activities eventually led Hamas to be designated as a terrorist organisation by the USA and the European Union.

When the Second Intifada began in 2000, Hamas intensified its actions and launched a number of suicide attacks in Israel itself. Hamas fighters participated in a number of raids and attacks on Israeli settlers and security forces in both the West Bank and the Gaza Strip. In fact, it was the action of their followers in the Second Intifada that made it even more violent than the first.

The Second Intifada died down in 2005 or so. In the ceasefire that followed, Israel announced its withdrawal from the Gaza Strip in 2005, and that itself was hailed as a great victory by Hamas. It grew in stature in the Gaza Strip and began to take over political power from Fatah – the Palestinian body that had administered Gaza earlier. When elections were held in the Gaza Strip in 2006, surprisingly, Hamas won by an overwhelming majority. Clashes broke out between Hamas supporters and members of Fatah which led to a break between the two major Palestinian parties. Eventually, Hamas took control of the Gaza Strip, but Fatah retained its hold in the West Bank. Incidentally, Israel had a role in the rise of Hamas. They actually aided and abetted it, hoping to divide and weaken the Palestinian cause. But as events would show, Hamas proved to be more dangerous than any other Palestinian body.

Hamas came into power in the Gaza Strip in 2006, promising development and improving the lot of the Palestinian people. But that was not to be. The hardliners became even more strident and they rejected the peace accord signed between the PLO and Israel which recognised Israel's right to exist. Yahya Sinwar – who would go on to become the head of Hamas, thundered, "Gone is the time when Hamas discussed recognition of Israel. The discussion now is about when we will wipe out Israel." The character sketch of Sinwar is in the attached appendix.

The Blockade of Gaza

With an avowed enemy in power in the Gaza Strip, Israel declared Hamas as a hostile entity and placed Gaza under a total land, sea and air blockade in 2007. A series of sanctions were imposed, including power cuts, curtailing of imports and exports, and control on the movement of persons and goods through the borders. The sea side was blocked by Israeli ships patrolling the Mediterranean shores. Relief vessels entering with humanitarian aid were not permitted to dock at Gaza. All movement in and out of the Gaza Strip could only be made through the Rafah Crossing on the Egyptian side and the Karen Shalom, Karni, Erez and Sufa crossings on the Israeli side. Egypt too supported the blockade, fearing that unfettered access would enable Hamas to cause the same instability on its soil that the PLO had caused in Jordan, Lebanon and Syria.

The blockade, which has been in force for 17 years now, has taken an immense humanitarian toll. Even dual-use items like fuel and cement have been curtailed and with reason. When the Israelis entered Gaza in 2023, they discovered over 500 kilometres of tunnels built with cement that should have been used for development and operated by fuel earmarked for civilian vehicles and generators.

In any case, the isolation of Gaza had already begun in 1994, when Israel constructed a 60-kilometre long fence all along the border as a security measure. When Israel withdrew from Gaza in 2005, it enhanced the system and developed it as a two layer, 7 metre high fence, with a 100-metre wide buffer zone on both sides of it to control movement. Sensors, cameras, remotely controlled machine guns and surveillance towers were established all along, and security balloons with cameras tethered over it. It even had an underground wall, almost 3-5 metre deep – complete with seismic sensors to detect tunnelling

– to prevent Hamas from tunnelling their way beneath it. Thus impregnable 'Iron Wall' was constructed at a cost of around $1 billion and considered impossible to cross, but as events would show, it would be breached with ease on that fateful day of 7 October 2023.

The Israel-Hamas Wars

- **The First Israel-Hamas War, 2009 – OPERATION CAST LEAD:** Hamas and Israel maintained an uneasy state of no-war-no-peace. Hamas attacks on Israel continued, as did Israeli attacks on the Gaza Strip right from 2007 to 2009. A truce was brokered in June 2008 but was repeatedly broken with each side accusing the other of violations. Finally, on 27 December 2008, Israel launched a massive assault on Gaza to strike Hamas infrastructure and their war-waging potential. For a week they pounded Hamas targets by air, and then launched a ground offensive on 3 January 2009 that reached the cities of Beersheba and Ashdod, but did not go deeper. On 18 January 2009, Israel unilaterally withdrew and a ceasefire was implemented. Thirteen Israelis and around 1,200 Palestinians perished in the three-week long conflict.
- **Second Israel-Hamas War, 2012 – OPERATION PILLAR OF DEFENCE:** In spite of the truce that followed Operation Cast Lead, tensions between Israel and Hamas continued to escalate. Rockets and mortars continued to be fired into Israel from Gaza which intensified in the first week of November 2012, when over 200 rockets were fired. Finally, on 14 November, Israel launched Operation Pillar of Defence, with targeted strikes at Hamas locations. The Hamas military chief ,Ahmed Said al-Jabari, was killed in a strike as the Israeli Air Force struck more than 1,500 targets in Gaza, including rocket launchers, weapon stocks, and Hamas infrastructure. In spite of the air strikes, rocket attacks by Hamas and its sister organisation, the Palestinian Islamic Jihad (PIJ), continued, hitting as far as Tel Aviv. Israel had mobilised its reserves for a possible ground invasion, but on 21 November 2012, a ceasefire brokered by Egypt came into effect, and the ground offensive was fortunately never launched.
- **Third Israel-Hamas War, 2014 – OPERATION PROTECTIVE EDGE:** This was the longest and bloodiest war fought between the two adversaries before 2023. The 2014 campaign was called Op Protective Edge by Israel

and 'The Battle of Withered Grain' by the Palestinians. It began in June 2014, when three Israeli teenagers were kidnapped and brutally murdered by Hamas operatives. In return, Israel arrested over 350 Hamas members and rounded up many more for questioning. Hamas retaliated by firing a series of rockets with the slated aim of forcing Israel to halt its persecution of Palestinians, release the arrested, and force it to lift the Gaza blockade.

Israel launched a series of airstrikes on Hamas positions on 8 July 2014, but the rocket attacks into Israel continued. On 17 July, Israel launched its ground invasion, hoping to destroy the Hamas tunnel system, from where the rockets were fired. The ground invasion located and destroyed 34 known tunnels and almost two-thirds of Hamas rocket launchers. But Hamas still fired rockets into Israel. At the end of 50 days of fighting, Israel withdrew with 67 casualties, claiming it had attained its military aims. Over 2,300 Palestinians and much of Hamas infrastructure perished as well, but they too claimed a victory saying they had forced the Israelis to withdraw. The inconclusive war was a forerunner of the Israeli offensive of 2023.

- **Fourth Israel-Hamas War, 2021:** The fighting and firing and raids never really stopped. It merely erupted on a larger scale from time to time. And the next eruption was in 2021. The trigger this time came in early May at the start of the holy month of Ramadan. The Supreme Court of Israel passed a verdict on the eviction of six Palestinian families living in East Jerusalem, forcing them to be removed from a land they had lived in for decades. The blatantly wrong judgement led to a string of protests in which Jews and Palestinians clashed on the streets. As the fighting and rioting spread, Israeli police chased some of the protesters in the compound of the al-Aqsa Mosque, and then fired teargas, rubber bullets, and stun grenades at them. This intrusion into the al-Aqsa Mosque – the third holiest Islamic shrine – raised a howl of protests across the Muslim world.

  As Israeli police continued occupying the compound of the shrine, Hamas gave an ultimatum to withdraw the security forces from the shrine by 6 p.m. on 10 May. Minutes after the ultimatum expired, Hamas and Islamic Jihad fighters launched a series of rocket strikes into Israel, hitting schools and residential complexes, killing civilians. Israel responded with air strikes into Gaza striking Hamas targets and hitting civilian infrastructure in which they were located. Over 256 Palestinians were killed in the strikes before

Egypt mediated a ceasefire on 21 May 2021, ending 11 days of fighting, in which, as always, both sides claimed victory.

The Preparation for Operation al-Aqsa Flood

The fighting between Hamas and Israel had never really ended. The simmering tension and constant firing had gone on for decades. Israel had not succeeded in truly breaking the war-waging potential of Hamas in any of the four rounds that had been fought earlier, though it did cause much damage and imposed a huge humanitarian cost.

After the last eruption in 2021, there was a period of relative calm. Hamas did not fire any rockets into Israel nor did they launch any attacks or raids. The Hamas Chief, Yahya Sinwar, changed tactics. He curtailed his rhetoric and convinced the Israelis that he was now only interested in peace and development for the people of the Gaza Strip and did not want to fight a war with Israel. His words and messaging convinced the Israelis. They allowed aid to flow into Gaza from Qatar and other sources for developmental work – much of it was siphoned off by Hamas for their own military use. They themselves pumped huge amounts of money into the Gaza Strip, hoping that they would be able to turn Hamas and the Gazans away from the path of conflict, and towards peace and prosperity. In a relaxation of controls, they even allowed Gazans to work in Israel, where salaries were ten times higher than what an average Gazan could hope to earn in the Strip. Over 20,000 Gazans now crossed the iron fence every day to work as gardeners, maids, plumbers, construction workers, plumbers and daily workers in Israeli kibbutzes and towns near the border. Amongst them were Hamas operatives who gathered vital information and familiarised themselves with the area inside Israel.

Hamas did not fire a single rocket into Israel in the preceding year. The few that were launched came from their sister organisation, the Islamic Jihad. But, there was an intensification of activities from Lebanon and the West Bank. Rocket attacks and raids from there began increasing. Perhaps it was a well-planned and coordinated effort to incorporate all these agencies in the attack that was to come. The ruse worked. Israel began shifting attention and resources towards the West Bank and against the Hezbollah in Lebanon, leaving the Gaza border thinly manned.

Hamas had been gradually stockpiling its rockets which they had been developing in their underground foundries, and also smuggling in from benefactors such as Iran. They were estimated to have built up a stockpile of around 50,000 to 60,000 rockets of all kinds, ranging from short-range Grads which could deliver a 45-kilogram warhead up to 48 kilometres to the more lethal M-75 and R-160 missiles that could strike up to 160 kilometres – capable of hitting Tel Aviv. They had also developed their own home-grown Qassam rockets – named after the al-Qassam Brigade that operated them. These rockets were a simple steel cylinder that could fire a load of explosives and metal ball bearings, propelled by a makeshift propellant of sugar and potassium nitrate to ranges of up to 30 kilometres. They were crude and inaccurate, but would serve the purpose of causing chaos and confusion. And while Hamas claims to have developed most of its arsenal indigenously, there is no doubt that it was aided by Iran – its main sponsor – that would have sent in vital know-how, components such as guidance and propulsion systems and even complete rockets which could have been smuggled in by sea or through the many underground tunnels.

As Israel grew lax, Hamas operatives began preparing for the deadliest attack ever on Israel. Hamas chief Yahya Sinwar and the head of its al-Qassam brigade, Mohammed Deif, who were the main architects of the plan had planned it meticulously down to the last detail. Even as training was underway, it was done in such secrecy that Israel's famed intelligence agencies, Mossad and Shin Bet, remained unaware of this plan. Information received by Israel from informers, and tell-tale signs about the forthcoming attack were ignored. Hamas built up its strength, even as it lulled Israel into a false sense of security.

And then on Simchat Torah Day – a holy day when Jews complete the annual reading of the Torah, and spend the day in prayer and reflection – Hamas launched Operation al-Aqsa Flood, the deadliest attack that Israel had ever seen on its soil. At 5.30 in the morning of 7 October 2023, a wave of almost 5,000 rockets were fired from Gaza into Israel. In the wake of these rocket attacks, around 1,000 Hamas operatives burst through the fence separating Israel from Gaza, broke through it in 22 places and attacked Israel. The next Israel-Hamas War had broken out – and this would prove to be longer, more brutal and with even more dangerous consequences than any of the previous ones.

Appendix

Yahya Sinwar: The Gaza Head of Hamas

Yahya Sinwar, the leader of Hamas in Gaza and one of the masterminds behind the 7 October 2023, attacks on Israel was born in the Khan Younis refugee camp to parents who had been displaced in the 1948 Arab-Israeli war. The camp was densely packed with impoverished families, who lived in poor conditions and relied on aid.

In 1985, prior to the formation of Hamas, Sinwar helped organize al-Majd, a network of Islamist youths who tasked themselves with exposing the growing number of Palestinian informants who had been recruited by Israel in recent years. In 1988, Sinwar was convicted for murder and sentenced to life in prison. While in hospital, his life was ironically saved when Israeli doctors operated upon him to remove a tumour in his brain.

During Sinwar's long incarceration, he maintained powerful sway over his fellow prisoners, using tactics of abuse and manipulation and help from his connections outside prison. He also spent much of his spare time studying about his Israeli enemies, reading Israeli newspapers and becoming fluent in Hebrew.

Sinwar's release came as part of the high-profile prisoner swap for Gilad Shalit, an Israeli soldier who had been abducted by Hamas in 2006. He was released in October 2011 in exchange for 1,017 Palestinian soldiers, including Sinwar. Sinwar was among the first set of Palestinian prisoners who were returned to the Gaza Strip. When he arrived, he was already sporting the emblematic green headband of the Hamas armed wing.

In April 2012, just months after his release, Sinwar was elected a member of Hamas's political bureau in the Gaza Strip. He made calls on militants to capture Israelis, prompting the USA to add Sinwar to its list of specially designated global terrorists. Sinwar was elected the head of Hamas in the Gaza Strip in 2017.

Sinwar's fiery rhetoric appealed to the hard-line militants. In one of his first public appearances, Sinwar told a group of young Gazans: "Gone is the time when Hamas discussed recognition of Israel. The discussion now is about when we will wipe out Israel." In his initial days, however, he focused on administration of Gaza, building up the potential of Hamas and strengthening ties with nations such as Iran, and like-minded organisations such as the Hezbollah.

May 2021 marked a turning point when violence boiled over after Israeli police entered the al-Aqsa Mosque in Jerusalem. Hamas responded by sending rockets into Jerusalem and southern and central Israel, prompting 11 days of intense fighting between Hamas and Israel. Sinwar's virulence surged after the incident. He called upon each person to "be ready to rise up as a gale to defend al-Aqsa." In rhyming Arabic, he would address the crowd: "We will come to you in a roaring flood, in rockets without end, and in a flood of soldiers limitless, in one tide after another."

It was an indicator of what he was planning. On 7 October, Hamas, launched 'Operation al-Aqsa Flood,' which led to the most devastating attack on Israel since its independence. It began with a barrage of rockets, which provided cover for at least 1,500 militants who infiltrated Israel at dozens of points along the heavily fortified border by using explosives, bulldozers, and para-gliders. They attacked military outposts, settlements and even an outdoors music festival killing around 1,200, and taking 240 hostages back to Gaza. It was the deadliest day in Israel's history. The assault showed hallmarks of Sinwar's tactics, and the taking of hostages echoed his preoccupation with prisoner exchanges.

Sinwar was the most wanted man for Israel and though hiding in the web of Gaza's subterranean tunnels is the top target for Israel in its invasion.

REFERENCES

'Hamas – Definition, History, Ideology and facts', *Britannica*, https://www.britannica.com
'Hamas and the Gaza War of 2014', A. Nishikida, https://ideas.repec.com
'Hamas: Background and Overview' Jewish Virtual Library, https://jewishvirtuallibrary.com
'How Hamas leader Sinwar plotted Israel's most deadly Attack' *Reuters*, 6 December 2023, https://www.reuters.com
'Israel and Hamas', *The Economist*, https://www.economist.com
'What is Hamas and why is it fighting with Israel in Gaza?', *BBC*, https://www.bbc.com
'Yahya Sinwar, Israel's most-wanted Terrorist' *ABC News*, 25 December 2023, https://abcnews.com
'How Hamas became Israel's Sworn Enemy?', *Le Monde*, 9 October 2023, https://www.lemonde.fr
'Gaza and the Israel-Hamas Conflict', *CNBC*, 9 October 2023, https://www.cnbc.com
'Why Hamas tried to Sabotage Peace Proposal', *Time Magazine* 8 October 2023, https://time.com
'Hamas, Fatah, Islamic Jihad, PLO' *The Indian Express*, 12 October 2023, https://indianexpress.com
'Yahya Sinwar: Who is the Hamas Leader in Gaza' *BBC*, 20 November 2023, https://www.bbc.com

11

Carnage on Simchat Torah Day: The 7 October Attacks

"We will come to you in a roaring flood, in rockets without end, and in a flood of soldiers limitless, in one tide after another."

—Hamas Slogan before the attacks

The Simchat Torah Attack

On the holy day of Simchat Torah, Jews celebrate the completion of their annual reading of the Torah. It is one of the holiest days of the Jewish calendar, a holiday to be spent in prayer and reflection. It was also the day that Hamas had selected to launch an attack into Israel a vicious attack with over 2,000 fighters that killed over 1,400 and led to over 240 others being taken back into Gaza as hostages. It was the single largest day of loss of life for the Jews since the Holocaust. In terms of per capita, the loss of life even exceeded the

9/11 attacks on the USA. This was Israel's 9/11 moment and perhaps it will change both Israel and the Middle East irrevocably hereafter.

At 6.30 in the morning of 7 October 2023, around 5,000 rockets were launched from Gaza into Israel. The sheer scale of the attack ensured that many of the missiles broke through the Iron Dome protective system and landed in Israeli territory, some as far as Tel Aviv. The crude and unguided rockets caused confusion and panic, and under cover of the salvos, at around 7.30, approximately 1,500 to 2,000 Hamas fighters broke through the security barriers surrounding Gaza and entered Israel at 22 different places. These fighters were from the al-Qassam Brigade, the military wing of Hamas, the Palestinian Islamic Jihad, the Mujahideen Brigade, the Abu Ali Mustafa Brigade and the al-Aqsa Martyrs Brigade, a conglomerate of disparate Palestinian groups under the banner of Hamas.

Israel had built its 'Iron Wall', a 65-kilometre long two-layered security fence that surrounds Gaza all around. Entry into Israel is only permitted through the select crossing places of Karem Shalom, Erez and Sufa. The fence has a 100-metre buffer zone on both sides where no one can enter without being challenged, and it also has a 5-metre-deep concrete and metal barrier beneath it, complete with seismic sensors to detect digging activity to prevent anyone from tunnelling their way beneath it. Around 40 surveillance and observation posts, each within mutual range of each other, dot the barrier, and an elaborate network of surveillance cameras keeps vigil day and night, seven days a week, 365 days a year. Seven observation balloons are also tethered overhead from where their cameras can monitor movement deep in the rear, and remotely controlled machine guns ensure that anyone approaching the fence without authorization will be engaged and fired upon instantly. This 1-billion-dollar surveillance system was designed to keep Gaza and the Gazans away from Israel and was reportedly 'impregnable.' This much-vaunted system was breached in minutes as Hamas fighters poured through it.

The Hamas fighters had been preparing for the attacks for years and knew the location of every surveillance camera, machine gun and communication system. In the initial phase itself, the cameras were disabled by snipers. Drones loaded with explosives slammed into the communications centres, and the remotely-controlled machine guns destroyed them. The weak spots in the fence were also identified, and blown apart with explosives. Through these weakened sections, armoured bulldozers simply smashed their way across and then Hamas fighters poured their way into the gaps and headed for designated targets in camps and settlements in the vicinity of the border.

Twenty-two such gaps were reportedly created, and fighters took also over the crossing places at Karem Shalom and Erez to pour through. They used other ingenious ways to breach the fence. Some flew in on hang gliders and powered gliders, and acted as pathfinders for the main force. They raced to the communications centres, cut off lines, and blew up exchanges to prevent any passing of information to headquarters and control rooms in the rear. Others used motor boats and rafts to enter. In an amphibious assault on Zikim, a detachment of Hamas fighters landed on the beach using boats and rubber dinghies, attacked the military base in the vicinity, and took soldiers prisoner.

Around 2,000 Hamas fighters entered Israel in a well-coordinated and rehearsed military operation. They raced towards the military base at Reim, where the headquarters of Israel's Gaza Division was located, overran it in a surprise attack and took several Israeli soldiers as captives. They had even claimed to have captured the commander of the Gaza Division, but that was later proved to be false. The terrorists set ablaze a Merkava tank and videos of

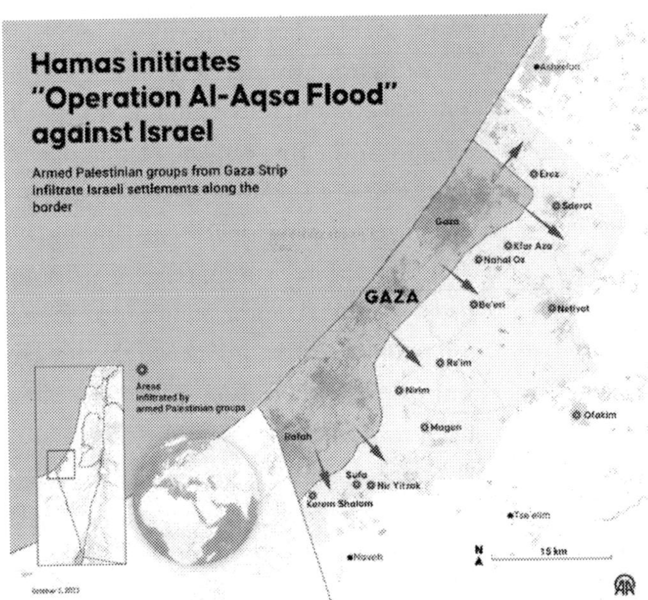

Hamas Initiates "Operation Al-Aqsa Flood" against Israel

them dancing around the smouldering tank with the bodies of dead Israeli soldiers on the ground were widely circulated. IDF forces regained control of the base later in the day, but the damage had been done. Six such military bases and installations were attacked on that fateful day.

The Hamas terrorists rushed towards the towns and settlements of Siderot, Ofakim, Beeir, Kfar Aza, Reim and others, penetrating almost 30 kilometres deep into Israel. In each case, their actions were part of a well-organized and impeccably coordinated plan. The terrorists knew the exact layout of the towns and even individual homes. Israel had recently relaxed its policy and allowed Gazans to move into Israel, work and return. Many of the attackers had been employed as daily workers in the border towns, and had commuted for months, gaining valuable information. They invariably targeted police stations, communications centres and security positions in the first attack. Then terrorists would race through the town on motorcycles and pick-up trucks firing indiscriminately all around. As panic-stricken residents fled to their homes, the terrorists entered their houses, and in a day-long orgy of murder and mayhem, sought out the occupants and killed them one by one. Towns such as Beeri lost 108 members – 10 per cent of its entire population – in this day-long attack.

The worst carnage took place at the Supernova music festival in the Negev Desert near the border town of Reim. Around 3,000 youngsters had gathered for a night-long, open air musical event in celebration of Simchat Torah. These unsuspecting youths were amongst the first targets. Hamas operatives flew in using para-gliders, at around 6.30 in the morning and landed in the vicinity of the festival. Some of the revellers who saw them landing even cheered, thinking it was part of the festivities. They cut off the electricity and destroyed the generators and took up positions. Around 50 gunmen then followed on motorcycles and pick-up trucks and raced through the crowd, firing indiscriminately. Other gunmen were in position around the exit and near the parking lot. As panic-stricken revellers fled, they were shot near the exits and in their cars. A few managed to escape by running into the open desert where they hid behind bushes and small trees, till they were rescued by Israeli forces. This gruesome massacre lasted for around five hours – almost till noon, as per recovered video footage – and claimed around 300 lives. Nearly 260 bodies were discovered at the site itself, and many more unaccounted for. Around 40 others were abducted and taken away to Gaza. Many of the victims were brutally raped, tortured and disfigured by the attackers in what was the most horrific attack of that day.

The Hamas attackers had cut off official communications between Israeli military stations, and it took some time for Headquarters to understand the true gravity of the situation. By then, frightened residents of border settlements had been passing messages back to relatives in the rear, and details of the attacks started unfolding. Israel launched a series of helicopter attacks on terrorist locations, but the militants were probably expecting them. They were told not to run but to mingle with the local population. This led to a number of 'friendly fire' cases in which Israelis were mistakenly shot by their own forces.

As details of the Hamas attacks emerged, Israel launched a wave of air and rocket attacks on Hamas positions inside Gaza at around 10.30 a.m. The Hamas HQ in Gaza City was struck by an air strike, which flattened it – along with the residential building in which it was based. Israeli commandoes also reached the beleaguered settlements of Okakim, Be'eri, Sderot, Sufa, Magen, Kfar Aza and others that Hamas had penetrated. Frightened citizens, hiding in cellars and bomb shelters, were contacted on cell phones and they guided the commandoes towards their locations, and also passed them information about the terrorists. Israeli commandoes began clearing the settlements house-by-house, flushed out the Hamas fighters, and began extricating civilians and rescuing hostages. Most of the Hamas fighters had already withdrawn into Gaza by then, but Israeli commandoes reportedly killed around 1,000 operatives, who still remained and battled the security forces as they approached. As the security forces entered town after town, the extent of the barbarity began emerging. Dead and mutilated bodies littered the streets; many more were found in homes and cellars. Body cameras recovered from dead terrorists showed how the Hamas fighters had gone from house to house, shooting at point-blank range, and killing women, children, the infirm and the elderly. Half-naked bodies were recovered which told of sexual torture and disgusting depravities. It took three days to clear the last vestiges of Hamas from Israel, but by then, the damage had been done. Over 1,400 were killed in the largest single day loss of life in Israel since its birth, and over 240 hostages carried away into Gaza. Israeli security had been breached as never before and it had lost its aura of invincibility – perhaps irretrievably.

How did Hamas fool the Israelis and execute the Attacks?

How could Hamas deceive Shin Bet (Israel's internal intelligence agency) and Mossad – arguably amongst the best Intelligence agencies in the world – so effectively? The last time Israel had been taken so much by surprise was exactly 50 years and a day earlier. Then, on 6 October 1973, the combined armies of Egypt, Syria and Jordan attacked Israel on the holy day of Yom Kippur. They breached the supposedly impenetrable Bar-Lev Line, pushed back the unprepared Israeli forces on three fronts, and pushed Israel to the verge of complete military defeat before it managed to finally retrieve the situation.

Israel was again taken by surprise on a holy day. Hamas chose the day of Simchat Torah – a holy day of prayer and rest when Jews complete the annual reading of the Torah – and as on Yom Kippur Day, caught them completely by surprise. Hamas had prepared for the attack for over two years. In an elaborate subterfuge, it convinced Israel that it was weary of war and was now focused only on economic development.

They also prepared meticulously for the attack. A mock Israeli settlement was created close to Gaza City where they practiced mock attacks and even prepared training videos of their manoeuvres. Yet, even as they trained, Hamas refrained from any action against Israel. Rockets and missiles were secretly stockpiled in the Gaza Metro – the 500-kilometre-long network of underground tunnels within Gaza – and no firing was done from Gaza into Israel for months preceding the operation. Through his broadcasts and speeches – very often in perfect Hebrew – the Hamas Chief, Yahya al-Sinwar, convinced Israel that his aim was to manage Gaza, rather than wage war, even as its military wing, the al-Qassam Brigade were training for the operation.

Even during training, (which must have gone on for months judging by the level of coordination) none of the operatives were told of the scale or the exact nature of the operation. All communications were made on secure lines and no mobiles, internet or radios were used. Fighters were merely told to assemble at designated points at specific times and travel in small groups on their own motorcycles and vehicles so as to not arouse suspicion. They were issued weapons and ammunition and briefed of their tasks only at the last moment. None but a handful of the top Hamas leadership was aware of the plan, and even Israel's formidable network of intelligence operatives which operated in Gaza and had even penetrated Hamas ranks, had any inkling of what was about to happen. The operation was coordinated in fine detail – as the scope of attacks across a 30-kilometre-long area shows – and the attackers seemed to be aware of the exact location and layout of the military installations and settlements they penetrated. Almost invariably, they blew up the communications centres at these locations, in the first phase itself, to prevent information from being relayed to the rear.

And how did Hamas breach the fence – the supposedly impregnable 'Iron Wall' within minutes. It is touted as the best surveillance system in the world. How was that breached? Hamas had collected the location and details of each camera and communications system and used armed drones to drop bombs on communications centres, surveillance systems and the remotely-operated machine gun posts. Snipers simply disabled the cameras before the operation, preventing any video information from flowing back which could have a activated the warning and protective systems. Perhaps there was an over-reliance on the high-tech system, because it was thinly manned, and though initial images of the ongoing attacks were streamed back, they were not noticed or detected in time. A sense of hubris and laxity had set in and the Israelis were confident that no one could breach their formidable barrier.

But information had been received about the attack, which was simply ignored by Israel. According to the *New York Times*, USA had given Israel detailed information about the attack plan almost a year earlier. This document called 'The Jericho Wall', provided the exact blueprint of the plan which was then executed. Surprisingly, Israeli intelligence simply dismissed it on the grounds that an attack of such a scale was beyond Hamas capabilities. Photo imagery had also detected a mock Israeli settlement which Hamas had created near Gaza City, where its operatives practiced the assault. Hamas training videos of how to cross the fence, how to attack a military base and to enter a settlement, how to take a hostage and other actions they would eventually execute, had also fallen into Israeli hands. These were dismissed as routine training activities of no great significance.

In June 2023, a young lady officer of an Israeli signals intelligence unit detected signal activity indicating a likely attack. However, when she reported it to her seniors, it was ignored on the grounds that she was too young and immature and her judgement was flawed. Egypt too had informed that something big seemed to be happening just three days before the attack but these signs too were ignored. The Israelis were like an ostrich with its head in the sand – refusing to see what was right in front of them, and hoping it would simply go away.

Even the internal situation in Israel was artfully exploited. Prime Minister Benjamin Netanyahu's divisive policies had caused wide divisions in Israeli society – especially the judiciary overhaul designed to reduce the powers of the judiciary over the government. These controversial measures had drawn tens of thousands of protestors out in the streets and formed a schism in civic society. The security forces were divided, with many reservists refusing to attend training if the reforms were pushed through. Netanyahu was focused on the survival of his fragile coalition government and had redeployed many of the security and intelligence staff to focus on the internal situation. As Netanyahu looked inwards, the threat from outside was coming closer.

In an interesting revelation, it was brought out that Israel had been allowing millions of dollars to flow into Gaza from Qatar. The money was designed to 'buy quiet' by sending a steady flow of money that would keep the Hamas focused on governing Gaza, and not entering into needless conflict with Israel. Apparently, Israeli intelligence officers even escorted Qatari officials into Gaza with suitcases containing millions of dollars in cash. This policy of propping up Hamas, at the expense of the Palestinian Authority in the West Bank, was designed to cause a divide between the two Palestinian bodies which would scuttle any talk of a 'two-state solution.'

What did Hamas hope to Achieve?

Hamas took advantage of all these factors to time their attack to perfection. Even as the first salvos were fired, Mohammed Deif, head of the al-Qassam Brigade – the military wing of Hamas – tweeted, "We announce the start of OPERATION AL-AQSA FLOOD with the first strike of 5,000 missiles and rockets that target enemy positions, airports, military fortifications ...."

The operation was designated 'Operation Al-Aqsa Flood' and designed to gather the attention of the Muslim world. Hamas wanted to draw attention to the entry into al-Aqsa Mosque – the third holiest Islamic site – by Israeli security forces, in May 2021. They also wanted to bring out the conditions of the Palestinians in the occupied territories of Gaza and the West Bank – most of whom lived in a state of siege under extreme hardship. Many had been forcibly evicted from their homes to make way for new Israeli settlements coming up in the occupied territories under Netanyahu's hard-line government. And, of course, they wanted to highlight the state of siege that Gaza had been in since Israel had imposed a blockade in 2007, and seek the release of the 5,400-odd Palestinians who were held in Israel jails.

However, the major issue was the growing acceptance of Israel by the Arab world. The Palestinian cause was being increasingly forgotten and their demands for their own state ignored. The 'Two-State Solution' was no longer even being talked about, and even the peace accords signed had conveniently pushed that aspect of the agenda to the future. It was becoming increasingly apparent that the world was losing interest in Palestine.

Moreover, Israel had re-established ties with the UAE, Bahrain, Sudan and Morocco and was slowly gaining acceptance in the Arab world with the signing of the Abrahams Accord of September 2020. Diplomatic ties had been established and economic and security linkages were being developed. With the Arab nations now accepting Israel, it was only Saudi Arabia – the most important Arab power that had to give a nod for Israel to be completely welcomed into the Arab world. An Israel-Saudi summit was now on the cards, which would normalize relations and bring the two major powers of the Middle East together after 70 years of hostility. With the leaders of the Muslim world now willing to sup at the same table as Israel, the Palestinian cause would soon be forgotten, and the two-state solution would be swept under the carpet, perhaps permanently.

Hamas was sure that an attack as horrific as this would invite a disproportionate Israeli response, and perhaps that is exactly what they hoped for. The Israeli response re-ignited the Palestinian issue and effectively scuttled Israel's rapprochement with its Arab neighbours. The heavy-handed Israeli response and the images of shattered buildings and civilian casualties are bound to evoke Arab sympathy and turn it from the victim to the aggressor. That would put Hamas and the Palestinian cause back in the limelight. Israel may succeed in its aim of destroying Hamas, but could eventually lose the larger war in the Middle East.

REFERENCES

'Analysis of the 7 Oct Attacks on Israel,' AOAV, 20 December 2023, https://www.aoav.org.uk

'Buying Quiet: The Israeli Strategy to prop up Hamas', *The Times of India*, 13 December 2023, Times Global.

'Documents reveal Hamas scale of Planning for Attack', *India Today*, 13 October 2023, https://www.indiatoday.com

'Gaza: Why the War won't end', *CSIS*, 2 November 2023, https://www.csis.org

'Hamas attack: A day of Hell in Israel', *Le Monde*, 30 October 2023, https://www.lemonde.fr

'How Hamas built a façade to attack Israel?', *BBC*, 27 November 2023, https://www.bbc.com

'Israel had 40-page document warning of 7 Oct 23'. 3 December 2023, https://www.livemint.com

'Learning from the Oct attacks on Israel', Wilson Centre, 17 November 2023, https://www.wilsoncenter.com

'Mapping the deadly Hamas attack in Israel', *Washington Post*, 7 October 2023, https://www.washingtonpost.com

'Mapping the Oct 7 Hamas attacks', *Map Mania*, 1 November 2023, https://www.mapmania.com

'Ruin and Death dot the map across Israel and Gaza,' *CNN*, 11 October 2023, https://www.cnn.com

'The Gaza Terror Offensive', Begin-Sadat Centre for Strategic Studies, 23 December 2023, https://www.besacenter.org

12

The Israeli Response: 'Operation Swords of Iron'

"*We are at War. And we will turn all places where Hamas is hiding into cities of ruin.*"

—Israeli Prime Minister Benjamin Netanyahu

The Israeli Response

"*We cannot always prevent the murder of workers in an orchard or sleeping families, but we can set a high price for our blood. A price too high for the Arab settlement, the Arab army and the Arab government to pay.... Retaliation operations are not for vengeance. It is an act of punishment and warning, that if that state does not control its population and does not prevent them attacking us – the Israeli forces will cause havoc in its land.*"

These words were spoken by General Moshe Dayan – the legendary Chief of Israel's Defence Forces (IDF) way back in 1955. But it is a philosophy that is applied even today. Unfortunately, Israel has been at the receiving end of terrorist actions right since its birth, and its response – almost as a survival instinct – has been to strike back hard at the perpetuators, irrespective of the damage caused. In its response to the Hamas attacks they seem to follow the same philosophy. As they struck out to take revenge and eliminate the Hamas – an action that could be easily understood and condoned – they lashed out at all the Palestinians in the Gaza Strip, as their air and ground attacks flattened over 60 percent of the infrastructure, displaced over 1.5 million Palestinians from their homes, and caused over 20000 casualties, in their quest to hunt out and eliminate the Hamas leadership and its cadres who had perpetuated the 07 October 2023 attacks.

That was the pitfall of the operation. As Israeli jets struck targets in Gaza, and images of shattered homes and dead women and children began flooding television screens and on social media, the perception of Israel as the victim slowly dissipated. Israel now began to be seen as the oppressor, as they smashed their way into Gaza from North to South. Maybe that is exactly what the Hamas leadership hoped for. Because as the war prolonged, world reaction turned against Israel. The awareness of the Palestinian cause and the creation of an independent state of Palestine began gaining ground. So even if Israel did eliminate Hamas – they would never be able to eliminate its ideology, and the Palestinian cause has come back to the public eye – just as Hamas hoped that it would, when they launched their attacks.

OPERATION SWORDS OF IRON

In the wake of the 7 October attacks, the Israeli response was fast and vehement. Israeli commando teams began moving towards the attacked settlements to clear areas taken over by Hamas, rescue hostages and frightened residents cowering in their cellars, and try to gauge the scale of casualties. The scenes that Israeli security forces encountered as they entered the area were horrific. Dead men, women and children littered the streets, many of the bodies badly mutilated. The women bore signs of terrible sexual assault, and were often brutalized. There were signs that the terrorists hoped to occupy the area and had come prepared for a long siege, with extra provisions, arms and ammunition, and in many of the settlements had to be cleared, street-by-street and house-by-house. It took the Israelis three days to clear the last vestiges of the terrorists from their soil.

At 1030, the same day of 7 October, Israeli jets struck targets in Gaza, hitting the Hamas Headquarters and flattening the residential building in which it was based. The very day, Israel called up over 3,00,000 reservists to beef up its 1,69,000 strong army for "a long war." The Defense Minister Yoav Gallant announced, "a full siege..., no electricity, no food, no fuel...nothing," of Gaza. Israeli cabinet approved a formal declaration of war for the first time in half a century and "OPERATION SWORDS OF IRON" was launched with the goal to "eliminate Hamas by destroying its military and governing capabilities, and bring our hostages back home."

It would not be easy. The military wing of Hamas – the Izz al-Din al-Qassam Brigade has over 25,000 fighters and over 80,000–90,000 sympathizers, who would be willing recruits for the battle. Their strength was complemented by another 6,000-8,000 fighters of sister organizations like the Islamic Jihad. The fighters were not as well trained or equipped as the Israelis, but held a wide array of automatic rifles, rocket propelled grenades, anti-tank missiles, machine guns, drones and a huge stockpile of rockets that continued firing into Israel throughout the war. And they had the defender's advantage of fighting in tunnels and built-up areas which would create immense collateral damage – and help turn world opinion against Israel.

Israel had been preparing for an invasion of Gaza for years. Specialist troops had been training for urban warfare in a center called 'Mini-Gaza' located in Southern Israel, which was an exact replica of Gaza City complete with a warren of tunnels and tightly packed buildings. They had created specialist teams of Engineers, dozers, tanks and infantry called Yaholom and canine combat teams called Oketz, specifically for this role. They had also formulated explosive gels and expanding foam that could be used in tunnels before the troops entered them. These would be essential to counter the "Gaza Metro"; the 500 odd kilometers of hidden tunnels, with numerous branches and arteries, that Hamas had artfully created and concealed beneath the ground of Gaza.

Operation Swords of Iron was planned in three phases. First, were an intense series of air and missile strikes to neutralize Hamas infrastructure;

then a ground assault to eliminate its leadership, cadres and war-waging potential; and finally, the establishment of a new security mechanism in Gaza, to preclude any return of Hamas. For three weeks Gaza remained in a complete state of siege, with no fuel or supplies permitted from the single crossing on the Egyptian border at Rafah. The blocking of fuel – though essential to the population – was a deliberate measure. It deprived Hamas of fuel to power the generators that ran the lighting and ventilation systems of their tunnels, forcing them to come overground. Israel pounded Gaza by land, air and sea for three weeks as it amassed troops on its borders to prepare for the invasion. The land offensive was delayed for three weeks, ostensibly at the request of USA which needed to beef up air defense resources for its bases in the region, should its troops be attacked in an expanding war.

As Israeli air strikes continued, the first mishap took place on 17 October, when a strike on the al Ahli hospital in Gaza City killed around 500 civilians, most of them patients and babies. The Palestinians said it was the result of an Israeli Air strike, but the Israelis provided evidence to show that the explosion was caused by a malfunctioning Palestinian rocket, that has hit the parking lot of the hospital and then exploded causing the damage.

US president Joe Biden visited the Middle East on 18 October to meet the heads of state in an attempt to defuse the situation. The meeting was a disaster. Although it would have reassured Israel about the US commitment to its ally, the Arab heads of states refused to meet him in protest against the hospital deaths that had taken place just a day before. The USA also sent two carrier groups into the region – the USS DWIGHT EISENHOWER, and USS GERALD FORD, perhaps as a show of force to prevent other powers entering the fray.

On 21 October, Israel issued a warning to all civilians of North Gaza – those living north of the Wadi Gaza, a dried up river bed that divides Gaza into the Northern and Southern regions - "Urgent Warning. Your presence north of Wadi Gaza is putting your life in danger. Leave immediately." Over 1.1 million civilians left their homes fearing an imminent Israeli offensive and trudged to what they hoped were safer areas in the south.

The Israeli invasion began with a series of raids and incursions into Gaza, perhaps to gauge the response and to try and identify the likely location of hostages. Over half a dozen minor raids were conducted, with the major one on 26 October, when approximately two battalions of tanks, armored dozers, infantry and engineers crossed the heavily fortified border fence and attacked suspected Hamas positions. They withdrew later in the night and the action was probably to assess the Hamas defenses before their ground invasion that was to follow soon.

The Ground Invasion

The ground invasion began on 28 October, as Israeli ground troops entered Gaza in three prongs – from the North, the North east and the South east – under an intense land, air and sea bombardment. They also targeted the internet, telecom and all other communication systems and effectively cut off communication between Gaza and the rest of the world, enabling it to control the flow of information and thus shape the narrative.

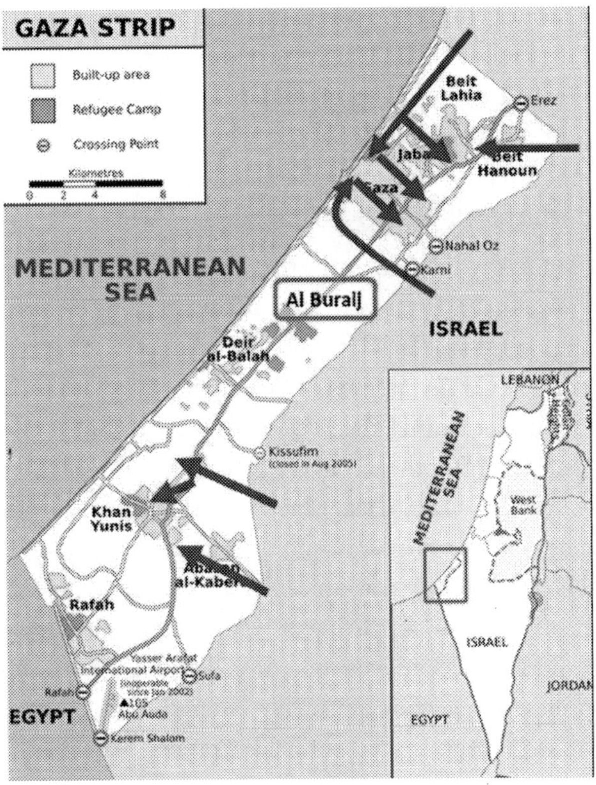

Gaza Strip

The offensive moved towards its primary target of Gaza City, where the main Hamas positions and leadership were based. A three-pronged advance, effectively cut it off. It also cut off the North-South highway which was the only avenue of escape for citizens fleeing the war. In the fighting, 16 Israeli soldiers were killed on 30 October and brought out the dangers of fighting in built up areas. Amongst the dead was Sergeant Halel Solomon, a person of Indian origin. But in the operation, the Israelis also managed to rescue Private Ori Megidish – a female soldier captured by Hamas during the 7 October attacks – in what was touted as the major step in rescuing the hostages.

One of the major aims of the war was the release of the 240 hostages taken by Hamas, and that was the most difficult task. Negotiations were ongoing for their release and two were released in a deal brokered by Qatar. Hamas claimed that another 50 were killed in Israeli air strikes. Determining the location of those hidden in tunnels, cellars and safe houses will be daunting. Hamas stated that it is willing to release all the surviving hostages in exchange for the 5900 Palestinian prisoners in Israeli jails. But Israel was not loath to take up that offer. In 2011, they released 1027 Palestinian prisoners in exchange for Corporal Gilad Shalit, who had been captured and held captive for five years. One of the prisoners released was Yahya Sinwar, who is their tormentor in chief now. They would definitely not want to take a similar step, nor give in to the Hamas in an action which will be seen as a defeat.

The intermingling of Hamas with civilians in the crowded area of Gaza, has caused immense collateral damage. Israel insists that Hamas is using civilians as human shields, and Hamas claims that Israel is deliberately targeting civilians. A bombing attack on Jabalia – Gaza's largest refugee camp killed Ibrahim Biari, a pivotal Hamas commander behind the 7 October attacks. But it also killed fifty refugees and wounded 150 others – many of whom had just come there from the war-torn north. In Gaza City, Israeli tanks closed in on Al Shifa and Al Quds hospitals – Gaza's largest hospitals – and surrounded it, claiming that it housed a Hamas communication center and armory, beneath it. For five days, it was cut off, with snipers firing at what they claimed were Hamas operatives within (and Hamas said were doctors), denying it fuel, and much needed medical supplies. When they eventually entered, Israeli troops showed photo evidence of well camouflaged tunnel entrances beneath the basement and huge stockpiles of arms and weaponry. But the attack on the hospital also caused innumerable deaths amongst the patients and new-born children. The placing of civilians and hospitals in the line of fire, has resulted in disproportionate civilian casualties – and is slowly turning world opinion away from Israel.

The Truce and After

Gaza had been besieged and pummeled for almost a month as Israel refused a ceasefire, and continued its relentless assault. Eventually Qatar and Egypt brokered a four-day truce on 23 November which came into effect the next day. As per the conditions of the truce, both sides agreed to stop firing, Israel permitted aid trucks to move in to Gaza, and most importantly Hamas agreed to release 50 hostages in exchange for 150 Palestinians in Israeli jails. The truce was extended by two more days in which 20 more hostages were released for 60 Palestinians, and then another day in which 12 more hostages were released. The prisoner swap seemed a good agreement and it was hoped that it would continue. However, both sides claimed repeated violations of the truce by the other, and when it expired on the morning of 01 December, Israel refused to extend it further. In fact, Israeli air strikes started eight minutes after the truce had expired, and the war went on.

Israel now focused on the South. None of the top Hamas leadership had been captured in North Gaza, and were believed to have fled to Khan Younis in the south. Israel issued a warning to all civilians to evacuate the south. This was almost impossible to do, since the civilian population had already been displaced from North to South and now there was no place for them to go - except the Mediterranean Sea or Egypt. And Egypt too, was not keen on accepting Palestinian refugees on to their soil.

By mid-December, Israeli tanks had entered Khan Younis, after intense combat with Hamas fighters. The Israeli army reported suffered the maximum casualties here as Hamas fighters used their local knowledge and moved from one location to another – often through the concealed tunnels – to fire anti-tank rockets at advancing Israeli tanks or lead advancing soldiers into ambushes. The Israelis used drones ahead of their advancing columns for early warning which prevented many casualties. Yet, in an unfortunate incident three hostages were killed by Israeli soldiers even as they approached them waving a white flag and calling out in Hebrew. This was a case of mistaken identity, with the soldiers justifying themselves by saying that it was a tactic used by Hamas, and hence they fired at the approaching hostages (and even chased one into a building where he was killed later) and brought out all the dangers of recovering the hostages to safety.

The Israelis also unearthed a vast network of tunnels – in a vast honeycomb of passages, featuring a drainage system, electricity, ventilation, sewage and communication. The floors were made of compacted earth, with the walls reinforced by concreate, and 1.5-centimeter-thick metal doors at the entrance. The Israelis had banned its soldiers from entering, fearing needless casualties and would send in remotely operated vehicles with cameras mounted on them, and even canine units to get advance information of the tunnels. Explosive gels and expanding foam were used to block the entrances, and the Israelis even pumped in sea water to flood the underground tunnels and force the Hamas cadres to emerge. Other tunnels were destroyed by simply covering them with rubble by blasting the building over them. The detection and elimination of the tunnels and the Hamas cadres within are the greatest challenge to the Israeli forces in this campaign.

The Rafah Offensive

By the end of December, Israel had overrun virtually all of Gaza, starting from the North, then moving to the South, and then moving back to North Gaza again, in an attempt to find and destroy the Hamas leadership. They claimed to have eliminated over 9000 Hamas cadres, but there is no way of differentiating a fighter and a civilian, and in any case, none of the top leadership were eliminated, and till end December, Hamas still retained the ability to fire rockets in to Israel.

Nor had the hostages been recovered. Many had been returned in prisoner swaps, but they were largely the women and children. Many were also killed by Israeli fire, and the really important ones, secreted deep in the tunnels. The professed aim of Israel to recover the hostages can be best done through talks and negotiation.

By then, 85 percent of its 2.3 million people had been displaced – first told to move from North to South, and then to move from South to North and then back again, as Israeli operations intensified in these areas. Over 45,000 people were killed and 53,000 wounded, with an additional 7000 missing, presumably buried beneath rubble. This is three times the number of civilian casualties caused by Russia in Ukraine all throughout the two-year long Ukraine war. The heavy civilian toll is higher than all other wars combined, but the only thing it has done is create a new generation of angry, resentful men, who remember this as another 'Naqba' – a catastrophe that has to be avenged.

Peace talks did continue in Cairo, conducted under the auspices of Qatar and Egypt, which stuttered on and off. There was hope that some sort of a cease fire could have been hammered out before the month of Ramadhan, but that was not to be. Hamas had put up a reasonable proposal, calling for a three-phase ceasefire, in which they would release 30 hostages in the first seven weeks, another set of prisoners in the next seven weeks, and the remainder in the next seven weeks. In return, Israel would announce a complete cessation of hostilities, and resume humanitarian aid, while a UN force would oversee the functioning of Gaza. It would also pave the way for a "final solution to the Palestinian issue."

The proposal was nixed by Israel which only offered a temporary ceasefire, while the hostages were released. It would leave them free to carry out offensive operations after they got their hostages back. The talks floundered on the subject of 'permanent' versus 'temporary' ceasefire, and the fighting continued.

And in that time, Israel was preparing for its next offensive – at Rafah, in the extreme south of Gaza, where over 1.4 million Gazans had fled to after the fighting in Gaza City and Khan Younis. Israel claimed that three Hamas battalions – the remnants of the 24 battalions Hamas had at the start of the war – were holed up there, along with their senior leadership. This itself would have created a humanitarian disaster of grave magnitude. Irrespective of world opinion, Israel closed the Rafah crossing, and prepared for the offensive into Rafah.

On 06 May 2024, the talks finally failed and the negotiators left in disgust. That same day, Israel blamed Hamas for the failure of the talks and launched their offensive into Rafah. The inhabitants were told to evacuate the town and move to safe areas along a coastal belt near the Mediterranean Sea, as the Israelis followed their usual playbook of launching massive air and missile attacks, and then sent in tanks and infantry into the area. All of Rafah was razed to rubble, and tanks prowled the streets and infantrymen combed the area. The end result was predictable. In spite of the massive devastation, and a displacement of over a million Gazans, there was little military gains. Few of the cadres were killed, only four hostages recovered, and none of the senior leadership apprehended.

In fact, even as the Rafah attack was continuing, Israel launched another attack in the north, towards Gaza City, stating that the Hamas cadres and leadership had fled there. This disjointed nature of operations, merely revealed the futility of these kind of disproportionate strikes on built up areas, and the fact that it got little in terms of military gains. In fact, the only this it attained was retribution to all Gazans for the horrors wrought by Hamas on 07 October.

But Israel did succeed in targeting the top Hamas Leaders. Marwan Issa, the Number 3 in the hierarchy was killed in March in an Israeli air strike in the Nuseirat refugee camp, where he had been hiding. Later, in July, Mohammed Deif, the head of their military wing – the Al Qassim Brigade died of wounds sustained during an air strike a week earlier. Israel also struck at Ismail Haniyeh, the Chief of Hamas, whom was assassinated in Teheran itself. These gave valuable political and symbolic victories to Israel.

But after a year of war, Israel is nowhere near its goal of eliminating Hamas or attaining its military aims. They are being increasingly seen as the aggressor and not the victim. They may eventually accept a truce for the return of hostages in exchange for a cessation of their actions. But, even if they do succeed in their aims, then what? Will they take over Gaza as they did earlier, only to withdraw? Will they hand it over to the Palestinian Authority to govern? Will they be forced to restart negotiations on "a two-state solution" which they have effectively stymied over the years? Eventually they may have to do all of that. And they would again have to start mending fences with the Arab world. Israel may succeed in its aim of eliminating Hamas – at least in its present form – but till they address the root of the Palestinian issue, the problem will remain and the Middle East will continue to stumble from one crisis to the next.

REFERENCES

"130 Hamas Tunnels destroyed in Gaza", *The Indian Express*, 6 November 2023, https://indianexpress.com

"2023 Israel-Hamas Hostage Crisis", *Wikipedia*, https://enwikipedia.org

"2023 Israel-Hamas War: How it Unfolded", *CNN*, https://www.cnn.com

"Five Potential next Steps in the Gaza War", *Rand Corporation*, 28 December 2023, https://rand.org

"Gaza Deaths surpass any Arab loss in Wars", *The New York Times*, 21 December 2023, https://www.nytimes.com

"Israel Hamas War Ceasefire", *The New York Times*, 24 November 2023, https://www.nytimes.com

"Israel Strikes back with Operation Swords of Iron", *India Today*, 07 October 2023, https://www.indiatoday.in

"Israel-Hamas War Highlights", 24 November 2023, *India Today*, https://www.indiatoday.in

"Israel-Hamas War of 2023", *Britannica*, https://www.britannica.com

"Major events during War between Israel and Hamas", *Reuters*, 28 December 2023, https://www.reuters.com

"Operation Swords of Iron: Israel Readies for next step", *The Economic Times*, 14 October 2023, https://www.economictimes.com

"Operation Swords of Iron", *The Rand Corporation*, 23 October 2023, https://www.rand.com

"Tunnels of Hamas Headquarters Destroyed: IDF", *ABC News*, 28 December 2023, https://www.abcnews.com

"What Gaza's death toll says about the War", *BBC*, 20 December 2023, https://www.bbc.com

"What you need to know about the Israel-Hamas War", Foreign Policy, https://foriegnpolicy.com

13

A Multi-arena War

"We are in a multi-arena war and under threat from seven sides – Gaza, Lebanon, Syria, West Bank, Iraq, Yemen, Iran."

—Israeli defense minister, Yoav Gallant

In the wake of the horrific 7 October attacks by Hamas on Israel, there came a concerted series of rocket and missile attack from Hezbollah in Lebanon, and an outpouring of fire and popular support from Palestinian militants in the West Bank. Shia militant groups in Iraq and Syria also joined the fray by striking at Israel and US targets in the region. And to add fuel to the fire, the Houthi rebels from Yemen began firing missiles and drones to express their own solidarity. Israel seemed to be under attack from all sides, even as it pressed on with its invasion of Gaza.

So much so, that the defense minister Yoav Gallant, warned his country

"We are in a multi-arena war and under threat from seven sides – Gaza, Lebanon, Syria, West Bank, Iraq, Yemen, and Iran."

Yes, Israel is under attack from all these directions. And the war is sucking in other parties as well. The longer the war goes on the greater is the possibility that it will engulf the entire Middle East in a wider conflagration.

The Iran and US Connections

One common thread binding all the present adversaries of Israel is Iran. Hamas, the Hezbollah, the Houthis and Shia militia of Iraq and Syria are all proxies, which have been armed and a sponsored by Iran. Although Iran denies any direct role, the rockets and weaponry provided comes from Iran itself – as does other aid and moral support. And Iran definitely has an act to grind with Israel. They are sworn enemies and the major poles of power in the Middle East, along with Saudi Arabia. The other Arab nations had begun the slow process of accepting Israel through the Abrahams Accord of 2020 – when UAE, Morocco, Sudan, and Bahrain re-established diplomatic and economic ties with Israel. A summit meeting with Mohammed bin Salman, the crown prince of Saudi Arabia, and Prime Minister Benjamin Netanyahu, was in the offing – but has now been pushed indefinitely. Scuttling the peace process that amalgamates Israel with the Arab world, suits Iran, since an Israel- Saudi-UAE coming together would have tilted the balance of power away from it.

And then there is Iran's nuclear program, which is so close to completion now (if it has not already been completed). After Trump walked out of the nuclear deal, Iran has recommended developing nuclear fuel, in the underground facilities of Natanz and Qom. A US-Israel attack on the reactor could set it back by decades, and it was perhaps one of Iran's major fears. That has not materialized so far and after the reactor goes critical, that window of opportunity would be lost. As it is, they have been a number of mysterious deaths of top nuclear scientists associated with the program, and the finger of suspicion points squarely at Israel. Keeping Israel weekend, not through direct war, but by continual attack from its proxies, and reducing US influence in the region, would definitely suit Iran.

The war has sucked in USA, which has rushed to the defense of its ally. In a clear-cut sign of support, it sent two carrier groups – USS DWIGHT EISENHOWER and USS GERALD FORD – into the region. This show of force was perhaps a signal to other parties such as Iran or Iraq, to not get directly involved in the conflict. President Joe Biden's frantic diplomacy has ensured that the Arab nations have stayed away from the conflict so far – short of providing the usual lip service. The Arab response to the Israeli devastation of Gaza – barring Turkey and Iran – has been surprisingly muted, and there has been no direct support from them towards Gaza. And while the USA has blocked outside interference, it has also ensured that Israel received emergency supply of arms and equipment, like 155-millimeter howitzer ammunition which is now being diverted from Ukraine towards Israel.

But though the USA successfully vetoed two UN resolutions calling for a ceasefire, so Israel could continue its offensive till the end, it is facing increasing internal and external criticism – and that too in election year. This has forced Joe Biden to acknowledge that, "the road to permanent peace in the Middle East lies in the Two-State-Solution" something that successive US administration had been in a state of denial for years.

The war has also deflected the USA from another theater – Ukraine. With Ukraine now conclusively on the back foot, Russia seems to be well on the way to attaining its military objectives. Ukraine is dependent on an increasing dwindling supply of aid, to continue to war, and there are questions being asked about the feasibility of continuing aid for a losing cause. The US policy failure in Ukraine has to be made up by ensuring the success of Israel. Else the USA will lose influence in this theater as well.

The war has become an arena of big power rivalry and that is what increases its stakes tremendously.

The Militia Wars

It is not clear whether the actions of the different militia groups supporting Hamas are being coordinated through design, or is just a spontaneous eruption. Most probably, it is a combination of both. But then, the actions of Hamas in Gaza and the West Bank, Hezbollah from Lebanon, militia from Iraq and Syria, and the Houthis from Yemen, have already put Israel at a greater multi-dimensional threat than at any time since 1967.

Hezbollah have stepped up their rocket attacks raids in to Israel – including cross-border attacks in the disputed area of Shebaa farms to attack Israeli posts and capture soldiers. This has forced Israel to focus attention on the northern sector to contain the Hezbollah. And though Israel has warned Lebanon that Hezbollah provocations could lead to the same retaliation that was seen in Gaza, this will be an even more difficult proposition. The Hezbollah are three times the size of Hamas, with around 100000 well-armed and motivated fighters, and an arsenal of over 1,30,000 rockets. Their attacks on Israel are more sophisticated than any other group, striking carefully coordinated missile and rocket attacks – even hitting the port city of Eilat – 350 kms away. The situation erupted dangerously when Saleh al Arouri, a senior Hamas official closely connected to Hezbollah was killed in an Israeli drone attack in the heart of Beirut. Hezbollah vowed "retaliation and punishment" and this could get Hezbollah even more involved in the fray. A northern front in Lebanon, while it is still engaged in Gaza will strain Israel tremendously. Yet there are many hawks – the Defence Minister Yoav gallant amongst them – who favour a pre-emptive attack to strike the Hezbollah in its bases in South Lebanon – like they did inconclusively in the 2006 Lebanon war.

The West Bank too, is dangerously close to eruption. The plight of their Palestinian brethren in Gaza has influenced passions tremendously – and the West Bank has seen more attacks than at any time in the past two years. Fatah and the Palestinian authority are playing a waiting game. While sympathizing with the Gazans, they will be secretly glad to see the end of Hamas – with whom they have been daggers drawn since they lost the Gaza elections in 2006. A Hamas defeat will give them an opportunity to regain power in the Gaza Strip again, and then as sole representative, press for a revival of the two-state solution.

The actions of Shia militia in Syria, Iran and Iraq are also coming closer home. Drone, missile attacks and raids have targeted US bases in Iraq and Syria, forcing them to launch retaliatory strikes, at suspected militant positions in this country. Brigadier Syed Razi Mansavi, a top Iranian advisor of the Islamic Revolutionary Guards, was killed by Israeli missile attack in the heart of Damascus. Even worse, over a hundred mourners were killed in a series of explosions within Iran as they gathered to mourn the anniversary of General Qassem Soleimani, who was killed by a US strike four years ago. This act, attributed to the Islamic State, now brings another party to the equations and revives Shia-Sunni passions at a dangerous moment. To add fuel to the fire, Iran fired missiles into Pakistan targeting the bases of Jaish al Adl – the Sunni militant group that had carried out the attack. All this increases the scope of the war.

The Threat to World Shipping

The most dangerous attacks have come from an unexpected source – the Houthis in Yemen. They too are affiliated to Iran and have been supported by it throughout the seven-year-long Yemen Civil War – which in effect was a proxy between Iran and Saudi. The Houthis – whose motto is "Death to America; death to Israel," began firing long range missiles into Israel in the first week of the war itself. Their attacks caused confusion more than anything else, but was a signal of their reach and ability to inflict damage.

The Houthis then used their strategic location, astride the Red Sea which allows them to control all movement through the Straits of Bab el Mandeb – through which 15 percent of the world shipping passes. They first targeted Israeli ships in the waters, and then expanded the scope to attack all shipping headed for Israeli ports, even launching missile strikes on the Israeli port of Eilat. Over two dozen attacks were conducted, forcing to take a longer route via the Cape of Good Hope in the southern tip of Africa, – a detour that added two weeks to the trip and increased costs.

The USA OPERATION PROSPERITY GUARDIAN – an international maritime force to ensure free and safe move of shipping through the waters, tried to keep the waters safe, but it This received mixed reactions. Many countries, including Saudi Arabia and UAE, distanced themselves from the venture so as not to be seen as taking sides in the conflict. But then things came to a head on New Year's Day when US helicopters shot and sank three Houthi boats in the first direct engagement between the sides. This was followed by a US and UK air and missile strike at 16 Houthi locations with over a hundred Tomahawk missiles, and air strikes by four British Typhoon aircraft. The Houthis are directly linked to Iran, and this increases the chances of an Iran-US confrontation.

Will the Conflagration Spread?

In three months of war, Israel has flattened 60 percent of Gaza's infrastructure, displaced 85 percent of its population, killed 20,000 (with 7000 missing-presumably under rubble) and wounded 56,000 without distinction of whether it is a Hamas fighter or a civilian. That is thrice civilian deaths caused by Russia's invasion of Ukraine.

Israel has promised to continue the war till it eliminates Hamas and recover its hostages. But the longer the war goes on, the more isolated it becomes. Should Iran galvanize all its proxies to a launch a coordinated series of strikes, it will force Israel into a multi-front war. It may even provoke an Israeli attack on Lebanon (like it did disastrously in 1982 and 2006). Also, should any of the attacks on US bases or ships cause inordinate casualties, it could bring USA in to direct conflict with Iran – maybe through a series of punitive strikes. Then there is even the wild card event of Iran, Turkey, Qatar or any Arab nation deciding to send a relief flotilla to Gaza Strip on humanitarian ground, which could clash with Israeli warships imposing the blockade. Any of these events could go out of hand and widen the confrontation to engulf the entire Middle East.

And Israel does not seem to have given much thought to the endstate they want to achieve. Return of the hostages and the destruction of Hamas is one of the aims. But so far Israel has been able to release just a handful of hostages through military action, though over a hundred have been released in the week-long negotiated truce. Around 8000 Hamas cadres have been reportedly eliminated, (who would be amongst the 22,000 dead) but none of the senior leadership like Yahya Sinwar, Mohammed Deif, Marwan Issa have been killed or apprehended after four months of war. Even if they are eliminated, they will merely be replaced by others. The idea of Hamas will go on.

Israel also wants to take over the security of Gaza after the war, but how? They tried it disastrously, till they were forced to withdraw in 2005 after the Second Intifada. At best, they could hand over the enclave to the Palestinian Authority – but the PA head Mahmoud Abbas is not keen on "riding into Gaza on a Tank" – and would not want responsibility for the battered enclave, till they get some guarantees from Israel and the world community.

And there is the question of rebuilding Gaza – now estimated to cost of $60 Billion - after the war; and resettling 1.5 million displaced Gazan. Who will bear the cost? There is also the major issue of a separate Palestinian state. Whether Israel likes it or not, it is back in the spotlight and will have to be addressed and satisfactorily resolved after the guns stop firing. Else the attacks and counter attacks will continue. This war would be just another bloody chapter in the continual cycle of violence engulfs the entire Middle East and threatens to inflame the world.

REFERENCES

"Hezbollah launch Rockets in support of Hamas", *Al Jazeera*, 14 October 2023, https://www.aljazeera.com

"Houthi Attacks close vital Red Sea Route" *CNN*, 24 December 2023, https://www.cnn.com

"Houthi Missiles strike Shipping, US hits back", *The Indian Express*, 18 January 2024, The World, https://www.indianexpress.com

"Iran Strikes terror bases in Pakistan" The Indian Express, 18 January 2024, *The World*, https://www.indianexpress.com

"Iran's Axis of Resistance and its Role in the Israel- Hamas War", *CBC*, 8 November 2023, https://ww.cbc.com

"Iran's Axis of Resistance", *The Economist*, 15 November 2023, https://www.economist.com

"Israel faces 'Multi-Arena War' from Seven different fronts", *The Australian*, 27 December 2023, https://www.theaustralian.com

"Israel-Hamas War: Attacks on Rise in the West Bank", *AP News*, 20 November 2023, https://www.apnews.com

"Israel-Iran Tensions", *BNN Breaking*, 26 December 2023, https://www.bnnbreaking.com

"The Israel-Hamas War", *CNN*, 26 December, https://edition.cnn.com

"The West Bank Smoulders", *Human Rights Watch*, 22 November 2023, https://www.hrw.com

"US announces Naval coalition to defend Red Sea Shipping", *The Guardian*, 20 December 2023, https://www.theguardian.com

"US led coalition warns Houthis", *Al Jazeera*, 29 December 2023, https://www.aljazeera.com

"What Houthi attacks in red Sea mean for Global Shipping", *BBC*, 29 December 2023, https://www.bbc.com

14

The Iran-Israel Confrontation

"Death to Big Satan, Death to Little Satan."

—**Iranian Slogan**

When Iranian missiles and drones struck Israel on the night of 13th April, it was the first time that any nation had hit Israeli soil since the 1973 war (less a flurry of missiles fired by Saddam Hussain in the first Gulf war of 1991). It was also the first time that Iran directly attacked Israel bringing their shadow war out into the open.

Iran and Israel have been in a state of animosity, bordering on open enmity, ever since the Ayatollahs came to power in Iran in1979. But though Iran proclaims, "Death to USA, Death to Israel," it largely relies on its proxies to carry out that threat. Hamas, Hezbollah, the Houthis, the Shia militia in Syria and Iraq are all sponsored and armed by them. Both sides view the other as an existentialist threat, but have refrained from direct attacks on each other – barring cyber-attacks, the killings of Iranian nuclear scientists by Israel and attacks on Israeli consulate members by Iran. However in most cases, the confrontation was through proxies and never directly claimed. It has now come out in the open.

The Iranian Attacks

The Iranian attack on Israel was in response to Israel's blatant attack on its consulate in Damascus that killed seven senior Iranian Republican Guards Corps officers. That attack had to be answered or else Iran would lose face, even with its own proxies. But their response seems deliberately designed to prevent further escalation. 'Operation True Promise' was a message more than anything else, and not meant to cause undue casualties. The Iranian communique at the UNSC announcing its strike stated that it did so using its inherent right of self-defence, and "The matter can be deemed concluded." The language itself indicated that they did not want any further escalation. Around 320 projectiles were launched, which included 185 drones, 110 ballistic missiles, and 36 cruise missiles fired from different locations in Iran, Iraq and Syria. It is significant that they used Shahed drones to start this attack. These antiquated drones puttering away at around 200 km/h, with a payload of just around 50 kgs, took 3-4 hours to fly in from Iran into Israeli territory – long enough to be easily detected and destroyed. They seemed to want to telegraph their intentions. By some accounts, information of the impending strike was also given to Saudi Arabia and other Arab nations to be passed on to Israel well in advance.

Israel claims that 99 per cent of the attacking projectiles were shot down, but a few did get through. The only target of note that was struck was the Nevatim airbase in the Negev desert, that houses the F-35 fighter squadron which had carried out the strike on the Iranian consulate a fortnight earlier. Iranian sources claimed that the base was completely destroyed, but satellite imagery revealed only minor damage, and the base continued being fully operational. This base was attacked with more advanced cruise and ballistic missiles that could get through its formidable network of David's Sling, Patriot and Iron Dome Air Défense systems – again a signal.

At the end of it, Israel claimed that the only damage was a 10 year old Bedouin girl who suffered shrapnel injuries from a destroyed missile. The mood in Israel is one of celebration, "We intercepted, we stopped, and we will win." But, stopping these attacks, cost them over 100 Arrow missiles and using $3 million missiles at swarms of cheap, incoming projectiles will definitely not be sustainable in the long run. Also there is a realisation that an even more dangerous enemy had hit them and Israel was under attack again.

There is another very significant aspect in that the Arab states of Jordan and Saudi Arabia actually helped Israel in detecting and countering the threat. Iranian missiles and drones had to overfly Saudi and Jordanian airspace en route to Israel. Saudi air defence detected them and passed information immediately back to Israel. Jordan actively engaged incoming missiles and drones and shot down quite a few with their own aircraft and air defence systems. The Arab nations were prepared to be seen as actively assisting Israel against another Islamic nation – even as Israel continues with its excesses in Gaza. This means that in the politics of the region, the proposed pact between USA, Israel, Saudi Arabia, UAE and other Arab states still holds, and could eventually come about after this war (Perhaps in return for Israeli concessions for a two-state solution as demanded by Saudi).

The Israeli Response

Although the Iranian strike was successfully countered without casualties, Israel seemed hell-bent on retaliating "at a time and place of our choosing." Israel insists that the best way to ensure their security is through retaliation and deterrence, so that their enemies never feel emboldened to try a similar strike again. They will use this same concept against Iran. Fortunately Iran and Israel are separated by over 1500 kilometres and ground action will not be feasible. But air and missile strikes are possible, as were selective assassinations, or cyber-attacks. Like Iran, Israel had to be seen as having retaliated, without really climbing up the escalatory ladder.

The Israeli retaliation came just three days later over the city of Isfahan and in Tabriz in North-western Iran. Israeli drones reported attacked the airbase over Isfahan, which houses its fleet of F-14 Tomcats. Isfahan is also close to the Natanz enrichment plant, the centrepiece of Iran's nuclear program. It is still not clear whether drones or missiles were used in the attack. Debris of Blue Sparrow air-to-surface missiles were recovered, indicating that they could have been missiles launched by Israeli aircraft away from Iranian airspace.

Iranian Air Défense reportedly destroyed the incoming projectiles without any damage, and the score line was now one-all.

In a way, both strikes were messaging indicating each other's capabilities to attack deep and it was hoped that the crisis would pass without wider escalation. But within Israel, the hardliners are increasingly harping on finishing Hamas, eliminating Hezbollah next, and then going for Iran – "the head of the snake." Another refrain that is being increasingly heard is, "What if one of the Iranian missiles had been a nuclear tipped one?" Israel may halt its actions with this retaliation, but should it contemplate eliminating Iran's nuclear capabilities at a later juncture, perhaps the USA will give a nod-and-a-wink, and even provide assistance to do so.

But striking Iran's nuclear facilities will not be easy. The major enrichment plans at Natanz, Fordow and Qom have been created deep underground, sheltered beneath mountains where even the most powerful bomb would not be effective. Also, the sizeable Iranian air defence is geared for an attack. A failed Israeli-US attack on its nuclear facilities may merely hasten Iran's nuclear programme (if it has not fructified already) or could lead it to obtain nuclear wherewithal from North Korea. Coupled with its impressive array of long range missiles, a smarting Iran could then become an even more dangerous foe.

For USA too, Iran is a sworn enemy, though it does not want an all-out war with it. Iran is too large and powerful to be directly attacked (as with Iraq). Its 5,60,000 strong army is strong and motivated, and in spite of sanctions, it retains a capable Air Force and Air Défense. And it has one of the world's most lethal array of missiles. Armed action would not be a feasible option, but the USA would definitely like to destabilise it further through sanctions and selective internal actions that would bring about regime change and perhaps replace the Ayatollahs with someone more amenable.

Although the direct actions between Iran and Israel seemed to have halted after the series of retaliatory strikes, the war with the proxies continues. Israel had intensified its actions with both Hamas and Hezbollah – and perhaps by eliminating them they will reduce Iranian influence. That would not be easy. And with Iran, the shadow war still lurks in the background and can explode at any time.

REFERENCES

"Assessing Israel's Strike on Iran," Center for Strategic Studies, 3 May 2024

"Deconstructing Iran's Massive Missile Strike on Israel," *NDTV*, 15 April 2024

"How Iran's attack on Israel was Stopped," *Reuters*, 15 April 2024

"Iran warns Israel of 'Obliterating War'," *Al Jazeera*, 29 June 2024

"Operation 'True Promise': Iran's Missile attack on Israel," Begin-Sadat Institute for Strategic Studies, 18 Jun 2024

"Teheran plays down reported Israeli Strike," *Reuters*, 19 April 2024

"The Iran-Israel War is just getting Started," *The Rand Foundation*, 25 April 2024

"Why have Iran and Israel Targeted each other?," *BBC*, 19 April 2024

15

The Assassinations in Beirut and Teheran

"We will get them, wherever they may be hiding."

Three Attacks, Two Assassinations

On 27 July, Iranian rockets fired by the Hezbollah from Southern Lebanon, struck a settlement in Israeli occupied Golan Heights. The rockets hit a field where children were playing football and killed twelve; in the deadliest attack on Israeli soil since 7 October. Three days later, Israeli jets hit the building of the Hezbollah Shura Council in a posh suburb of Beirut, killing Faud Shukr, the top Hezbollah military commander who was responsible for the strike. His killing in the heart of Beirut, was a clear message of intent.

Barely 24 hours later, Ismail Haniyeh, the chief of Hamas was assassinated in the Iranian capital of Teheran. Just hours before, he had attended the swearing-in ceremony of Iran's new President Masoud Pezeshkian, and was seen on television beaming with supreme leader Ayatollah Khamenei. The strike was a deliberate affront to Iran, carried out on a state guest in their own capital, staying in a government guest house guarded by their elite Iranian Revolutionary Guards. Although Israel did not comment on it (less a cryptic 'We shed no tears') nor claim responsibility, all indicators pointed squarely to it, and predicably Iran vowed revenge.

Initial accounts indicated that the attack came from a "Airborne guided projectile." But it emerged later, that the likely cause of the explosion that ripped through Haniyeh's room at 2 a.m. in the morning could have been a bomb that had been planted in the guestroom much before, just waiting to be activated at just the right time. The special guest house was used for high profile guests like Haniyeh and indicated the depth of infiltration in the most secure zones. That in itself carried a message to Iran. The targeted deaths of Fuad Shukr in Beirut and Ismail Haniyeh in Tehran raised the stakes in the Gaza war.

Haniyeh was the political, and not the military face of Hamas, but was its senior most leader. He was considered to be a more moderate face, and was the representative of Hamas during the peace talks. His killing dealt a major blow to the peace process, but then, Israel did not seem too serious about the ceasefire in any case, unless it was purely on their terms. But on the flip side, Israel got a symbol of victory, which could enable them to be persuaded by the US to accept a ceasefire.

With his death, the top leadership of Hamas had been eliminated. Israeli air strikes killed Marwan Issa in Gaza in March 2024. Mohammed Deif, the head of their military wing also reportedly died of wounds sustained during a Israel strike on 13 July (which also claimed 90 other Gazans). This left only Yahya Sinwar on the hit list – holed out in Gaza, perhaps in one of the underground tunnels – but he seemed to be 'dead man walking.'

The mood in Israel was buoyant after what was seen as a major achievement. Netanyahu could claim to have attained some of his war aims at least, and came closer to his professed aim of eliminating Hamas. Yahya Sinwar was the next target, after which they could declare victory in Gaza, and perhaps wind up operations there. It would free troops for subsequent operations – perhaps in Lebanon against the Hezbollah and also give Netanyahu the political capital to continue in his chair for some more time.

A New Phase of the War

But even if Hamas is now leaderless and broken, and Gaza has been reduced to ruin, the war is entering a dangerous new phase. It is unlikely that Iran will take this direct affront lightly. They will lose all standing if they do so. Iran had attacked Israeli territory in April in retaliation for an attack on their consulate in Beirut which killed senior IRGC commanders. That was in a series of ineffectual drone and missile strikes, that were more face-saving than anything else. This strike was on their own capital, at a national event targeting a state guest, and they will be forced to retaliate. In the words of their Supreme leader Khamenei, Iran will "seek vengeance as a sacred duty, in which the Zionist regime can expect severe punishment." In an emergency meeting of the Supreme National Council, Khamenei reportedly ordered, "A direct strike on Israel."

Another flurry of missile and drone strikes would follow. Perhaps Israeli embassies and diplomats could be targeted overseas. Their 'Axis of Resistance' – Hamas, Hezbollah, Houthis and other militia – would be activated to launch coordinated attacks along multiple fronts on Israel. The Hezbollah would be in the forefront of these actions. Israel and the Hezbollah have been trading blows for the past 10 months and these are likely to intensify. Israel itself, seems to be preparing for an all-out war with Hezbollah, as part of its strategy to ensure long term security. Netanyahu has promised retaliation on Lebanon, "That will make Gaza look like a picnic ground in comparison." A Israel-Hezbollah war would devastate southern Lebanon. Israel could target the Hezbollah leader, Hassan Nasrullah, or even invade Southern Lebanon to seize area up to the Litani River, as a buffer zone against future attacks. But defeating an organisation as strong and well-armed as the Hezbollah would be easier said than done – as their experience with Hamas has shown.

But Iran would not be passive in the case of such a war. They too, could launch their own strikes, use the Houthis to block the Red Sea shipping lanes and attack Israeli diplomats and missions abroad. The US too would stand by Israel – irrespective of any moralistic stance they proclaim – and send additional troops and warships into the region. Each of these actions could draw the region closer to all-out war, which would be much worse than the Gaza conflict, and drag the region into a wider war which could engulf all of the Middle East.

REFERENCES

"A Hamas Leader killed in Iran during Visit," *The New York Times*, 30 July 2024
"Hamas Political Chief Assassinated in Iran," *Al Jazeera*, 31 July 2024
"Hezbollah Top Commander killed in Beirut Strike," *Axiom*, 30 July 2024.
"How Hamas Leader Ismail Haniyeh was killed in Iran," *The New York Times*, 04 August 2024
"The Shadowy History of Israel's Attacks," *Al Jazeera*, 15 April 2024
"Who was Fuad Shukr: The Hezbollah Commander killed by Israel," *Al Jazeera*, 31 July 2024
"With its latest Assassination, Israel is testing Iran," *The Economist*, 02 April 2024

16

Israel and the Hezbollah

"Israel is our enemy. Its destiny is in our motto, 'Death to Israel'."

—Sayed Hassan Nasrallah, Head of Hezbollah

"It is inevitable," is the standard refrain that one hears in Tel Aviv about the likelihood of a war between Israel and the Hezbollah. It is made with a mix of resolution and resignation, reflecting the divisions within Israel itself on the conduct of the war. As the Gaza war meanders inconclusively Israel readied itself for an even more dangerous conflict in Lebanon.

Hezbollah was the first to fire rockets and missiles into Israel, as a sign of solidarity with Hamas after Israel attacked Gaza. Since then, cross border raids, rocket and missile attacks and artillery duels had become a daily feature along the Israel-Lebanon border. The attacks reached a crescendo in June which saw over 650 strikes by both sides. This forced Israel to evacuate over 70,000 settlers from the border areas, and push additional forces to contain the damage.

In retaliation, Israel struck Hezbollah targets not only along the border, but deep into Lebanon. They killed Abu Taleb, the high-ranking commander of Hezbollah forces in South Lebanon, prompting a flurry of 240 rocket and drone attacks into Israel in retaliation. In July, The Hezbollah launched an attack on an Israeli settlement in the occupied Golan Heights, killing 12 children who were playing football. Three days later Israeli jets hit a building in Beirut, killing Faud Shukr, a top Hezbollah commander who was responsible for operations in Southern Lebanon, getting immediate retribution.

The Northern Front saw its major escalation when Israel launched over 100 jet strikes in Southern Lebanon on 25 August, in what they termed as "Self-defence pre-emptive strikes." Hezbollah hit Israel with over 320 drones and missiles in their largest attack of the war, raising the prospects of a wider conflagration considerable.

Israel has to only see how its Gaza campaign has panned out to realise the dangers of a campaign against the much larger Hezbollah. Gaza has been reduced to rubble, but Israel is no closer to destroying the Hamas ideology or getting back its hostages, then they were at the start. The IDF began the campaign by attacking Gaza City in the north, then Khan Younis, and moved towards Rafah in the extreme South without any tangible results. Even now, Israel has decimated 21 of Hamas' 24 battalions, but its ideology remains as strong as before – and perhaps even more appealing. Cracks have emerged between the military and the political leadership, with the IDF stating publicly, that "the idea of destroying Hamas, is throwing sand in the eyes of the public." The Hamas leadership is intact and the hostages cannot be caught back unless there is a truce. However, Netanyahu flatly refuses a permanent ceasefire, insisting on continuing the pointless war till "final victory."

Already, Prime Minister Netanyahu has announced that the fighting in Gaza is winding down, freeing troops for the Northern border to confront Hezbollah. Netanyahu and his hardliner allies are gung-ho for an all-out war with Hezbollah, proclaiming, "We can fight on several fronts, and are prepared to do that." Israel has threatened to destroy the state of Lebanon to its foundations, "Where Gaza would look like a paradise in comparison," if Hezbollah continues its actions. Hezbollah, on their part, insist that they will stop their attacks only when a ceasefire is declared in Gaza. Thus, the longer that Netanyahu holds out against the ceasefire, the greater are the dangers of war erupting on its northern borders.

Plans for the impending Israeli offensive into Lebanon have already been formalised and approved, and all it needs is the signal to launch. Yet, it would be more difficult than they imagine. Israel may bomb Lebanon back into the Stone Age, like they did with Gaza, but destroying Hezbollah – or even defeating it militarily - is quite another story. The Hezbollah is thrice as strong as Hamas, and holds over 100,000 well-armed and motivated fighters in their ranks – many of them battle-hardened veterans of the Syrian war. It also has a carefully built-up stockpile of over 1,50,000 long range rockets and missiles, which can strike as far as Tel Aviv and Eilat, and simply swamp Israel's air defence. Israel ground invasion would be even more dangerous. During the 2006 invasion of Lebanon, Israel had four fresh and fully equipped divisions in Southern Lebanon, but were still held in a series of delaying battles all the way to the Litani river, and eventually forced to withdraw. Hezbollah succeeded in fighting the IDF to a standstill and destroyed quite a few of their prized Merkava tanks. Hezbollah is stronger and better prepared now, while the IDF is stretched thin with ongoing actions in Gaza and the West Bank. It could just end up biting more than it can chew.

After nine months of war, the army is tired and overstretched. The three divisions committed there have suffered 300 dead and over 4000 wounded – with many more showing PTSD. The equipment needs maintenance and stocks of ammunition are running low. Israel would need to reorganise themselves after they finish the task in Gaza, to be ready for a fresh offensive in Lebanon. And Gaza is still unfinished.

Israel set out to eliminate Hamas to "ensure security" without having a clear end-state in mind. They seem to have no idea or what they hope to achieve against the Hezbollah, except "To ensure long-term security." They hope to eliminate Hezbollah, like they set out to eliminate Hamas, but the Gaza war has revealed the improbability of that. There is a nebulous idea of creating a 70 km wide security zone along the Israel-Lebanon border that would serve as a buffer zone to prevent further Hezbollah attacks on Israeli settlements along the border. But that is easier said than done. It would involve long-term occupation which will be difficult to sustain. So the end-state of this war would also see Lebanon bombed into rubble, but the Hezbollah still holding out, and Israel finding itself more insecure than before.

There is also the roles of the principal sponsors – USA and Israel. The USA – in spite of open differences with Netanyahu – will stand by Israel. It has released additional stockpiles of weaponry, and even sent an amphibious assault ship, 'USS WASP,' along with a contingent of marines, to add to the two carrier groups already operating in the region. That is a clear signal of deterrence. Iran has been in the backdrop after its exchange of missiles with Israel in April, but it would not remain passive, should its main proxy be attacked. All this could lead to rapid escalation and perhaps even raise the question. After the Hezbollah, what will be the next target in Israel's quest for "long-term security?"

REFERENCES

"Fears that Israel and Hezbollah are headed for all-out War," *The Guardian*, 24 August 2024

"Hezbollah launches Missiles at Israel, prompting attacks on Lebanon," *Deccan Herald*, 25 August 2024

"Hezbollah says 'First Phase of Attack' is over," *BBC*, 24 August 2024

"How Israel and Hezbollah stepped back from the Brink of War," *The Washington Post*, 25 August 2024

"Is Israel Underestimating Hezbollah and its Military Capabilities?," *Zee News*, 24 August 2024

"Israel and Hezbollah exchange Strikes," *CBS News*, 25 August 2024

"The Coming Conflict with Hezbollah," The Center for Strategic and International Studies, 21 March 2024

"What is Hezbollah and will it go to War with Israel?" *BBC*, 24 August 2024

"Why did Israel, Hezbollah attack each other?" *Al Jazeera*, 24 August 2024

TAIWAN

17

Taiwan: A Looming Confrontation

"The reunification of Taiwan – by force, if necessary – is an inevitability."

—Xi Jinping

Will China Seek to Reunify Taiwan by Force?

Will they? Won't they? Will China attack Taiwan and seize it by military force? And will the USA intervene? And if so, what will be the consequences? These are questions that have plagued policymakers across the world. Even as the wars of Ukraine and the Middle East occupy centre stage, there is a graver confrontation looming in the Indo-Pacific – a likely invasion of Taiwan.

A rising China under Xi Jinping has asserted itself across much of the China Sea, citing 'historical claims.' It has initiated a confrontation in Ladakh that saw Indian and Chinese blood being spilled along the Line of Actual Control, for the first time in 40 years. It has chased Philippine, Vietnamese and Japanese fishing boats from their traditional fishing areas, using water cannons and ramming trawlers. They have constructed islands and military bases in disputed waters, and they have denied freedom of navigation in the international waters of the China Sea. And of course, they have suppressed the Uighurs of Xinjiang Province with an iron hand and Taiwan by denying them basic human rights. Tibet, Xinjiang, Senkaku and the China Sea are all part of the 'core interests' of China. But it is Taiwan which is the jewel in the crown for their aspirations to form a 'Greater China.'

Ever since the nationalist government forces of Chiang Kai-shek were defeated in the mainland by the communists in 1949, and then fled to Taiwan to establish their own government there, reunifying the island with the Chinese mainland has been a 'sacred duty' for Chinese leaders. Taiwan – or, to use its official name, The Republic of China – has retained its independent system of democracy, as opposed to China's authoritarian communist rule. But it has not yet declared itself an independent state. And though China has resorted to a range of measures to push Taiwan into re-joining the mainland, it has not resorted to actual war. Not yet.

Perhaps the enormous cost and casualties, and the probability of failure have prevented the Chinese from an actual assault to force reunification. There is also the likelihood of the USA entering the fray in defence of the democratic island. However, as China's economy slows, world reaction to its policies increases, and Xi Jinping's own position becomes insecure, perhaps he would like to regain his pre-eminence, by becoming the great Chinese leader, who got the breakaway island back into the Chinese fold. With the world pre-occupied with the wars of Ukraine and Gaza, can he choose this moment to strike? The PLA has been conducting an unprecedented series of exercises, practising an air, ground and naval invasion of Taiwan. Any of these exercises could well be converted into the real thing. Will they take this gamble?

Both the risks and the stakes are high. If Taiwan is re-unified with the Chinese mainland (by force, if necessary) it would add 58,000 square kilometres to its area and over 23 million trained and educated people to its population. Taiwan's strategic location at the junction of the East and South China Sea will provide a springboard into the Pacific Ocean, and will mark a tectonic shift in power. Most importantly, they will attain a stronghold over the world's superconductors – the tiny chips that power everything from mobiles to missiles to computers and cars. Taiwan produces 60 per cent of the world's semiconductor chips, and the Taiwan Semiconductor Manufacturing Corporation alone provides over 80 per cent of the world's most advanced chips. No other nation, including the USA, has been able to attain that expertise. Should China get control of the world's semiconductor production, it will have a stranglehold to control the world economy for decades.

Will China take the chance? If it does, how will the USA react? Will they actually go to war for democratic values in an island 12,000 km away? A war, which will wreak havoc and which they are not definite of winning? A USA-China conflict over Taiwan, coupled with the one in Ukraine and Gaza could engulf the entire world in war, and could well bring in the start of World War III.

Taiwan

The island of Taiwan came under the Qing Dynasty of China in the 17th century till the Sino-Japanese war of 1895, when Japan defeated China and took over the island. It remained under Japanese rule till 1945, when it was given back to China after the defeat of Japan in World War II.

In China, during the late Forties, the civil war between the Communist Party of Mao Zedong, and the nationalist forces of Chiang Kai-shek raged for years. The communist forces eventually took over Beijing and the entire Chinese mainland. Chiang Kai-shek and the remnants of his nationalist party – known as the Kuomintang (KMT) – fled to the island of Taiwan, where they established their own government. The KMT has been Taiwan's most prominent political party and has presided over the island for much of its 75-year long history.

The island of Taiwan lies 130 km from the Chinese mainland. Around the main island are a series of smaller islands, some of them like Kinmen and Matsu, just 3 kilometres away from Chinese shores. Taipei, the capital city, lies in the northern part. The main island is dotted with beaches, which could be suitable for an amphibious landing. The population is largely Han Chinese with strong historical, ethnic and cultural ties to the mainland, but the present generation is staunchly Taiwanese, and want to develop their own distinct identity. They are proud of their democratic values which they want to preserve. The movement to preserve its democracy and way of life has intensified after seeing the harsh clampdown which China imposed upon Hong Kong, when they took it over in 2019. Most Taiwanese were happy with the status quo of "one nation, two systems," but now, more and more of the youth favour outright independence.

China does not quite view it that way. For them, Taiwan is an inalienable part of China and its unification through peaceful means, coercion; even armed attack is an inevitability. Under Xi Jinping, the movement to reunify the island by force has intensified. He has repeatedly called upon the PLA to be prepared to take the island by force by 2027 – a year which could be a watershed moment. That is when China would have built up to peak strength and have its greatest window of opportunity. Beyond this, Taiwan would also become stronger and more difficult to subdue. More importantly, the new generation of Taiwan would have taken over, who does not favour any reunification, and could even declare themselves an independent nation.

Though Taiwan is fiercely independent, it has not antagonised China by declaring itself as an independent state. It has been recognised as a sovereign country by only 13 countries (including the Vatican) and even the USA, India, Russia and most European nations do not recognise it as such. For China, Taiwan is still part of China with a separate system of governance, "One country two systems." So, it goes ahead with a series of threats, inducements, coercion and actions just short of war, hoping to get Taiwan to willingly reunify with the mainland. Should Taiwan not do so, the possibility of military action can never be ruled out.

Should China attack, how will the USA respond? Much depends on the outcome of the wars in Europe and the Middle East. If Putin gets away with his aims in Ukraine, it could embolden Xi Jinping to try a similar gambit in Taiwan, knowing that the West would not get involved directly. The USA is now diverted in the Middle East and Europe, and has been deflected from the area of its main threat – the Indo-Pacific. Like his friend, Putin, Xi Jinping could seize the 'once-in-a-century moment' to attack Taiwan and seize it by military force. If he does take the gamble, how will the USA respond?

China, Taiwan and the USA

The USA – the champion of democracy and human rights (notwithstanding its own record of violations across the world), has always stood for Taiwan's democratic way of life, as opposed to China's Communist autocracy. However, as it turns increasingly inwards, will it fight for democratic ideals in an island 12,000 kilometres away? And will it shed American blood for its ideals?

The USA has no mutual defence treaty with Taiwan like they have with Japan and South Korea. On the contrary, since the 1979 Taiwan Relations Act, it has explicitly recognised the island as part of China under the 'One China, Two systems policy'. It maintains a policy of 'strategic ambiguity' towards Taiwan, which is at the heart of the delicate balance between the USA and China. At the same time, the USA has armed and aided Taiwan and provided it with F-16 fighters, 155-mm howitzers, tanks, ships and submarines to make the island capable of defending itself. US aid and arms deliveries to Taiwan are another sore point with China. The USA has no forces on the island itself, but holds bases in Guam and Japan, which can respond should Taiwan be threatened.

USA-China relations have gone rapidly downhill since 2014 – ever since Xi Jinping took over. It was not just the trade wars. China's aggressive actions in the China Seas had led President Obama to make the famous, 'Pivot to the Indo-Pacific.' The alliances of QUAD and AUKUS were part of measures to counter an increasingly assertive China, as the US actions to move ships and aircraft in areas illegally claimed by China, to maintain the principle of 'freedom of navigation.'

A series of events have also strained relations. When Nancy Pelosi – the Speaker of the US House of Representatives visited Taiwan in August 2022, it raised a howl of protest from China, which called the move 'a dangerous provocation.' President Joe Biden, too raised a hornet's nest when he announced publicly, "US forces will defend Taiwan in the event of a Chinese invasion." It was a direct affirmation of US support and was repeated four times in different forums. But even then, it is not clear whether the USA will actually respond.

Chinese and Taiwanese Forces

If one looks at the forces of China and Taiwan, there is a vast disparity. Taiwan's standing army of 169,000 is dwarfed by China's 2 million strong armed forces. But Taiwan has over half a million reservists who can be called up rapidly for military duty. As it is, President Tsai Ing-Wen had enhanced the conscription service of all young men from 18 to 36 years from four months to one year – to provide a greater pool of trained manpower. These could be called up to defend their country in the event of an invasion.

	China	Taiwan
Total active forces	**2,035,000**	**169,000**
Ground forces	965,000	94,000
Navy	260,000	40,000
Air force	395,000	35,000
Reserves	510,000	1,657,000
Tanks	4,800	650
Aircraft	3,348+	691+
Submarines	59	4
Naval ships*	86	26
Artillery	9,550	2,093

*Only includes ships classified as principal surface combatants, such as aircraft carriers, cruisers, destroyers and frigates

Source: The Military Balance 2023, IISS

Taiwan has built up its armed forces substantially with a purchase of $ 1.55 billion of new hardware from the USA in 2023. These include air defence systems, anti-ship missiles, and anti-missile systems, along with tanks, F-16 fighters, ships and submarines. A lot hinges on Taiwan's defensive forces being strong enough to delay the enemy; prevent him from landing, or decimate the invasion force by cutting it off from its long supply chain extending 130 kilometres across the Straits of Taiwan. Buying time till the USA arrives, is the heart of the Taiwanese defence strategy.

A Chinese invasion will not be easy. They will require a force of around 300,000 to 500,000 men, 4,000 ships, 2,100 planes, and around 3 million tons of equipment – even greater than those required for the Normandy landings. These will have to be assembled in secrecy, then ferried 130 kilometres across the Straits of Taiwan. The assaulting force would then have to establish a beachhead, and then move with additional forces across the difficult mountainous terrain to seize ports and cities, especially the capital, Taipei. All this, while contending with a likely US response from the Pacific. The Chinese vulnerabilities of crossing the 130-kilometre long channel, and maintaining its forces on the other side, can be exploited.

How and when could the Flashpoint erupt?

The most likely date for a Chinese invasion is anticipated to be around 2027. But with the Ukraine and the Middle East wars, Xi Jinping may be tempted to use the US pre-occupation with these wars to play his cards earlier. One key event is the Taiwanese presidential elections in January 2024. If an anti-unification and pro-independence party like the Democratic Progressive Party comes into power, it could spur the Chinese to take action before it is too late.

The US elections of November 2024 is another vital factor. The run-up to the elections and the period of transition that would follow will be one when the USA would be focused inwards, and attention diverted towards the elections. China could use this to act at a time when they feel the US administration would be divided and indecisive.

The capabilities of the PLA are also a major factor. By 2025, the PLA would have built up its strength to be able to invade Taiwan. Their navy has already expanded rapidly to become the largest navy in the world, with 350 vessels, even surpassing the US naval strength of 293 ships. The US Navy, of course, has a distinct edge in technology and sophistication. But with US forces engaged both in Europe and the Middle East, its forces would be divided.

The war for Taiwan has been ongoing for a while now, with the Chinese following a strategy of coercion and threats, just below the threshold of war. For years the PLA has been ramping up its aggression, by intruding into Taiwan's air defence identification zone and entering Taiwan's waters and air space. In 2023 itself, there were over 2,000 air and naval violations ofTaiwanese territory, including 103 in a single day in September. Taiwan has been struck by cyber attacks and disinformation almost on a daily basis.

China could perhaps start the operations by seizing islands close to the mainland like Matsu or Kinmen. This would be like the salami slicing tactics practised by the USSR during the Cold War. It would enable them to test the waters, gauge the Taiwanese and US response and also back down without loss of face if things don't go well. Incidentally, in the 1950s, China shelled the island of Kinmen and massed troops in preparation for an attack, but backed down when the US sent a large fleet into the area.

Concurrently, China could launch a complete blockade of Taiwan using some pretext. Naval ships and fighter aircraft would deter ships and aircraft entering Taiwanese waters and airspace. Perhaps even missile tests could be conducted in the area to block the passage of commercial shipping. This will enable China to establish a stranglehold before the actual invasion.

The actual invasion could start with intense bombardment directed at military assets and key installations to soften up Taiwan's formidable defences. Air strikes could be launched at Taiwanese bases. China would seek to establish complete air and naval ascendency over the 130–kilometre wide Straits of Taiwan, so that its amphibious forces could cross with impunity. The initial assault forces would establish beachheads on both sides of the island – aided by paratroopers who would act as pathfinders for the invasion force. Once the beachhead(s) is/are established, the main invasion force would follow, enter the beachhead and then move inland to capture Taipei and other critical targets.

The crux of the operation hinges on how the USA will react. For 2-3 days, once, China establishes its beachhead, it will be difficult to evict them. Delaying the US forces is thus a critical part of the plan. China will establish an air and naval screen along their first and second island chains to prevent US forces entering the area, and keep them away by firing long-range missiles. Should the US keep its commitment to Taiwan and respond to the Chinese aggression, they will have to engage the Chinese navy and air force and then get closer to interdict their follow-on and supply forces crossing the Straits of Taiwan. There would be a series of air and naval battles fought along the first and second island chains, as the Chinese navy keeps the US fleet at bay. The outcome of these will decide the course of the war. It all depends on the US response, and the speed with which they respond. But the outcome will be more than the battle for Taiwan. It will actually be a battle for world supremacy.

Let us have a look at a likely scenario and see how this war could pan out.

18

A Chinese Invasion and the US Response: The Battle for Superpowerdom

"US forces will defend Taiwan in the event of a Chinese invasion."

—US President Joe Biden

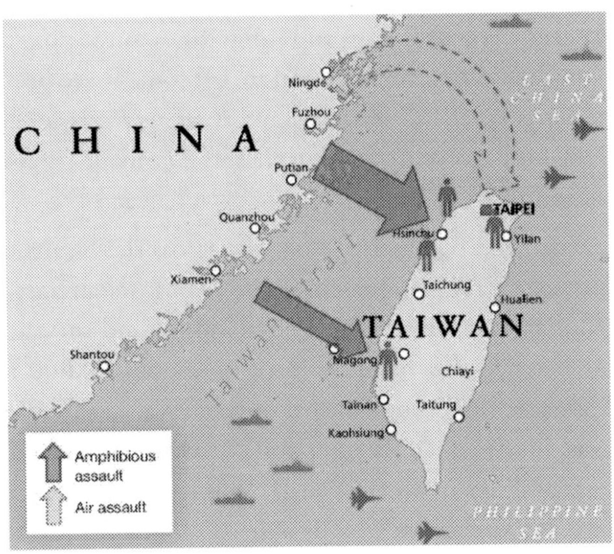

The Preparation and Planning

It is the year 2024. The war in Ukraine is not officially over, but Russia has occupied over 18 per cent of Ukrainian territory and amalgamated the provinces of Kherson, Zaporizhzhia, Luhansk and Donetsk, in a *fait accompli* – in much the same manner that they did with Crimea in 2014. The Middle East is in turmoil, with the truces and ceasefires between Israel, Hamas and the Hezbollah being repeatedly broken. The skirmishing continues there. Though these conflicts have receded to the back pages, they are smouldering and still occupy the time and attention of US policy makers.

In Taiwan, a new government has taken over which follows an anti-unification and pro-independence hard line. Polls in Taiwan show that over 54 per cent of the population now want independence and only around a fifth favour reunification with China. Taiwan is also modernising and strengthening its armed forces and seems to be slipping away from China's domain.

For the Communist Party and Xi Jinping himself, it is a delicate situation. Xi is under increasing pressure for the failure of policies such as the Belt and Road Initiative, the slowdown of the Chinese economy and its isolation in much of the Western world. More worrying, after decades of the 'one-child' policy, its population is reducing and aging rapidly. The only upside is that the PLA has reached peak strength. The Chinese navy is now the largest in the world with a fleet of over 400 ships and submarines, surpassing the USA navy in quantity, if not quality. Its missile and rocket forces have been built up, its nuclear arsenal is primed and ready. The PLA seems ready for an invasion of Taiwan, and the only worrying factor is that its commanders and troops have not seen actual combat, or have any battle experience.

The PLA has been conducting exercises across the Straits of Taiwan for months, rehearsing a mock invasion of the island. Its aircraft have entered Taiwan's territorial waters over 100 times a month and they have tested the Taiwanese air defence and radar. A force of about 300,000 men with six amphibious brigades has been deployed opposite Taiwan for months now, as part of an invasion fleet of 4,000 ships and 2,000 aircraft – a force larger than the Normandy landings in World War II. This force has been practising and rehearsing for years. They are now ready to heed Xi Jinping's repeated extortions to be ready "to perform your sacred duty" and take over Taiwan by military force.

At a conclave held in utmost secrecy in Beijing, the leaders meet to discuss the likely invasion of Taiwan. Xi Jinping is all in favour of seizing the 'once-in-a-century-moment' and his word holds sway. The very next day, the PLA is warned to prepare for an impending invasion of Taiwan in mid-October, when the tides and weather conditions would be most suitable. It is also timed with the US presidential elections due in November, when the USA would be occupied with its internal affairs.

The Prelude

The actual plan, along with different contingencies, had been in place for years and only needs to be fine-tuned. Surprise is the key to get an early foot hold and then exploiting it. The troop ships, escorts and aircraft, along with additional civilian ships and aircraft required, assemble in plain sight near the embarkation ports. They know they will be detected, but since they have been practicing this action for months, the USA and Taiwan will mistake it for yet another exercise.

US satellites and intelligence had been monitoring Chinese actions for months earlier. They detect these activities, and even though there is more frenetic activity than usual, most feel it is just another exercise. An important clue comes when US intelligence detects the stockpiling of blood plasma and the activation of civil hospitals along the Chinese mainland. It could be a sign of the real thing.

US intelligence conveys this information to Taiwan, indicating that Chinese activity could be more than routine military exercises. By then, Chinese jets and ships have been intruding into Taiwanese space every day, coming deeper with each foray. Taiwan has been subject to a series of cyber attacks that have intensified in recent times and have disrupted their internet, telecom and financial services. A flood of Chinese propaganda also swamps television, digital and social media warning that the "disastrous policies of the capitalist regime will hurl the Taiwanese people towards ruin." They urge the Taiwanese to go back to "their historical roots on the sacred soil of our motherland, where you belong."

Taiwan intelligence officials do not take the US warnings seriously. They have been subject to invasion scenarios for years and have been lulled into a false sense of security. They dismiss it as routine Chinese activity and the President rejects calls to mobilise the 300,000 reservists to augment the 169,000 strong army.

The trigger comes when a flight of J-10 fighters intrudes dangerously close and is intercepted by Taiwanese F-16 fighters. A dangerous game of 'I dare' ensues, with each side coming dangerously close to the other in an attempt to scare them away. Then the inevitable happens. A Chinese J-10 crashes with a Taiwanese F-16 that sends both aircraft plummeting downwards. The F-16 pilot ejects to safety. But his Chinese opponent is not so lucky and plunges into the waters of the Straits of Taiwan along with his aircraft.

The Chinese media howls in protest and accuses the Taiwanese pilot of shooting down the Chinese aircraft with a missile while their pilot was "performing routine self-defence manoeuvres inside own territory". The political, diplomatic and propaganda war reaches a crescendo. Xi Jinping himself warns that Taiwan's aggression would not be allowed to go unpunished. Three days later, China launches its carefully calibrated invasion of Taiwan.

The Invasion

In the first action of the war, a Chinese flotilla, along with paratroopers, lands on the Kinmen and Matsu islands – just 3 km from the Chinese mainland. The few defenders on the islands are rapidly overrun, and the radar station and communication centres taken over. The two islands are blocked from the main island of Taiwan as Chinese marines gain complete control of the island in two short days.

This naked aggression is a sign that the Chinese mean business. The Taiwanese air force and navy try to respond, but are kept away by a large Chinese force aggressively patrolling the Straits of Taiwan. The first dogfights of the war take place, with losses to both sides. But in spite of world condemnation, China takes over and holds on to the islands. Then they announce a referendum. Unsurprisingly, they claim that over 98 per cent of the population voted for "reunification with our beloved homeland." Images of the local population cheering and celebrating the reunification in obviously forced and stage-managed parades are beamed daily to the Taiwanese people and across the world. The Chinese claim that the Taiwanese people want to join China but, being oppressed by "the Fascist government under its capitalist masters," embark on the "sacred duty to re-unify the island with China."

Concurrently, the PLA navy establishes a blockade around Taiwan, barring ships from entering its ports, and preventing commercial flights from overflying the island. While Taiwan is blocked from all sides, the Chinese navy takes up positions along the first and second island chains to block the approach of the US Navy.

The USA is in a quandary. The anticipated assault has arrived. But in election year, the domestic population is in no mood to fight for an island 12,000 km away. The idea of shedding American blood would be politically damaging. Even the generals do not want to get involved in a war which could cause immense damage and have horrific consequences.

However, in a rare show of decision, the US government decides to stand by their pledge to defend Taiwan in case of Chinese aggression and sends two carrier groups to the area. They warn the Chinese to withdraw their blockade and announce their intention to deliver much-needed humanitarian aid to Taiwan. US bases and Guam and Okinawa are activated. The USA also forms a 'coalition of the willing' to counter Chinese aggression. Japan and South Korea were treaty bound to join, and reluctantly agree. Australia refuses to get directly involved, but agrees to provide its ports and bases for use by coalition forces. The European nations, especially Germany and France, sympathise, but claim to be too preoccupied with the Russian threat to spare any troops or equipment for the Indo-Pacific theatre. Only UK agrees to send two warships and a squadron of Tornado fighters. NATO members flatly refuse to get involved in a war that is ' way beyond our jurisdiction.' India, is supportive, and hopes 'peace will prevail.' It refuses to get involved directly, but intensifies naval patrolling in the Indian Ocean, and places troops in Ladakh and Arunachal Pradesh on high alert, to counter any fallout of this big power confrontation.

However, before the USA can send its forces into the region, the Chinese launches a massive air and missile attack on Taiwanese ports, air bases and military installations. The Taiwanese Air Force has been expecting such an attack and its aircraft are dispersed in hard shelters and suffer relatively little damage. After the first wave of Chinese attacks, they are still able to take to the skies and deny China the air superiority that it seeks.

At the same time, a flotilla of around 400 ships, carrying 40,000 men, crosses the Median Line dividing the Taiwan Straits, and enters Taiwanese waters. A screen of fighters and naval warships protects them, but the Taiwanese navy and Air Force attack the invading force with great determination, sinking 20 of the landing craft and their escorts. But the odds are against them. The

Chinese have an overwhelming superiority and succeed in approaching the beaches of Jinshan, Jialutang, and Kaohsiung on the eastern and western sides of the island. As the invasion force closes in, a battalion of paratroopers land near Jinshan – the northern beach closest to Taipei – to secure a foothold. The paratroopers suffer immense casualties, but ultimately succeed in securing a tenacious toehold on the beach.

That toehold is invaluable when the main amphibious force hit the beaches. Three beaches are hit simultaneously – two in the eastern part of the island and one in the west. The assaulting force is countered by heavy fire from the coastal batteries and well-prepared Taiwanese defences. Many of the landing sites also have obstacles and remotely operated guns to deter a crossing, and anti-ship mines guard the approaches. Around 10 per cent of the amphibious landing craft are sunk even before they touch land. But while dogfights rage in the skies, the ground forces try to establish their beachheads. They are repulsed in two locations, but one of the amphibious brigades finally succeeds in landing at Jinshan – where they link up with the paratroopers there and slowly consolidate a beachhead, through which additional forces are pumped in.

The US Response

Although they USA has been expecting this full-fledged invasion, they delay their response for two crucial days, hoping that the Taiwanese would be able to repulse the attacks. They still hope that the confrontation would be over without an actual exchange of fire between Chinese and US forces. In that time the Chinese manage to land around 20,000 troops in their beachhead, which is being gradually expanded. The majority of the invasion force still waits at the mainland – waiting for the beachheads to be consolidated so that they could storm through them to capture Taipei and other cities deeper inland. The first wave of Chinese follow-on troops, along with their escorting warships and fighter aircraft begin crossing the 130-kilometre wide Straits of Taiwan. The limited Chinese capability in landing craft means that the subsequent assaulting groups have to be ferried across in waves and would take another 4 to 5 days to build up completely on the island.

That is the period when the Chinese are the most vulnerable – when they have a force holding on to its beachhead on the island, when part of the force is being ferried across the Straits, and a part is waiting in the mainland to be carried across. It is also the period when US forces approach the area, reinforced by another carrier group. The USA gives a clear warning to the Chinese leadership that their invasion will be considered an act of war, and that the USA will intervene if they do not withdraw. The Chinese leadership had miscalculated. They were sure that the USA would not intervene, but the USA reacted actively, recognising this battle as not just for Taiwan, but for world supremacy in the 21st century.

The Chinese leadership decides to cripple the US fleet, before it can become fully operational in Taiwanese waters. US bases in Guam and Okinawa are struck by a barrage of missiles that cause over 300 casualties and damage ships in harbour. The US Seventh Fleet, approaching from the Pacific, is hit by a salvo of DF-26 missiles – long range hypersonic carrier killers that had been developed by China, specifically for this contingency. The missiles strike the fleet while it is still 2,000 kilometres away, and while the air defence systems of the carriers barely manage to intercept the incoming missiles; three escort ships are hit and badly damaged. Two are sunk and a third is towed away to harbour.

The USA realises that it would be difficult to break the blockade of Taiwan. It thus focuses on destroying the invasion force by cutting off the flow of supplies and manpower as they try to cross the Straits. US long-range bombers and missiles target the Chinese fleet and the invasion force during their crossing. Their superior intelligence and precise targeting allows them to strike with pinpoint accuracy – hitting the limited landing craft and forcing subsequent waves to return to the safety of their bases on the mainland. Chinese supply ships carrying much needed replenishment to their troops on the island are also targeted. The USA, however, does not strike at any target on the Chinese mainland believing it could escalate the war beyond control.

However, in spite of enormous casualties, Chinese ships and aircraft manage to ferry additional troops to the main Taiwan island and build up forces there. The Taiwanese have fought a grim defensive battle and contained the Chinese in their beachhead, But the beachhead is now three kilometres deep and five kilometres wide, and within it the Chinese inducts another assault division which is tasked to make a lightning strike at the capital city, Taipei – which would paralyse the Taiwanese government and force it to capitulate.

That is when the fatal flaw in the plan comes in. None of the troops had seen battle, and none had been exposed to hostile enemy fire earlier. It is a traumatic experience for most of them. Their commanders too are not battle-hardened to cope with this situation. The Chinese advance was slow and timid, and overly cautious. They move out timidly from their beachhead in a uncoordinated advance, and are pummelled with artillery fire. They are unable to even break the screen established by the Taiwanese ground forces that are fighting in well-prepared defensive lines around the beachhead. The Chinese breakout fails and they are forced back to their beachhead, to which they cling on. The Taiwanese forces establish a defensive perimeter around it to prevent them from attempting another break out.

With the situation on the ground under control, the USA now shifts strategy to actively destroy the Chinese navy. In a series of naval battles fought around the first island chain, the USA slowly gets the upper hand. In a decisive encounter, it also attacks the Chinese aircraft carrier *Liaoning*, with long-range anti-ship missiles, sinking it in a major victory for the Allied forces.

That is the turning point of the war. China no longer tries to follow up on the invasion of Taiwan, but focuses on keeping the US fleet away. Their submarines and long-range missiles cause heavy damage on allied naval forces – even damaging an aircraft carrier, which is towed back to safety, but declared inoperable thereafter. A second aircraft carrier is also hit by a long-range missile, but fortunately the damage is contained. After three weeks of intense air and naval battles, the allied forces succeed in gaining dominance. Their ships and aircraft can now sever the supply lines from the Chinese mainland to the 30,000-odd Chinese troops still holding their beachhead in Taiwan. China threatens to use nuclear weapons and even contemplates a nuclear strike on the US Seventh Fleet or at US bases in Guam – but fortunately does not do so, fearing retaliation. Clashes even occur in outer space, when a Chinese anti-satellite missile destroys a US communications satellite. The debris created by the blast continues to speed on a low Earth orbit for years thereafter, rendering it unusable.

After two months of intense naval and air engagements, both sides finally agree to talk and call a truce. China withdraws its forces from Taiwan, but is allowed to keep Kinmen and Matsu islands. The Taiwanese Parliament also formally agrees to renounce independence and adhere to the principle of

'One China, two systems.' China renounces the use of force, but remains confident that the Taiwanese would eventually "re-join with their homeland."

Both sides claim victory in the war, but in reality, both suffer incalculable damage. As per a war game conducted by the Centre of Strategic and International Studies, a confrontation such as this could cost the USA and its allies over 350 aircraft and 40 ships – including one or two aircraft carriers. China was expected to lose around 200 to 250 aircraft and almost 150 ships, including most of its invasion force. But more than the materiel damage is the long-term costs. The war would reduce the GDP of China by up to 25 per cent, and the US GDP would drop from 7-10 per cent. The clash between the world's two largest economies would cripple supply chains and plunge the world economy into recession.

This scenario that has been painted is just one of the many that could unfold. Things could take a different turn. The USA could refuse to respond to a Chinese invasion of Taiwan and merely impose sanctions. Should the USA refuse to get involved, it is estimated that Taiwan would be able to stave off the invasion for just 2-3 weeks and fight on the island for perhaps a month or so before being forced to capitulate. China would suffer very high losses of men and materiel, but once it absorbs Taiwan, its pre-eminence as a global power is assured. It would be able to control the Indo-Pacific, dominate the semi-conductor industry and be the unchallenged power in the region – if not the world. If the USA does not take on the challenge, it will lose its status as the world's superpower, and perhaps its terminal decline would be hastened.

The looming war is seen as a question of not 'If,' but 'When.' Most identify the probable dates in the window between 2024 and 2027. The world is reeling from the wars of Ukraine and the Middle East. This superpower confrontation in the Indo-Pacific could have far greater consequences. It would reactivate all other theatres and bring the world to another World War – one which will have even more horrendous consequences than the previous ones.

REFERENCES

'A Potential Timeline for Conflict', *Global Guardian*, 12 December 2023, https://www.globalguardian.com

'China and Taiwan: A really Simple Guide', *BBC*, 6 April 2023, https://www.bbc.com

'Explained: What if China invades Taiwan in 2026?' *WION*, 10 January 2023, https://www.wiones.com

'How prepared is Taiwan for a War with China?', *Al Jazeera*, 10 October 2023, https://www.aljazeera.com

'How will China take over Taiwan? Five Scenarios', Bloomberg, 5 November 2023, https://www.bloomberg.com

'Invading Taiwan would be a Logistical Minefield', *The Economist*, 6 November 2023, https://www.economist.com

'Is a Chinese Invasion of Taiwan the most likely scenario?', Stimson Centre, 27 October 2023, https://www.aljazeera.com

'Is China planning to Attack Taiwan?', https://www.thediplomat.com

'Reunification with Taiwan through Force', Centre for Strategic and International Studies, 22 November 2022, https://www.csis.org

'Taiwan Wary of Conflict with China in 2027', *The Guardian*, 21 April 2023, https://www.theguardian.com

'Ukraine War may affect How and When China Invades', Business Insider, 20 July 2022, https://www.businessinsider.com

'Will China really Invade? Caution and Optimism in Taiwan', *Nikkei Asia*, 4 December 2023, https://www.asianikkei.com

Index